PIRATE GOLD

Brian Lister is a trusted and respected radio consultant, working with numerous radio groups. He previously co-authored a guide to *Managing Radio* with two colleagues from Sunderland University where he is a visiting lecturer. With a diverse, multi-skilled background in BBC, commercial and community radio Brian currently specialises in radio licence application projects, station launches, programming consultancy, interim management and training. His passion for radio is life-long, initially involved in broadcasting through land-based pirate radio and setting-up a hospital radio service, he became manager of University Radio Essex while studying for his electronics degree. He then trained with BBC Radio as a studio manager, working at Broadcasting House and with the overseas services at Bush House. Joining Metro Radio for the launch of the Tyneside radio station in 1974 he went on to manage commercial radio stations in Teesside, Harrogate, Darlington and Sunderland. He was also a founding director of community radio stations in Sunderland and Teesdale. As development director for The Local Radio Company he wrote many successful Ofcom licence applications for the group and other organisations. He has since worked with a variety of radio businesses and projects including Jazz FM and Lyca Media. In the 1970s he served on the National Executive of the broadcasting union ABS and in the 1990s was a board member of the Commercial Radio Companies Association. Brian was a trustee of the Public Service Broadcasting Trust and is an active member of the Radio Academy.

PIRATE GOLD

The real story behind the offshore radio stations of the 1960s

Brian Lister

Sound Concepts

© 2017 Brian Lister

All rights reserved

No part of this book may be reproduced in any form or by any electronic or mechanical means including information storage and retrieval systems, without permission in writing from the author.

ISBN 978-0-244-01718-7

First published 2017

Sound Concepts
37 West End, Sedgefield, TS21 2BW. England.

Cover: Red Sands fort in 2017, photo by the author.

CONTENTS

INTRODUCTION   1

Chapter One
BRITANNIA WAIVES
THE RULES   3

Chapter Two
THE VOICE OF AMERICA   18

Chapter Three
THE VOICE OF SLOUGH   26

Chapter Four
CONS PIRACY   41

Chapter Five
TOWERS OF POWER   62

Chapter Six
OIL ON THE WATER   81

Chapter Seven
CASH CASINO   99

Chapter Eight
LAISSEZ FAIRE   130

Chapter Nine
SHIVERING SANDS   140

Chapter Ten
MARINE OFFENCES   156

Chapter Eleven
RED SIGNALS   173

REFERENCES   198

INDEX   204

INTRODUCTION

It is sometimes said: 'if you can remember the 1960s you weren't really there.' That could be one of the reasons why so many of the facts stated in this book are contradicted by other sources. Indeed in some cases the other sources may be correct. However it is certainly true that many of the commonly held myths about the offshore broadcasters are the result of clever marketing, political spin, commercial expediency or official secrecy at the time and have remained largely unchallenged ever since.

The 2009 Richard Curtis comedy film *The Boat That Rocked* (retitled *Pirate Radio* in the USA) was a fun romp, more about the social attitudes of the 1960s than about the realities of running a radio station in the North Sea. It did however reflect the general public perception of a group of young rebels getting themselves a ship and sticking two fingers up at the establishment, particularly the stuffy BBC.

Much has been written about this era, in books, magazines and on the internet, mostly by people who were directly involved in the stations. Their accounts are valuable and illuminating but often reflect a version of events promulgated at the time. I have deliberately written this from the standpoint of a keen observer, a dedicated listener to the sixties stations whose career, and indeed life, has been shaped by the lessons I learned then.

As a teenage listener in the sixties I was happy to conflate the emergence of the UK pirate radio stations with the left-wing liberation struggles going on at the same time: civil rights protests, anti-war movements, student unrest and more liberal attitudes to sex and sexuality. Fifty years on, I now appreciate the reality: the people behind the early offshore stations were frequently motivated by a very different political agenda and often the ships and forts were simply pawns in much bigger power games.

This book has been compiled from a large collection of notes, conversations and insights collected over those fifty years. Indeed some of the notes are in my young handwriting from as far back as 1964.

I tried to find the source for that quip about remembering the sixties, but according to the *Quote Investigator* website: 'Many people think they remember who said this. The problem is they disagree: Paul Kantner, Robin Williams, Paul Krassner, Pete Townshend, Grace Slick, Timothy Leary, and many others have been credited with the saying. Of course, no one who was there really remembers.'

CHAPTER ONE

BRITANNIA WAIVES THE RULES

Most people with an interest in UK radio know the story: For some 40 years the British Broadcasting Corporation had held a monopoly in radio broadcasting to the UK. A young Irishman who managed a couple of bands became frustrated that he couldn't get them airplay on the BBC. He decided to do something about it. He bought a ship and, at his father's small port in Ireland, converted it into a transmitting station. Radio Caroline was born. Others copied the model and pirate radio became an essential component of Britain's 'swinging sixties'. In the end the government, under pressure from copyright holders and the BBC decided it had to act and made them illegal.

Except it wasn't like that.

Radio Caroline came on-air on 28 March 1964, just four months after the world had been shaken by the assassination of President Kennedy. The President, generally popular around the world as a charismatic breath of fresh air in the White House, reflecting the rising hopes of a young generation in the early sixties, was far less popular in some conservative sections of US society. He was shot while driving in an open-top car through central Dallas and died almost immediately.

There are sufficient conspiracy theories in this radio story without my adding to the already substantial controversy over the Kennedy assassination. Suffice to say that a lone gunman called Lee Harvey Oswald was very promptly arrested and charged with the murder of the leader of the free world. Just two days later, while being paraded in front of reporters and cameramen, Oswald was himself shot dead by Dallas nightclub owner Jack Ruby.

When Ruby was arrested, directly after the shooting, he immediately asked to speak to one man. He wanted to see his close friend Gordon McLendon, the owner of major Dallas radio station KLIF who was involved in right-wing politics and had CIA connections. Ruby had called McLendon's ex-directory home phone number and visited the KLIF studios on the day of the assassination. At the Dallas police headquarters he posed as a KLIF reporter to get close to Lee Harvey Oswald and kill him. Gordon McLendon went on to be instrumental in the setting up of several European pirate radio stations. His name surfaces regularly in this book.

Radio Caroline founder Ronan O'Rahilly was later to claim that the station had been named after the late President Kennedy's daughter. This is one of the many 'alternative facts' surrounding the story of the offshore stations, statements that suited a purpose at the time and have remained largely unchallenged ever since.

Caroline wasn't even the first ship-borne radio station in the UK. Fully 35 years earlier, in the early years of the BBC, a steam yacht called the Ceto sailed from Dundee carrying a broadcast transmitter and all the equipment needed to broadcast music and advertising.

The *Daily Mail* chartered the ship intending to broadcast, from outside British territorial waters, publicity for the paper and its sister publications the *Sunday Dispatch* and *London Evening News*. The idea was that, throughout the summer of 1928, the Ceto was to anchor off coastal towns and holiday resorts and beam entertaining programmes to the local area. However AM transmitting equipment was still very primitive and getting a reliable medium-wave signal to land proved very difficult as was playing brittle 78 rpm discs in rough seas.

After some initial tests off Scotland the radio project was abandoned and the ship instead was fitted out with powerful amplifiers and speakers through which popular gramophone records and advertisements for the three papers were blasted at the beaches from closer to the shore as the Ceto moved round the coast.[1]

And Radio Caroline, if it wasn't the first, was certainly not the best of the sixties pirate stations. The initial programming was not the non-stop top-40 sound those of us who used to listen with transistor radios under the bedclothes like to recall. True, they were playing music from what the BBC then liked to call 'gramophone records' all day every day, but the Caroline selection of music was far more *Housewives Choice* than *Pick of the Pops*.

It was the arrival of rival stations with American programme directors that generated the non-stop pop sound we who listened at the time fondly remember. Within weeks Caroline had direct completion from a neighbouring ship on a neighbouring frequency with a harder-edged sound. By the end of the year a well-funded competitor brought an even more powerful, polished and punchy format imported from Dallas and Caroline really had to up its game.

In the background, watching all this unfold, were government agencies alarmed to see their control over popular media starting to ebb away.

During the 1950s the country, and thus its BBC, was living in the shadow of the second world war and its devastating impact on our economy and infrastructure. The BBC was not ready to embrace the British cultural revolution of the 1960s. But after fifteen years of austerity, including food rationing and compulsory national service that extended well into the fifties, the public, especially those born after the war, was ready for a change. If the fifties had been lived in shades of grey everyone now wanted colour. Youth culture was stimulated by an increase in disposable income among teenagers and the desire to experience things their parents had never dared to dream about. New fashions, greater mobility, pop culture, Beatlemania - these were all manifestations of the new world of the early sixties with which 'aunty' BBC was struggling to cope.

In order to understand how and why the offshore broadcasters suddenly blossomed it is necessary to take a brief look at the dramatic changes taking place in Britain in the early 1960s. This is a story of the coming together, at a particular place and time, of a wide range of individuals, special interests, international politics, changing attitudes, new technology and the legacies of the recent war.

The development of the UK pirates relied on strange alliances between people from very different backgrounds and with very different political beliefs. The list of key players ranges from the wife of the US President, an American evangelist preacher, the managers of struggling pop groups, and a theatrical agent, to some notorious London gangsters. And through it all the shadowy presence of various state security agencies is constantly in the background.

At the start of the sixties the government still maintained considerable powers over what the public could see or hear, and how we could communicate. Although commercial television had been introduced in regional stages from 1955 onwards it was tightly controlled by the government-appointed Independent Broadcasting Authority and the commercial companies were not themselves broadcasters but 'programme contractors' under contract to supply programmes to the IBA – which was legally the broadcaster and could pull the plug at any time.

Even theatre stage performances were censored by the establishment. A law passed in 1737 gave the Lord Chamberlain the statutory authority to veto the performance of any new plays and to prevent any play from being performed for any reason. Theatre owners could be prosecuted for staging a play that had not received prior approval. While, by 1843, the Theatres Act had restricted the powers of the Lord Chamberlain so that he could only prohibit the performance of plays where he was of the opinion that 'it is fitting for the preservation of good manners, decorum or of the public peace so to do' this law remained in place throughout most of the swinging sixties. The Lord Chamberlain of the Royal Household of the United Kingdom having refused a licence, it was not possible to stage the hippy musical *Hair* (in which some members of the young cast briefly appeared nude) until the law was repealed in 1968,

In a similar fashion all means of communication between British subjects, apart from face-to-face conversations, were controlled by a state monopoly under a senior government minister, the postmaster general. The PMG was responsible, among many other things, for the Royal Mail, Post Office telephones and all radio and television licensing. You could not buy or rent a telephone instrument from anyone other than the Post Office and every kind of transmitter – even for a remote controlled model – required a specific individual licence. As we will see his powers (and the PMG was always a he) even extended to being able to forbid ship-to-shore radio calls for the offshore stations and to deny them listings in the telephone directory! But by the start of the sixties cracks were starting to show in the paternalistic, conservative, controlling, edifice of government which had been born of two world wars and in the shadow of the atomic bomb.

D H Lawrence's novel *Lady Chatterley's Lover* had been published privately in 1928 in Italy, and in 1929 in France and Australia. An unexpurgated edition was not published openly in the United Kingdom until 1960. The book soon became notorious for its story of the relationship between a working class man and an upper class woman, its explicit descriptions of sex, and its use of the word fuck. Perhaps it was the depiction of class and the fact that as a paperback it was more widely available to the general public that spurred the crown into acting against it.

Penguin Books was prosecuted under the Obscene Publications Act 1959 and the trial took place in Number One Court at the Old Bailey over six heavily reported days in late 1960.

An enduring memory of the case, illustrating just how out of touch with everyday life the establishment had become, was the prosecution's initial address to the jury. Mervyn Griffith-Jones explained they must decide if the book was obscene and if so whether its literary merit amounted to a 'public good'. Inviting the jury to consider whether it would deprave or corrupt he asked: 'Is it a book you would have lying around your own house? Is it a book that you would even wish your wife or your servants to read?'

When Penguin won the case the resulting publicity ensured the book sold three million copies and ushered in a liberalisation of publishing in the UK. Some see the trial as marking the start of the permissive society and the swinging sixties.

When a maverick entrepreneur started a pirate radio station broadcasting from a wartime fort in the Thames estuary just a few years later he gained considerable publicity by featuring readings of the sexual passages from *Lady Chatterley's Lover* in its late night programmes.

The ability afforded by offshore radio for people and organisations to transmit to huge audiences without any government control came as a shock to the British establishment. While government pronouncements focussed on international frequency agreements, music copyright and dangers to shipping, their real concern was more fundamental. From the start of the BBC broadcasting infrastructure had been constructed in such a way that, in the event of a major public disturbance or emergency, the government could immediately take control of all transmissions. This was not only built into the BBC's Charter and all transmitting licences but was also physically built into the transmission network. The facility to shut down the regular studios and take control of all transmitters from remote locations was introduced during the second world war. It would obviously have been invaluable had the country been at risk of being overrun by invading German troops. This system formed the basis of the Wartime Broadcasting Service (WTBS) set up after the war to face the threat of an attack with atomic weapons. It was possible at very short notice to remotely switch the lines feeding BBC transmitters so their programmes came from secret studios in government bunkers – and there would be nothing the regular broadcasters could do to stop it.

When commercial radio was finally established in the UK from 1973 onwards this system was extended to the new commercial radio operators. As with the commercial television stations licensed from the mid-fifties, the companies were not allowed to own and operate their own transmitters. I came to understand one vital aspect of this arrangement when the radio station I was working for went off the air after a Post Office cable was damaged in a most unlikely location. A Post Office engineer explained, under conditions of strict secrecy (which I imagine no longer apply) that our transmitter feeds were required to be routed via a 'hardened' switching centre where, at a moment's notice, our programmes could be replaced by the government.

Even the little campus radio station I managed at the University of Essex in 1970 had a similar arrangement – although I knew nothing about it until after I had left the University. Apparently the Home Office had quietly asked the University authorities to install a secret switch in a service cupboard below our studios which could shunt our transmitter output into a dummy load, rendering it inaudible in the event that those in power didn't like what we were broadcasting.

Against this background you can see why the British establishment were appalled to discover that independent-minded operators, some representing foreign interests, could set up high-power transmitters so close to our coast.

The BBC's plans during the Cold War were very detailed and specific. A bombproof studio and office block had been built at the rear of Broadcasting House during the war, it was later absorbed into the original extension (recently demolished to make way for New Broadcasting House). Known as 'the Stronghold' the studios and control room were designed to allow the government to broadcast during a period of heightened tension right up until a nuclear attack. It was linked to other underground studios in government bunkers and elsewhere, including the BBC's own nuclear bunker under the BBC technical training centre at Wood Norton near Evesham that had four radio studios and accommodation for up to one hundred staff.

The main cable carrying the key long wave service from Broadcasting House to the giant Droitwich transmitter (then normally carrying the Light Programme, now Radio 4, but crucially audible across most of the UK) was diverted through the Wood Norton bunker giving it direct access to that transmitter and others around the country. There was a special network of 54 local medium wave transmitters, some of which were mounted in mobile trailers that were provided with emergency generators and some degree of fall-out protection. In the mid-sixties, as a schoolboy on holiday, I visited a remote BBC transmitting station at Burghead near Inverness. In addition to the ancient high-power long and medium wave transmitters in a corner of the old stone-built transmitter hall there was a shiny new Marconi medium wave transmitter sitting idle. When I asked what it was for I was told I was not supposed to see it, it wasn't there, and the subject was changed.

The intention was that the government would make the decision to trigger the Wartime Broadcasting Service at a late stage in a pre-war crisis. All normal broadcasting, including BBC and commercial television, would stop and the channels would start advertising the new frequencies for the WTBS. After an hour the WTBS would take over with one national radio programme, containing emergency advice and information originating from

Wood Norton. In addition studios were constructed in the regional civil and military bunkers which were linked to the local transmitters in order that regional commissioners could opt-out to broadcast local messages.

The text of a WTBS information announcement, intended to be broadcast in the first hour after WTBS had been triggered, makes chilling reading, especially if you imagine it being intoned by a traditional formal BBC voice: 'Here is an important announcement about the broadcasts you will be able to hear after (time). At (time). all normal radio and television services of the BBC and IBA will cease. They will be replaced by a new single radio service known as the Wartime Broadcasting Service. We will give you details of the new service, and the wavelengths and frequencies you should tune to, in a few moments. Please have a pencil and paper ready to take down this information.'

The national broadcasting system, particularly radio which could continue to be received after mains supplies and televisions had ceased to operate, was central to the government's plans for controlling the civilian population in the event of any major upheaval. Evidence of how tightly successive post-war governments had tried to restrict access to the airwaves was provided in August 1985 when *The Observer* published details of the secret system used by the BBC since 1937 to vet potential employees. The system meant that all new recruits, not only to news and current affairs posts but also film editors, directors, producers and graduate trainees in radio and television, were vetted by MI5 before being offered a position. A 'security liaison officer' on the first floor of Broadcasting House submitted the names of the job applicants directly to C Branch of MI5. They were then passed on to the F Branch 'domestic subversion', whose F7 section looked at political extremists, MP's, lawyers, teachers and journalists. MI5's conclusions were passed to the BBC's Personnel Department.

If MI5 said a person was a security risk that could be enough to blacklist them from working in broadcasting for ever. Others, who perhaps were on record as having attended a protest meeting, once had a subscription to the *Daily Worker,* or had friends who were CND activists or communist party members, had their personnel files stamped with a symbol that today would be seen as looking like the graphic on an extra fast-forward button, three connected triangles in a row, then described as a Christmas tree. A head of department wanting to employ someone with a 'Christmas tree file' had to review the intelligence supplied by MI5 before giving them a position. If going ahead with the job offer they might be required to keep the applicant away from sensitive areas or subjects.

When I left the BBC to join one of the first wave of legal commercial radio stations in 1974 I had an 'exit interview' with the head of personnel. I had no idea of its significance at the time but I was fascinated by the symbol stamped at an angle on the front of the buff folder containing all my employment records. It was only when reading the *Observer* article years later that its meaning became clear. I had been a student at Essex University during the disruptive period of the late sixties/early seventies and had been a member of the Students Council. I had also attended a couple of protest marches including an anti-Northern Ireland internment rally. As far as I was aware I had done nothing to draw myself to the attention of the authorities or Special Branch but, apparently, I'd done enough to earn myself a Christmas tree.

After the *Observer* story revealed that an MI5 man was working at the heart of the BBC the official line was that it was simply related to the BBC's contingency plans for a wartime and emergency broadcasting service. The BBC claimed that only a few members of staff, who would be involved in sensitive areas or would require access to classified information went through the vetting procedure. In fact it had become common practice to put all graduate trainees through 'the formalities' in order to decide where they might, or might not, be deployed in the future. In my case I was never asked to work on those aspects of the World Service where the Official Secrets Act was known to be invoked.

The system was of course absurd and cumbersome. As early as 1939 the BBC director general complained of 'the failure of MI5 to okay our artists at reasonable speed.' Among big names known to have been falsely flagged by the system were folk singer Ewan MacColl, actor Michael Redgrave, film and TV director Roland Joffe, drama producer Kenith Trodd, TV journalist Anna Ford and even future BBC Director General Sir Hugh Greene. Nevertheless the vetting failed to stop the BBC from employing Soviet spy Guy Burgess as a radio producer.

In 2013 veteran radio personality Paul Gambaccini claimed that earlier in his career the BBC had marked his personnel file with a Christmas tree simply because he was gay. He told the *Daily Telegraph*: 'The country was still obsessed with the Cambridge spies. To some people, a gay man was a potential security threat and might betray his country to the Soviet Union. Utter balderdash!'[2]

If it seems implausible, fanciful, that some of the characters in this story could have ever met, let alone worked together in a common cause, we must bear in mind the seismic shifts taking place in society in the 1960s. While it was still the case that most major issues or business deals of any import were sorted out in the smoke-filled rooms of London's gentleman's clubs, changing social attitudes and more permissive laws were encouraging contact between the classes which might have been unthinkable twenty years earlier.

One example was the legalisation of betting shops and gambling. Anyone who grew up in the east end of London in the middle of the twentieth century knew exactly how to place a bet on a horse race. Newspaper vendors and other traders would take the bet which would be transferred in a locked and ingeniously timed box by a 'bookies runner' back to the base of an illegal bookmaker. Many of these characters remain well-known names above betting shops on the high-street or online today.

And, of course, if you were upper class and knew the right people there were always opportunities for more hard-core gambling. Famously, in the late 1950's John Aspinall had organised gambling parties for society's elite in Belgravia and Mayfair.

In his book describing a gambling scam involving Aspinall, Douglas Thompson writes: 'England was coming out of its post-war gloom and London was fast becoming the most exciting and glamorous city in the world, the upper classes had unlimited amounts of money to squander and there were opportunities for chancers at every level.' [3]

Throughout the late fifties into the sixties, Aspinall's gaming tables hosted top society figures including well-known names ranging from Ian Fleming and Lucian Freud to Lords 'Lucky' Lucan, Derby, Boothby and the Duke of Devonshire. The stakes were high. There were games where the standard bet was £1,000 (more like £25,000 in today's money) During the course of one evening one Lord was reputed to have lost £300,000 (the equivalent of almost £7 million today).

These were the places where those responsible for setting and enforcing Britain's laws came into contact with others who, in business or the underworld, were keen to subvert the same laws to make a fast profit. The now infamous London gangsters Reggie and Ronnie Kray built their empire on income from 'protecting' these upmarket illegal gambling parties.[4]

In May 1961 a new Betting and Gaming Act allowed betting shops to open for business and relaxed some of the rules on other types of betting. Over the next five years around a thousand casinos opened. Loopholes in the law allowed almost anyone to open a casino and as a result, many of the them became a cover for criminal activity.[5]

When, in 1962, John Aspinall opened the Clermont Club at 44 Berkeley Square in Mayfair, the club's original members list read included five dukes, five marquesses, twenty earls and two cabinet ministers. It also attracted a certain kind of right wing businessmen with a mission which might today be defined as to 'Make Britain Great Again', these included the likes of Jimmy Goldsmith, Tiny Rowland, Jim Slater and David Sterling who would, according to Decca Aitkenhead: 'gamble wildly in gracious rooms and plan business schemes to bring them the wealth and power they imagined they deserved'.[6]

Reggie and Ronnie Kray quickly took advantage of the new law and acquired a posh Knightsbridge nightclub called Esmerelda's Barn (as part of a crooked deal with slum landlord Peter Rachman). They converted it into a gambling club which attracted many of the same influential people who had frequented Aspinall's, with the addition of the Krays underworld contacts and a procession of A-list celebrities.

Interestingly, when John Aspinall later opened a casino under his own name it was based at 27-28 Curzon Street, a little patch of Mayfair just off Park Lane which will feature regularly in this story.

Perhaps nothing represents the change in British attitudes to those in power more than the late Saturday night BBC TV programme *That Was the Week That Was.* A live satirical show which ran during 1962 and 1963, it was presented by David Frost and devised, produced and directed by Ned Sherrin. The programme thought nothing of naming names and mocking the pomposity and hypocrisy of those in powerful positions

It was very different to anything before seen on British television and with hindsight the BBC was remarkably brave to broadcast it. The programme not only mercilessly lampooned previously respected establishment and political figures including, notably, the prime minister Harold Macmillan, but it broke most of the then conventions of broadcast television. Director Ned Sherrin made no attempt to hide cameras, lighting, microphone booms and the backstage crew. The bare studio walls were frequently visible, giving the show a fresh, modern and exciting feel. Although still a child, I was allowed to stay up to watch it and can still feel the excitement that anything could happen, from the opening bars of Millicent Martin's signature tune, with topical lyrics each week, through to the end (which happened whenever the cast and crew had run out of material). This was spontaneous, irreverent, open-ended live television which regularly attracted an audience of twelve million.

Unexpectedly the programme was gifted a rich seam of material when the conservative secretary of state for war was forced to resign from the government and from parliament after lying to the House of Commons over his involvement with 19 year-old would-be model Christine Keeler.

The 'Profumo affair' centred on a brief sexual relationship in 1961 between John Profumo, and Christine Keeler. Public interest was heightened by reports that Keeler may have been simultaneously involved with Captain Yevgeny Ivanov, a Soviet naval attaché, thereby creating a possible security risk. Keeler knew both Profumo and Ivanov through Stephen Ward, an osteopath and socialite, and the exposure of the affair generated rumours of other scandals and drew official attention to the activities of Ward, who was charged with a series of immorality offences. Reasonably feeling that he was being used as a scapegoat to distract attention from other figures in high places, Stephen Ward took a fatal overdose during the final stages of his trial, which found him guilty of living off the immoral earnings of Keeler and her friend Mandy Rice-Davies.

Press coverage of the Profumo affair highlighted both the hypocritical attitudes of parts of Britain's elite and their ability to mix seamlessly with the more unsavoury sections of society when it suited their purposes.

Soon another scandal was to highlight how members of the establishment were able to close ranks to defend their interests across distinctions of class or politics.

In July 1964 the *Sunday Mirror* ran a front page story under the headline 'Peer and a Gangster: Yard Probe'. The paper had been tipped off that Scotland Yard had virtually completed an investigation into a homosexual relationship between a peer 'who is a household name' and a notorious London gangster 'involved in West End protection rackets'. The *Sunday Mirror* did not name names but it was widely understood in high places that the peer in question was Lord Robert Boothby, the former Conservative MP for East Aberdeenshire and a familiar television celebrity, and that the gangster was Ronnie Kray.

The following week, the *Sunday Mirror* repeated the story with more detail adding that it had in its possession photograph of the gangster and the peer taken at the peer's Mayfair flat. This second article effectively identified Lord Boothby and by now copies of the photograph, showing Ronnie Kray sitting with the lord on the sofa in Boothby's Eaton Square flat, were circulating widely in Fleet Street and Westminster. In much the way that today's super-injunctions have no effect overseas, on the continent the identities of the two were being published, as usual it was only the British public who had to be protected from such revelations about their superiors.

Surprisingly, Tory Robert Boothby's reputation was spectacularly rescued by two major Labour Party figures. The Labour Party was just weeks away from fighting a general election but their leader Harold Wilson rushed to the aid of the lord, encouraging the prominent lawyer Arnold Goodman and respected QC Gerald Gardiner to represent Boothby in a libel case against the *Sunday Mirror*. Gardiner was later rewarded with the post of Lord Chancellor and Arnold Goodman soon received his peerage. The reasons for the incredible closing of political ranks did not become fully clear until the release of cabinet papers under the thirty-year rule in 1995. It emerged that left-wing journalist Tom Driberg, one of Wilson's closest allies who would go on to become chairman of the Labour Party, had also been compromised in his relationships with the Krays and Boothby. Homosexual acts between men were illegal in the UK until 1967.

With the establishment now in full cover-up mode, Lord Boothby publicly denied having any kind of close relationship with Ronnie Kray, he launched a libel action against the *Sunday Mirror*. The Metropolitan Police Commissioner, Sir Joseph Simpson, denied that there had been any investigation. The *Sunday Mirror's* sources suddenly did not wish to give the paper any more information and the paper therefore had little evidence to support its story.

Plainly the authorities did not want to see the case go to court, a parade of witnesses discussing Boothby's private life and whether he had ever met with the Krays would not have been helpful, and therefore Goodman concentrated on getting an apology and retraction from the newspaper. The law of libel to this day creates a rare situation where it falls on the accused to prove his innocence, the publisher must produce hard evidence to support any suggestion of wrongdoing. With Goodman's political allies and opponents, the police, security services and the criminal underworld united in a cover-up the paper was in an impossible situation. The *Sunday Mirror* had to agree to settle out-of-court and, publishing a front page apology, paid Lord Boothby then unprecedented damages of £40,000 (more like a million in today's money).

As a result the story of Boothby and the Krays was buried and many people in powerful positions needed it to stay that way, otherwise they would be implicated in a cover-up which could, if revealed, do them greater damage than the original accusation would have done. An unexpected consequence was to make the Kray twins seem untouchable, suddenly less troubled by the police or press and able to call in favours from the likes of Boothby whenever they were in a sticky situation. A couple of years later Reggie Kray still felt able to tell the owner of a pirate radio station that he had enough influence over the government to prevent any legal action against them.

If the more liberal political, social and cultural climate was preparing the ground for a big change in radio broadcasting so too was a kind of liberalisation of radio technology. This was the point in time where the transistor was first starting to take over from the radio valve (vacuum tube for US readers).

In the nineteen fifties and early sixties war surplus shops sprang up all over the country, selling massive amounts of army, navy and airforce equipment which had been stockpiled at the end of the war and was now being sold off by the government. There were streets in London, notably Tottenham Court Road and Edgware Road, where traders specialised in surplus electronic equipment and components. The navy and air force had been dependent on directional beacon transmitters many of which operated on or around medium wave frequencies. The navy also used frequencies just above medium wave for ship-to-shore communication. It was possible in an afternoon to buy everything you would need to put together a quite powerful medium wave transmitter. I did and was later prosecuted for it. So it's no surprise that all the entrepreneurs who set up stations cheaply on the abandoned wartime forts in the Thames estuary started out using such war surplus gear, modified for the new purpose.

The better funded ship-based stations used professional broadcast transmitters imported from the USA but these, like the modified military gear, used valves throughout – those seductively glowing glass tubes filled only with metalwork in a vacuum.

This was the technology found in almost every British home in the 1950s. The radio set was either a large mains powered stand-alone device housed in an ornate wood or Bakelite cabinet or, increasingly, formed part of an early incarnation of the media centre – the radiogram. The dials of these radios were adorned with the names of potentially receivable stations, beyond the BBC Home Service, Light, Regional and Third Programmes the other stations were identified by their home city – an illuminated glass dial engraved with exotic locations ranging from Paris and Luxembourg, Hilversum and Athlone, to Warsaw and Reykjavik. The contraption required the attachment of a wire antenna, the longer and higher the better to receive any of those foreign stations, and it needed to warm up before use.

While such cumbersome and inflexible valve based equipment was not really a problem at a fixed transmitting station, or even when properly installed on a ship (indeed many high power broadcast transmitters to this day still use valves) the old mains powered radio set in the lounge, with all its connotations of being controlled by a pipe-smoking father figure as the family sat around 'listening-in', was not really conducive to the wind of change about to sweep through the media.

The typical portable valve radio of the fifties was no better, about the size and weight of a lunchbox, and contained one or more torch batteries to heat the valve filaments and a heavy high voltage battery to power the signal circuits. If you were lucky the batteries would last for a few hours.

Just in time for the swinging sixties, radio receiving technology was about to take its own radical leap forward. The transistor had been invented in the USA in 1947 by a team led by William Shockley at Bell Laboratories. The goal was to replace the bulky, inefficient and unreliable valves with something much smaller using solid-state technology. Wartime work on electronic computers - including the Colossus used by Alan Turing to break German codes at Bletchley Park during the second world war – showed that they needed literally thousands of power-hungry valves. Those attempting to create the first commercial electronic computers after the war desperately needed an alternative.

The earliest mass-market broadcast radio receivers had been known as crystal sets. With no amplification they were barely capable of translating a strong AM radio signal into enough audio energy to power a pair of headphones. The circuit was based on a thin adjustable wire that lightly touched a crystal of appropriate mineral (usually galena) and which passed electric current in one direction but not the other – hence 'semi-conductor'. The early transistor was similarly constructed from a crystal of germanium, but with two gold point contacts touching the surface. This developed into a bi-polar transistor which was capable of mass production. While radio receivers using the new technology had already been demonstrated in the early 1950s it wasn't until Texas Instruments introduced the TR1 in November 1954 that the first mass-produced transistor radio was sold in any significant numbers. Using only four expensive transistors (one as a mixer-oscillator, two as intermediate-frequency amplifiers and one as an audio amplifier) the quality of reception was not great although the style and size of the pocket-sized radio was attractive. The radio was not cheap however, retailing at around 50 dollars.

In 1957 a small Japanese company, the Tokyo Telecommunications Engineering Corporation, introduced an improved six-transistor radio under their new brand name, Sony. The TR63 was smaller than the Regency TR1 and, with inspired marketing, recognising that this was to become a style icon, it was available in four colours: lemon, green, red, and black. The company produced its own transistors and miniature components and, because the radio needed a new battery design to produce the ideal voltage, started using the still-familiar PP3 nine-volt battery. With six transistors to play with - the extra two providing push-pull output to the tiny loudspeaker – the audio was higher quality and, importantly, much louder. The circuit became the basic standard for the next ten years or so.

Listeners learned that, although the cheap radios were not very sensitive or selective, the internal ferrite-rod aerial was very directional and rotating the set could improve reception of weaker signals considerably. The high resonant frequency of a small speaker in a thin plastic box gave the radios a characteristic tinny sound and, although most included an earphone jack and a cheap single earpiece, the favoured solution amongst teenagers was to hold the entire radio directly against the side of the head, with the speaker pressed tightly against the ear.

Following the huge success of the Sony pocket-sized radio other manufacturers, particularly in the far east, started flooding the market with their own versions. By the time the first pirate stations opened in the UK the typical price for an imported pocket-sized AM only radio had dropped to around £10 to £14 (and by the end of the decade was down to around a quarter of that). While this represented a lot of cash in the early 1960s, equivalent to hundreds of pounds today, I suppose the personal radio was the equivalent of a smart-phone now. It was certainly at the top of most teenagers' Christmas lists.

Just as in today's digital age the real advances in media come about when compatible advances in hardware and software coincide. So, as the Beatles *Please Please Me* was replacing Frank Ifield's *The Wayward Wind* at number one, a new kind of radio listening was becoming readily available to a wide public.

CHAPTER TWO

THE VOICE OF AMERICA

In 1952, amid great secrecy, a 338 foot US Coastguard cutter was fitted out with broadcast transmitters and sailed across the Atlantic. Positioned off the coast of Greece, for ten hours each day the station beamed programmes from the Voice of America in 16 languages into communist eastern Europe and the Middle East.

The ship, the USCGC Courier, was very well equipped with a high power 150 kW RCA medium wave transmitter and two Collins 207B 35 kW shortwave transmitters. Above the deck a range of sophisticated antennas enabled the ship to broadcast on a wide range of frequencies. In addition the station could launch an antenna almost one thousand feet above the ship using a barrage balloon filled with 150,000 cubic feet of helium. However the Courier did not boast proper studio facilities, in common with other Voice of America stations programmes were originated in Washington DC and sent out by shortwave radio links or were pre-recorded on tape.

Originally it was planned to deploy seven similar ships around the world, able to move to an international hot-spot and begin putting out the American view of world events within a matter of hours, mainly to counter Soviet cold-war propaganda. It is thought that work on others commenced but only the Courier was put into service in Europe.

In 1958, taking inspiration from the Courier, and well ahead of its time, a small Scandinavian fishing boat was converted to broadcast on the FM band. Radio Mercur started broadcasting on 93.1 MHz from the Danish-owned Cheetah anchored outside territorial waters between Stockholm and Malmo. Despite the more limited range of FM signals the station put a decent signal into parts of Sweden and later in the year, when the transmitter power was increased, the frequency was changed to 89.5 Mhz to avoid interference to an existing Swedish station.

Programmes were pre-recorded in Copenhagen and broadcast between 6am and midnight daily. Later the Cheetah also began to broadcast in Swedish under the name Skånes Radio Mercur using airtime leased from the Danish company. Much like the position in the UK at that time, Swedish state radio was limited to broadcasting 'pop' music for one hour per day so the non-stop music on Mercur was a huge success.

At the start of 1961 Radio Mercur acquired a larger radio ship and named it Cheetah II. With space for two transmitters it was able to broadcast simultaneously in Danish (on 88 MHz) and Swedish (on 89.5 MHz). Previously known as the Mosken the larger ship had been built in Norway in 1924 and used as a ferry between the Norwegian fjords and islands.

The original Radio Mercur ship, Cheetah I, went to Norway for repairs and improvements to its radio facilities and was sold to Britt Wadner who used it to launch another Swedish offshore station called Radio Syd.

By 1962 all the Scandinavian governments had passed laws to outlaw their offshore stations. The Danish authorities took immediate action and sent police out to seize the vessel and Radio Mercur duly closed down. Britt Wadner then bought the Cheeta II to replace her original ship.

While now being outside the law and despite the prosecution of a number of advertisers Radio Syd managed to stay on the air until January 1966. Although Britt Wadner had spent some time in prison the eventual closure was as much to do with the extreme freezing Baltic weather as the Swedish anti-pirate laws.

Meanwhile in 1959 a project which became known as Radio Veronica had also been converting a vessel, the ex-German lightship MV Borkum Riff, for radio broadcasting. The station name, Veronica, came from the original project title VRON which stood for 'Vrije Radio Omroep Nederland' or Free Radio Broadcaster Netherlands. 'Free Radio' was within a few years to become the accepted description, among their supporters, for offshore pirate stations Europe-wide.

In April 1960 Radio Veronica began test transmissions on 185 metres from a position in international waters three and a half miles off the Dutch coast. Wasting no time, and suggesting the frequency off the high end of the medium wave band was interfering with shipping signals, the Dutch authorities started jamming the signal by broadcasting noise on the same channel. The wavelength was switched to 182 metres, which was worse, and then to 192 metres – which became Radio Veronica's permanent home.

Programmes were pre-recorded in Hilversum and sent out to the ship on the twice-weekly supply tender. Hourly news and weather bulletins were broadcast live from the ship. The shows were mainly pop music with some specialist oldies, jazz and country & western programmes. A 10 kW transmitter put a strong signal into the Netherlands but the station could also be heard across part of Belgium and on the east coast of England.

Despite all this home-grown offshore radio activity, back in the summer of 1960 a shadowy group of American businessmen had arranged for a pair of brand new broadcast transmitters to be dismantled into some six thousand separate parts and secretly shipped to Denmark.

Their brainchild, Radio Nord, broadcast for little over a year between March 1961 and June 1962 from an American owned and operated ship anchored in international waters off Stockholm, Sweden.

One of the leading figures in the consortium was Gordon McLendon, the radio friend of Jack Ruby, the murderer of Kennedy's alleged assassin. Despite his politics McLendon has always been something of a hero-figure to radio anoraks. He is generally considered to be the man who brought strictly formatted radio to the mass market, an innovative radio programmer who perfected the Top 40 radio sound. Born in 1921 he attended school and a Military Academy in Atlanta, Texas before going on to make his mark at Yale. During the second world war he was commissioned as an intelligence officer in the Office of Naval Inteligence.

According to radio folk-lore at the age of 25 McLendon purchased local station KNET, the following year moving to Dallas and launching KLIF. Unable to afford the rights to audience-winning live baseball coverage he made a name for himself by recreating the games using sound effects and wire copy. So successful was this strategy that within a few years his reports were heard on over 400 stations in his Liberty Broadcasting System network.

Top 40 radio was the brainchild of Todd Storz, owner of radio station KOWH in Omaha, Nebraska. According to the commonly-told story Storz noticed that juke-box users in a local café selected a relatively small number of songs very regularly, so he decided to play only the top current songs on his station in heavy rotation. After buying WTIX in New Orleans he produced the first proper Top 40 sequence in around 1953. This is the format regarded as having been perfected by Gordon McLendon at KLIF in Dallas and which was imported to the UK with the early pirates.

While taking nothing away from Storz and his programming genius, in reality the now familiar format had a rather longer gestation. Since the 1940s many smaller independent radio stations had been broadcasting a format of 'music and news' – essentially a disc-jockey programme interspersed with regular news reports. Storz developed Top 40 radio from this cheap and popular model by defining explicit rules for the selection of the music played on KOWH as early as 1949. Over the next four years his stations refined the format, removing any non-pop material which had previously been included to broaden the audience appeal and choosing a 'best' recording of a hit song rather than playing various cover versions. In 1956 the Storz stations introduced the first truly limited playlist, guaranteeing that the most popular songs were heard most often.[1]

Strict music selection was important to the format. Previously disc-jockeys had, within reason, made their own choice of music. Now a programme director aimed for a single, coherent 'station sound'. This required central selection and scheduling of the records and attention to the choice and presentation of other programme features. To this day new radio programmers are told that a successful radio format requires that the size of the universe of available songs is greatly reduced. While this conflicts with the oft-quoted desire of the audience for a greater variety of music the experience of a great many radio services over half a century is compelling.

Management control of the station playlist also put a stop to the informal 'payola' scandals in which prominent disc-jockeys were known to have taken cash from record companies in return for plugging particular songs.

Gordon McLendon is also widely credited with having established the first mobile news units in American radio, the first traffic reports, the first jingles, the first all-news radio station, and the first 'beautiful music' programming (at KABL Oakland, California in 1959). He also was among the first broadcasters in the United States to permit the transmission of editorial opinions. McLendon especially attracted attention for his criticism of French president Charles De Gaulle. His stations also aired an influential political radio show financed by a well-connected Texan oil billionaire Haroldson Lafayette Hunt who had made his fortune in the early 1930s by getting hold of one of the biggest oil fields in America. The programme, *Life Line*, aired strongly conservative anti-communist views and among its contributors was Dallas nightclub owner Jack Ruby.

In 1959 McLendon had formed a company with other Texas broadcasting and political interests to invest in a radio ship to broadcast to Sweden. Key among his supporters was Clint Murchison Jr, who early in 1960 had used his family's oil fortunes to found the Dallas Cowboys football team and to promote US political interests. Murchison and McLendon remained in the shadows and allowed Murchison's long-time friend Robert F Thompson to take credit for actual ownership of the station while day-to-day management was vested in Swedish/Finnish movie executive Jack Kotschack.

Why these successful and shrewd Americans should want to sink money into such a venture is bewildering. If they wanted to open up a new market in Europe for American-style commercial radio why pick Sweden, with its relatively small population and tiny advertising market already served by another station? Why not anchor of the coast of France, Italy, Germany or the UK and reach a far bigger audience in a more widely spoken language?

By May 1960 the hold of the former cargo vessel MV Olga had been expensively converted to create studios, a transmitter room and additional crew quarters at the Norder Werft shipyard in Hamburg, West Germany. The ship was renamed Bon Jour and sailed to Copenhagen where the pair of 10 kW LTV-Continental Electronics transmitters were re-assembled and installed and a 125-foot aerial mast fitted.

After several months of technical problems due to storm damage Bon Jour anchored near Stockholm and began test transmissions on on 7 February 1961. Radio Nord started broadcasting fully from her intended anchorage on 21 February.

Within days the Swedish parliament passed legislation permitting their authorities to confiscate the broadcasting equipment should the Bon Jour return to a Swedish port. Around the same time the Swedes were also pressing Nicaragua to withdraw the ships registration. The ship was leased by a company called Nord Establishments of Liechtenstein, a company financed by Clint Murchison, and was registered under the Nicaraguan flag because Murchison was a close personal friend of the dictator Anastasio Somoza whose family ruled Nicaragua. Without a flag to sail under any ship at sea is open to being seized by any nation so, to be on the safe side, the Texan owners changed her name to MV Magna Maria and registered her in Panama.

A small nation of just three million, Panama has the largest shipping fleet in the world, greater than those of the US and China combined. The vast majority of ships flying Panama's flag belong to foreign owners wishing to avoid the stricter marine regulations imposed by their own countries. The 'flag of convenience' offers the ability to employ cheaper foreign labour and to pay no income taxes. Among the first ships transferred to Panama's register were two US passenger ships wishing to serve alcohol to passengers during Prohibition in 1922.

In what was later to become a standard model Radio Nord was owned and operated by a series of front companies. The ship itself was owned by The Superior Shipping Co. (registered in Managua, Nicaragua) while Nord Establishment (registered in Vadez, Liechtenstein) leased the ship, engaged the marine crew and technicians, was responsible for transmitting the station and received all advertising income. Meanwhile a separate company, Radio Reklam Productions AB (registered in Sweden), sold airtime on the station and was also responsible for the actual production of programmes, the hire of on-air staff and radio technicians.[2]

As with the earlier Voice of America ship the programmes were generally pre-recorded on land, and were delivered to the ship by tender, or were dropped near the ship from light aircraft in waterproof containers.

Although ostensibly broadcasting to southern Sweden (so why call it Radio Nord?) the ship's signal was sufficiently powerful to be heard as far away as Leningrad, Finland, Estonia, northern Poland and East Germany. It is now clear that the chosen location in the Baltic Sea was ideal for reaching an audience behind the Iron Curtain. It seems likely that the rapid action by the Swedish government thwarted the original intention for the ship to become an apparently privately funded operation broadcasting propaganda to Eastern Europe.

When the Swedish government introduced a further law outlawing offshore broadcasts Radio Nord closed down and in July 1962 the Magna Maria sailed to Spain for repairs and then, after a brief spell in the North Sea, to Galveston in Texas. We'll hear more of her later under her next name, the Mi Amigo.

Meanwhile back in the states a company called the Gibraltar Steamship Company (which did not own any steamships and whose president was Thomas Dudley Cabot, formerly the US Department of State's director of the Office of International Security Affairs) was inspired to set up a commercial radio station on a small island off Honduras which had been claimed by the CIA on behalf of the USA.

The station, named Radio Swan after the Swan islands on which it was based, acted like any other commercial broadcaster, broadcasting in Spanish with music, news and sponsorship from major advertisers such as Kleenex and Phillip Morris. The real target audience was not, of course, the tiny indigenous population of Swan Islands (in 2014 the population numbered ten people), nor of Honduras, who claimed the islands were theirs anyway, but the much larger prize of the nearby island of Cuba.

A 50 kW AM transmitter was brought to the island by the US Navy in 1960 from its previous posting to Radio Free Europe. It was joined by a 7.5 kW shortwave transmitter. The programmes, on 1160 kHz AM and 6000 kHz shortwave included airtime purchased by anti-Castro political groups in the USA. One of the largest programme sponsors was the Radio Church of God whose *The World Tomorrow* programme presented by Herbert W Armstrong appeared every weekend. As we will see later T*he World*

Tomorrow was carried by many other stations around the world who appeared to have a connection with the CIA.

In April 1961 the real purpose of the station became clear - it had been intended to help in the aftermath of a US invasion of Cuba. During the period immediately prior to and during the abortive landings at the Bay of Pigs the station switched to an all-news format including obvious coded messages. The station even described itself as 'assisting those who are fighting Castro within Cuba'.

The station was removed from the islands in the late 1960s and its main transmitter was whisked away for use in the Vietnam War.

Please do not infer from anything in this book that I wish to question the motives of the majority of people who worked on or for the later UK offshore stations in the sixties. Most did it for perfectly sound reasons and many for the best of motives – they wanted to have fun making great radio. As they were clandestine operations anyway it is not really surprising that it is hard to pin down details of the CIA's connections with the pirate stations. Most of their projects were undertaken through a series of front companies and organisations, some established for other purposes many years before. It is entirely plausible that even some of those individuals directly involved were not in a position to see the full picture.

What we do know is that from the early 1950s the CIA sponsored a so-called 'grey' broadcasting programme under which apparently commercially-funded radio stations around the world radiated material suiting American interests.

The colour coding is revealing. 'White' stations were those that operated legally and openly and identify themselves for what they were – the Voice of America, say, or Radio Moscow, or the BBC World Service. 'Black' stations were defined as 'broadcasts by one side that are disguised as broadcasts by another'. They came into prominence during the second world war when, for example, a British transmitter would mimic the style of a German station, even taking over the same frequency when the service shut down during an air raid, and include subtle items designed to sow doubt and dissent among the unaware German listeners. Their 'grey' broadcasts were far more subtle, ranging from whole clandestine stations allegedly operated by dissident groups in areas unfriendly to the USA to individual programme items planted in western-style stations intended to gather wide audiences for an American view of the world.[3]

As a flexible grey broadcasting programme required a quick response in new trouble spots around the world, the lengthy and costly process of installing transmitters and programme links (in 1960 the CIA was told it could take a year and two million dollars to set up a high power broadcasting station to cover the Caribbean area) was unacceptable. The obvious solution was to build up a fleet of ready-made broadcasting ships that could be swiftly deployed around the globe. But, to fit the grey philosophy, these had to appear to be owned and operated by independent private concerns.[4]

Given the doctrine of matched force prevalent during the Cold War years it would be very surprising if the communist countries of the Soviet bloc had not operated a similar policy. That's for a later chapter.

CHAPTER THREE

THE VOICE OF SLOUGH

It is often forgotten that the BBC started life as a commercial radio operation. At the end of the first world war British 'radio hams' started demanding opportunities to restart wireless activities, and the companies manufacturing early radio sets were keen to provide programmes for the public to receive on their new devices, much like the manufacturer of a games console today needing to ensure a supply of suitable software to play on it. In 1920 the postmaster general issued a transmitting licence to the Marconi company factory in Chlemsford, Essex. Station MZX was allowed to use a ten-watt transmitter to broadcast for no more than thirty minutes per day. Soon the London Marconi station 2LO was broadcasting live music during the evening hours and other stations were also coming on air. By 1922 the General Post Office (GPO) had issued another license to Marconi to operate station 2MT – announcing itself on-air phonetically as 'Two Emma Tock' - from the Marconi factory research facility in the Essex village of Writtle. However all the other manufacturers wanted to operate their own stations, as did other interested bodies, and by 1922, the GPO had received nearly one hundred applications for broadcast transmitting licences. Anxious to avoid the same chaotic expansion experienced in the United States – where the unregulated airwaves were full of interference from competing stations - the GPO proposed that it would issue a single broadcasting licence to a company jointly owned by a consortium of leading wireless receiver manufactures. To be known as the British Broadcasting Company Limited the company was to be financed by a royalty on the sale of wireless receiving sets from approved manufacturers.

    The British Broadcasting Company was formed by combined interests of Marconi's Wireless Telegraph Company; British Thomson Houston Company; General Electric Company; Western Electric Company; and Burndept Ltd. (representing the interests of 28 smaller companies). By the end of 1922 there were permanent BBC stations in London, Birmingham, Manchester and Newcastle. These were initially operated under the companies' existing licences, the BBC itself received its first formal broadcasting licence from postmaster general Neville Chamberlain in January 1923. During the year further stations opened in Cardiff, Glasgow,

Aberdeen, Bournemouth and Sheffield and some programmes started to be shared between stations using Post Office land-lines.

This pragmatic arrangement seemed to suit everyone, keeping this dangerous new communications medium under government supervision while simultaneously closing the door to the stations being funded by commercial messages as in the USA – an arrangement vigorously opposed by the powerful and influential British newspaper proprietors who did not want to see their advertising revenue becoming diverted to commercial radio stations and which was seen by others as an example of American vulgarity.

The snag was that the British Broadcasting Company financial model did not really work. Quite apart from the fact that radio enthusiasts could avoid the BBC levy by building their own receiver from a kit of parts (hence the term 'radio set' which we still use today) the income from a once-only licence fee was inevitably going to start to dwindle once every home had a radio receiver.

By 1925 the future of broadcasting needed further consideration, wireless manufacturers were anxious to exit the loss making consortium, more money was needed to fund rapid expansion and the BBC was keen be seen as a public service rather than a commercial enterprise. As has happened every few years since the start of the original BBC, a government appointed committee was formed to discuss the issues. The recommendations of the Crawford Committee were published in March the following year and were still under consideration by the GPO when the general strike broke out in May 1926. The strike interrupted newspaper production and the BBC suddenly became the primary source of news for a national audience. As a result the BBC thrived, and the end of the strike was followed by the Government's acceptance of the Crawford recommendation that the British Broadcasting Company be replaced by a non-commercial organisation operating under a Royal Charter: the British Broadcasting Corporation. The BBC in its present form came into existence on 1 January 1927 with a coat of arms including the motto 'Nation shall speak peace unto Nation'.

Throughout the general strike the BBC had been under the command of its original general manager, John Reith, a dour Scottish Calvinist engineer who combined an overbearing paternalism with an astute political sense. The crisis placed the BBC in a delicate position. On one hand Reith was acutely aware that the Government might exercise its right to take over control of the BBC and use it as a mouthpiece of government at any time, but on the other he was anxious to maintain public trust by appearing to be acting impartially and independently.

While the BBC likes to recall its handling of the general strike by emphasising the positive impression created by its balanced coverage, in practice Reith suppressed a number of viewpoints supportive of the strikers. Jean Seaton, professor of media history and the official BBC historian has characterised the episode as the invention of 'modern propaganda in its British form'.[1]

Following the General Strike John Reith was rewarded with a knighthood and was appointed the BBC's first Director General.

From the start John Reith had made no secret of his aspirations for the BBC. In his 1924 book *Broadcast over Britain* he made a clear distinction between giving the public what they wanted and providing them with what he thought they should have. He believed that the BBC had a duty to inform the electorate; that it should halt the secularizing of Sundays - which should be reserved for the official religion of the country, the Church of England; that the BBC should be a 'servant of culture' with no 'vulgar Americanisation' of the airwaves; and that making money should not be the object of broadcasting, it should be a public service.[2]

To this day, the BBC claims to follow the Reithian directive to 'inform, educate and entertain'.

Reviewing progress through 1927 the *BBC Handbook* stated: '...the standard of the everyday programmes of entertainment had risen appreciably – and all this had gone hand in hand with a perfecting of technical resources which had brought efficient and faithful reception within the reach of any one who was normally careful in choosing and maintaining his set'. But the business of listening-in was not to be taken lightly: 'What was still more important was the realisation of the constant growth of a body of listeners who completed the work of the programme-builders by giving to their programmes careful and instructed listening and criticism.'[3]

One practical result of this puritanical approach to broadcasting was that the BBC provided no light entertainment on a Sunday, and no 'jazz' music at any time. The BBC Sunday schedules were overwhelmingly religious, with no entertainment or light music allowed. According to the 1929 *BBC Handbook* despite objections in the press the public found this perfectly acceptable: '...there began a determined and widespread attempt to arouse public opinion to insist upon sweeping changes in Sunday programmes. It was alleged that the religious character of these Sunday programmes was unpopular, and that, on the lowest terms, an "entertainment" alternative should be made available. Careful examination of the problem provided no evidence of any substantial dissatisfaction with existing arrangements. On the contrary, the opinion was confirmed that the services and concerts on Sunday represented the most highly and widely appreciated part of the work of the BBC.'

Of course listeners could receive signals from further away. It is a feature of medium wave frequencies that the signals are deflected by the ionosphere when it is not illuminated by the sun, as a result stations from over the horizon become receivable in the evenings and overnight. Not for the last time the BBC seemed blissfully unaware that listeners were voting with their tuning knobs.

One person who did appreciate what was going on was Captain Leonard Frank Plugge. He was the same age as Reith but his attitude to broadcasting could not have been more different. The businessman and conservative politician realised that radio listeners all over the country were listening to overseas stations rather than the BBC on a Sunday. They might not understand the language but they could enjoy the music. By now there were five million radio receivers in the UK and, seeing a commercial opportunity, Plugge formed the International Broadcasting Company (IBC) and started leasing airtime on foreign transmitters which could be beamed towards the British Isles.

IBC's English language commercial broadcasts began with talks broadcast from Radio Paris using a transmitter on the Eiffel Tower. A typical example was a fashion feature sponsored by a London department store. By the 1930s IBC had built studios and offices in Portland Place directly across the road from the side entrance to the new BBC Broadcasting House and could boast a full schedule via Radio Normandy on the coastline of France and through many other continental transmitters. Playing music banned by the conservative BBC, especially on Sundays, these overseas broadcasts stole a significant proportion of the BBC audience.

Captain Plugge's success at the IBC soon inspired other investors to construct a powerful commercial radio station in Luxembourg with antennas specifically designed to target the British Isles. Using its monopoly powers over communications to the full the GPO refused to allow IBC or Radio Luxembourg to use landline links of the type then being widely used to distribute BBC programmes. The only solution, other than to move the entire production operation overseas, was to record programme items on acetate discs in London and ship them out to the stations. Magnetic tape recording was only to come into general use after the second world war. However Plugge found an ingenious alternative, using the optical soundtrack recorders used for movies, and was thus economically able to fill his schedules with soap operas and entertainment shows pre-recorded in London.

The war brought all this to an end. Radio Luxembourg closed down in September 1939 on the instructions of the government of the Grand Duchy. The IBC transmitter in Normandy continued to operate for some time but was put out of action by the RAF and French troops just before it could fall into the hands of the invading German army.

When the Germans invaded Luxembourg in May 1940 they handed the Radio Luxembourg facilities to the Großdeutscher Rundfunk. The station was also used to reach the British Isles with the famous propaganda broadcasts of William Joyce, popularly known as Lord Haw-Haw.

Luxembourg was liberated by American forces following the D-Day landings in 1944 and the station fell under the control of the US Army. It became 'the voice of the Supreme Headquarters Allied Expeditionary Force' on behalf of America, Britain, France, Belgium and Luxembourg. However in addition to this 'white' broadcasting operation the transmitter also became home to Nachtsender 1212, a black propaganda radio station operated by the Psychological Warfare Branch of the US Office of War Information (OWI). The station claimed to be broadcasting from within Nazi Germany and initially gained a loyal Nazi audience by broadcasting material favourable to the official German world view. But, as allied troops advanced into Germany the station began to include mischievous, misleading or completely untrue stories into its broadcasts, suggesting that support for the Nazis was beginning to crumble.

At the same time the British were beaming a similar black broadcasting station into Germany. Soldatensender Calais masqueraded as an official entertainment service for German troops while undermining German military morale with subtle misinformation.

Captain Plugge's IBC never returned to the air but following the war Radio Luxembourg was handed back to the Grand Duchy and the English-language service attempted to restart transmissions to the United Kingdom as a full-time commercial radio station on the long wave band. Long wave frequencies are able to travel far greater distances in daytime than medium wave signals, following the curvature of the earth. However in post-war Britain advertising revenue was in short supply and the broadcasting hours in English were rapidly reduced.

THE VOICE OF SLOUGH

By 1951 the English programmes of Radio Luxembourg had all been moved from long wave onto the medium wave frequency of 1439 kHz – which became far better known as the wavelength 208 metres. Due to the action of the ionosphere the 208 signal could only be heard reliably in the UK after dark and the English-language programmes typically started after 6pm, although this varied between summer and winter. While the signal was very prone to fading and interference it still offered a welcome alternative to the stuffy BBC content.

A British company, Radio Luxembourg (London) Ltd, controlled the programme content and sold the advertising time but was still not allowed to send the programmes live from its studios in Hertford Street, London. As a result programmes were either disc-jockey style shows presented live by announcers resident in the Grand Duchy or were pre-recorded in London and flown out to the station for transmission.

Perhaps as a result of the need to record separate programmes and the need to have these sponsored, a style of programming evolved based around 15 minute segments. A sponsor would effectively own the programme block and could include not only their commercial message but whatever editorial content they deemed appropriate. Originally this included soap-operas, comedy and variety shows, many hosted by big name presenters who also appeared on the BBC, but these gradually lost their popularity as television, particularly commercial television, spread across the UK in the late 1950s.

By 1963 Radio Luxembourg was almost exclusively targeted at the growing teenage market, listening to pop music on their new transistor radios under the bedclothes at night. The Radio Luxembourg schedules I remember from the early sixties were largely filled with short programmes each sponsored by one of the big record labels, mainly EMI and Decca. Not surprisingly each show featured music from the label's own current catalogue and, in order to pack in as much product as possible, individual songs were usually, and very annoyingly, faded after a minute or two.

Conventional spot advertisements were also carried and one regular advertiser and his home town became national household names purely on the back of his Luxembourg spots. Horace Batchelor promoted his 'Infra-Draw' method of winning money on the football pools in spots he voiced himself, inviting listeners to write for details to a post office box in Keynsham near Bristol. He always took the time to spell out the town name: 'Keynsham – spelt K-E-Y-N-S-H-A-M'.

31

The main reason why we put up with the weak, frequently distorted and fading signal from Luxembourg was the almost total lack of authentic pop music on the BBC services. At this time, the early sixties, there were just three national stations: the Home Service was talk-based (it grew into today's Radio Four); the Third Programme (now Radio Three) was dedicated to serious and classical music and cultural talks; and the Light Programme that had to handle the whole range of entertainment programming for a wide audience. Then, as now, funding from a compulsory licence fee meant that the BBC had to demonstrate that it had something for everybody. It tried to achieve this by putting different styles of music on at different times and on different days. Pop music was perceived as only for young people and it was broadcast mainly in two programmes at the weekend. *Saturday Club*, presented by Brian Matthew, included studio performances by big-name bands and a maximum of eight pop records between 10am and noon each Saturday morning, and on Sunday afternoon there was Alan Freeman's *Pick of the Pops* – an actual top twenty chart show.

At other times if you heard a current pop song on the BBC at all it was probably being performed by one of the BBC's talented, well-meaning but bland house bands rather than being played from the original disc.

The BBC's attitude to playing popular records had its roots in the Reithian principles of its founder. Although John Reith had left the BBC in 1938 his notion that the BBC existed not to give listeners what they wanted but rather what (he thought) they needed still governed most thinking in Broadcasting House. But there was a second, more practical problem with playing 'gramophone records' on the air.

Copyright law generally meant that a broadcaster had to obtain the appropriate rights to a recording before broadcasting it to the public. Following a 1934 High Court ruling, when a Bristol café was successfully sued in a test case by the Gramophone Company for playing records without payment, Phonographic Performance Limited (PPL) was set up by EMI, Decca and most of the other labels to collect 'royalties' on behalf of its members and to pass a proportion of the fees to the musicians who had performed on the records. The public broadcast of recordings also fell under the remit of PPL and the organisation soon entered into copyright negotiations with the BBC.

In the UK broadcasting rights were (and still are) held by the Performing Right Society (PRS), representing songwriters, composers, arrangers and publishers of musical works, PPL representing the performers of recorded music and the record companies, and the Mechanical Copyright Protection

Society (MCPS) who were concerned with preventing the unlicensed copying of recordings. In addition the BBC, as arguably the biggest single employer of musicians in the UK, had established a close relationship with the Musicians Union.

All the copyright bodies believed that unlimited broadcasting of 'gramophone records' would result in a reduction in sales of discs and less employment for live musicians, while the Musicians Union was also concerned to maintain the employment of a large number of musicians and singers in the wide range of BBC orchestras and house bands.

The result was the introduction of what became known as the 'needle time' agreement. This restricted the amount of music the BBC could broadcast from the grooves of publicly-issued records.

From 1935 the BBC was permitted to broadcast just 14 hours a week from records in return for an annual fee of £20,000. By 1959 the allowance had been raised to 28 hours per week for all BBC radio, but this had to be shared across all three networks. Even had the Light Programme been allocated half of this total it would still have been limited to playing an average of two hours – of any kind of music – from records per day.[4] Following the appearance of the offshore pirate stations the needletime limit was increased to 75 hours per week across all stations but, in the early to mid-sixties, the Light Programme schedule was still filled with programmes featuring a BBC house band or orchestra playing an assortment of popular tunes from the second world war onwards.[5]

Even with the launch of Radio One in 1967, and some increase in the amount of needle time allowed, the BBC was required to fill large amounts of its airtime with its own home-grown recordings. These were often promoted as a 'session' specially recorded with the original artists – at least generating a storehouse of priceless live recordings from the great musicians of this era.

As late as 1973 I spent an afternoon working in a small Broadcasting House studio where the legendary pop music producer Mickie Most was attempting to recreate a perfect copy of one of his current hits for broadcast on BBC Radios One and Two. This involved us playing the single repeatedly to compare the sound while bouncing tracks between old-fashioned two-track tape machines and demanding countless re-takes from the bemused musicians. All so the listeners wouldn't know it wasn't the hit single!

Even later, when the first legal commercial stations on the mainland started from 1973 onwards, stations were still limited to playing records for 50% of their airtime with a maximum of 9 hours per day. For this privilege a station could expect to hand over something like 10% of its commercial income to the copyright bodies.

By the late fifties the position of the record companies had already been revealed as rather hypocritical as they were always pushing for greater BBC airplay for their own artists and paying to broadcast their recordings on Radio Luxembourg!

Contrary to the popular belief that pirate radio was the brainchild of Radio Caroline founder Ronan O'Rahilly in 1964, the growing success of the pop music format of Radio Luxembourg and news of the Scandinavian pirate ships stimulated interest in offshore broadcasting to the UK as early as 1960.

1961 saw the announcement of plans for an offshore station aimed squarely at the English listener. A Slough journalist had bought a 65 foot former fishing boat and made some basic modifications, adding diesel generators and so on, to make it the base for a radio transmitter. His idea was to anchor it as close to London as possible but outside territorial waters near the Nore lightship three miles off Southend-on-Sea. The plans kept resurfacing under different names: GBLN, Radio Ellen, Radio LN, or, most bizarrely, The Voice of Slough. Readers who know their London will know that Slough is to the west of London, you would not choose to get there via Southend - and would be even less likely to want to.

The man with the plan, John Thompson, originally came from the UK but had emigrated to Canada becoming a reporter on a local newspaper and eventually a DJ on a Vancouver radio station. His 70 ton ship, the Ellen, was quietly fitted out in Scotland and intended to transmit on 306 metres using an old RCA 1 kW transmitter. Programmes were to be mainly music and news aimed at a young audience and studios were built in two wooden huts in Buckinghamshire to prepare pre-recorded programmes to be taken out to the ship by speedboat.[6]

John Thompson formed a company, The Voice of Slough Ltd., with three other individuals: Canadian millionaire Arnold Swanson as technical advisor, Robert Collier, a wholesale newsagent, as company secretary and a mysterious man called Leon Taylor.

According to press reports at the time advertising would be sold at £3 for 25 words in peak time.[7]

Through mutual contacts the American evangelist Herbert W Armstrong, whose programme *The World Tomorrow* was broadcast on the CIA's Radio Swan, committed to buying large chunks of airtime. Although the station never made it on-air the nightly broadcast of this programme on the Voice of Slough was even advertised in the Radio Church of God's magazine *The Plain Truth*.

The station failed to appear on-air, apart from one test transmission which is generally thought to have originated using the 1 kW transmitter on land in Slough. There seemed to have been issues with HM Customs and the seaworthiness of the Ellen which never made it down from Scotland. Frustrated at the lack of progress Swanson split from Thompson in January 1962 with backing of £100,000 to start his own station GB-OK.

The Amalgamated Broadcasting Company was formed to front the GB-OK project with a registered office at Swanson's home, in Thame, Buckinghamshire. A London office for the Amalgamated Broadcasting Co. was also established at 151 Fleet Street, EC4, but commercial airtime on the planned station was to be sold through another company, Adanac Broadcasting Agency, which also operated from the same two addresses.

Studios were built in a bungalow in the grounds of Swanson's large home, Notley Abbey, which he had recently purchased from Sir Laurence Olivier and Vivien Leigh following their divorce. A glossy sales pack was produced, DJ's were recruited and a second-hand Marconi 5 kW transmitter was purchased. Some test programmes were recorded by DJ Ed Moreno (later to broadcast on Radio Caroline and Radio Invicta).

Swanson knew that the record companies had objected to the Voice of Slough plan to tape their records as part of the programmes taken out to the ship and unsuccessfully tried to reach an agreement with them. Perhaps for this reason the GB-OK publicity mentioned programmes being prepared at studios in Dublin, although whether these really existed is open to question.

The plan was to broadcast on 388 metres from a location just outside territorial waters near the Nore, the same location as had been planned for the Voice of Slough. The sales pack claimed the station would reach a potential audience of eleven million listeners in a 150 mile radius from the south east to the midlands with the new sound of a 24-hour American-style music format with news bulletins at the top of every hour.

As on Radio Luxembourg, commercial sponsors could pay to be associated with segments of the schedule and peak time advertising spots were quoted at £16 for 20 seconds. By March 1962 Arnold Swanson claimed to be making good progress in signing up advertisers and their agencies.

Earlier in the year a 84 year old teak lightship 'Lady Dixon' had been purchased and taken to Pitsea, Essex to be secretly fitted out. The plan was to re-name her 'Bucaneer'. Unfortunately she got stuck in the Essex mud and all attempts to pull her out failed. While she was waiting to be refloated the ship gathered some press attention and soon the Post Office started taking an interest. In March the Lady Dixon was finally freed and towed to Sheerness for more work. What exactly happened next is not clear but it seems that GB-OK fell foul of the terms of Section 1(1) of the Wireless Telegraphy Act 1949 which made it an offence not only operate an unlicensed transmitter but also to install such a device. When it was later reported that she was ready and just needed a tow to the Nore to begin broadcasting the ship was raided by the Post Office and the equipment confiscated.

Swanson had now spent over £15,000 on the project and after the raid decided that the old light vessel was not worth any more investment. Instead he announced that he had bought an old tank landing craft which he intended to fit out as a radio ship at a cost of £30,000. The new craft was to have a stronger transmitter giving the station a projected coverage area as far north as Manchester.[8]

Nothing more was heard of that project but the key players certainly continued working towards setting up a UK offshore radio station. After Radio Nord closed down the American-owned ship – before heading across to Texas - briefly stopped off the Essex coast to broadcast a test transmission as 'Radio LN' on 306 metres. You'll recall that 306 metres was John Thompson's chosen wavelength for The Voice of Slough and that Radio LN was one of his alternative names (Ellen was the name of Thompson's wife). It is thought that this was an attempt to get Thompson and his friends to take an interest in the expensively fitted-out US-backed radio ship. John Thompson appears later in this story as one of the people behind Kent's fort-based station Radio Invicta which also used the same 306 metre wavelength..

Meanwhile during 1960 and 1961 a venture known as CNBC (the Commercial Neutral Broadcasting Company) had leased airtime on the Dutch pirate station Radio Veronica. Broadcasting for a few hours each morning, the station was run by a Canadian disc jockey called Doug Stanley, who had previously worked for the British Forces Network in Germany, while advertising was sold by Ross Radio Productions, a company run by the future Managing Director of Capital Radio, John Whitney, which produced sponsored shows for Radio Luxembourg.

CNBC gained quite a lot of press attention and questions were raised in Parliament. The Labour party was against the commercialisation of broadcasting and asked what the Conservative government would do about it? The Lord Privy Seal, future prime minister Edward Heath, was instructed to contact the Dutch government about trying to stop the station, but the

Dutch radio authorities said that as the ship was outside territorial waters they could do nothing.[9]

At this time Radio Veronica was using a fairly low power transmitter and the small size of the ship would not allow any substantial improvement in power or antenna efficiency. Although the 192 metres signal could be received quite well along the English coast from Margate to Hull it did not penetrate very far inland. While CNBC – 'Your friendly host off the Dutch coast' - lasted for less than a year it, and of course the evocatively titled Voice of Slough, formed the basis for a lot of what was to follow

CNBC Programmes were originally recorded on land in the Netherlands and taken to the ship via the nearby port of Scheveningen but the plan was to record shows in a studio at their headquarters in central London for shipment out to the Borkum Riff. The offices were at Royalty House in Dean Street, since 1995 the home of the trendy 'Soho House', a well-known private members' club for people in the creative industries. In the sixties Dean Street was a centre of the creative, advertising and film industries and to some extent retains that image today.

Watching all this unfold from the offices of a music empire less than a hundred yards away from the CNBC offices in Dean Street was Allan Crawford. Crawford had been employed in Australia and London by Southern Music Limited at a time when the music business revolved around the sales of sheet music. He left to set up on his own in London, formed the Merit Music publishing company and, seeing the way the music industry was changing, the Crossbow, Rocket and Cannon record labels that featured session musicians imitating the biggest pop hits of the day.

At a time when UK top ten hits were often themselves cover versions by our own acts of the original US recordings Crawford had come up with a good money making scheme. Embassy records had since the mid-fifties offered cheap copies of hit songs through a deal with Woolworth stores, Crawford took the idea further, selling mail order EP discs each with six cover versions of current hits for less than the cost of one original single. (Later Crawford went on to create the *Top of the Pops* series of albums)

Allan Crawford had been showing a great interest in offshore stations since 1960 and was known to be discussing plans with the Texans. Meanwhile, frustrated that he could not get any airplay for his records on the BBC, Crawford arranged for his recordings to be plugged on CNBC.

Crawford was soon to be putting together a much more substantial, viable and famous offshore broadcasting project. The next three years were to see more developments in British radio broadcasting than had been seen in the previous three decades.

A note on frequencies and wavelengths

Although the BBC had started to simulcast its main services on FM in the fifties, the vast majority of radio listening in the sixties was on medium wave, also known as the AM band because the stations all used amplitude modulation - the oldest and most straightforward way to send speech and music over a radio wave. The majority of the new pocket-sized transistor radios flooding the market in the early sixties were only capable of AM medium wave reception.

A well-known complication of medium wave broadcasting is the effect of the earth's ionosphere at night time. During daylight signals on these low frequencies pass straight through the ionosphere and out into space with the result that only stations up to, or a short way beyond, the horizon can be heard. But at night medium wave behaves more like the short wave bands and signals bounce around the globe. Certainly in the UK even the cheapest transistor radio would pick up stations from all over Europe. This was the effect which had made stations like Radio Luxembourg popular before the pirate era.

In practice any radio signal carrying modulation covers a range of frequencies around the nominal 'carrier' frequency and, as with digital technology today, the desired quality of the audio governs the 'bandwidth' required. There was only room for some 120 channels across the medium wave band. Europe now had many times that number of broadcast transmitters and to minimise mutual interference fixed frequencies 9 kHz apart had been allocated by international agreement. The same channel would often be used by a dozen different stations in different countries. There were no empty frequencies and the offshore stations, like squatters, had to find the best location and try to make it their own. Inevitably this meant that some services which were perfectly clear in daytime became unlistenable in the evenings and a generation of listeners armed with transistor radios with built-in ferrite rod antennas became adept at rotating their set to minimise the interfering signals.

At this time radio stations in the UK customarily identified their position on the dial by giving a 'wavelength'. Radio Luxembourg was famously on 208 metres while many older listeners will always identify BBC Radio One with 'two-four-seven'. I guess we should be grateful that our great grandfathers, despite being British, did not choose to give the stations' dial positions in feet and inches. In the USA and elsewhere the AM stations always branded themselves with a frequency measured in thousands of cycles of radio energy per second, kilocycles per second, later simplified to kilohertz or kHz. In the UK VHF FM stations – who would all be on around just three metres – have always been identified with a frequency in megahertz (MHz) just as in the USA.

The relationship between wavelength and frequency is strictly mathematical, governed by the speed of light or, in this case, the speed at which radio waves travel in free space. As light travels at approximately 300 million metres per second we can convert a frequency in kilohertz into a wavelength in metres by simply dividing the figure 300,000 by the frequency in kilohertz. Thus a station broadcasting in the middle of the medium wave dial on 1,000 kHz could equally accurately be described as broadcasting on 300 metres. For example the Voice of Slough on 306 metres (a channel later used by Radio Invicta) would have been using a frequency of 980 kHz.

In this book I have used both types of terminology, generally being guided by how the radio station publicised its own wavelength or frequency. However, as with so much about this era of broadcasting, people were not always telling the exact truth, marketing, or simple poetry, being more important to these buccaneering entrepreneurs than the laws of physics.

Since all radios were tuned by hand (even the push-buttons of some car radios had to be initially set by knob-twiddling) and tuning-dial pointers were hopelessly inaccurate, the wavelengths given by many stations were, to be polite, purely illustrative. For example it was pleasantly alliterative to say 'Radio Caroline on 199' and later 'on 259' even though this did not correspond to the exact frequencies. This was all vaguely absurd as the majority of imported transistor radios had been designed for the American market and were calibrated in kHz, the little tuning dial bearing seemingly irrelevant numbers ranging from 530 to 1600 or often the impenetrable 5 to 16.

For the new radio stations, quite apart from a desire to find a channel relatively free of interference, the choice of transmitting frequency was also influenced by the laws of physics. The optimum length for a basic radio transmitting antenna is a quarter of a wavelength and ideally, to prevent wasted energy going upwards, such an antenna should be vertical. On low frequencies such calculations can make a big difference to antenna design, an optimum antenna at the high frequency end of medium wave band can be a third of the size required at the low end. These calculations suggested that it would be easier to pick frequencies with lower wavelengths. Considering the relative popularity of Radio Luxembourg on 208 metres, nearby channels between 208 and the top end of medium wave at 188 metres seemed attractive. It was no coincidence that the original stations, such as Caroline, Atlanta and Sutch all gravitated to this end of the band.

However in physics you never get anything for nothing and as the need for maximum population coverage became more critical the fact that lower frequencies (longer wavelengths) could give greater daytime range became more significant. The BBC long wave transmitter on 200 kHz (now 198 kHz) used this effect to cover much of northern Europe from a single site. The second-generation stations started to move down the band, with Radio London on 266 metres, Radio City on 299, Britain Radio on 355, and Radio 390.

CHAPTER FOUR

CONS PIRACY

So, by the start of the 1960s there were a number of people showing interest in setting up their own radio stations. The growing interest was mainly driven by one of three things: frustration at being unable to get pop records played on the BBC (especially among bands and managers not signed to the big four, Decca, EMI, Philips or PYE); dislike of the BBC as a concept (mainly among right-wing thinkers, the public corporation model having been copied in the nationalisation of various industries); or frustration at not being able to use British airwaves to promote a different agenda (notably from the Americans who were used to buying their way onto the air elsewhere).

During the second world war many of the brightest young minds of the 1940s had been pressed into service in the top brass of the military and the intelligence services. And these same men (and they were almost all men) were now heading businesses and organisations across the social spectrum. The old-boy network was well established and extended to contacts with our cousins across the Atlantic. These were the peak years for the principle of 'it's not WHAT you know, it's WHO you know.'

One name central to this story is Major William 'Oliver' Smedley. After distinguished service as a paratrooper and gunner in the second world war, winning the Military Cross in the battle for Normandy, Smedley became a Liberal politician and established a large number of campaigning organisations concerned with free trade and a reduction in government control over business, opposing the spread of socialism and central planning.

Major Smedley's organisations included the Cheap Food League (against all types of protection and subsidy in agriculture) and the Council for the Reduction of Taxation. In 1955 he met Antony Fisher and together they founded the Institute of Economic Affairs (IEA), an influential think tank which to this day promotes free market economics.

The orginal Brexiteer, Oliver Smedley resigned from the Liberal Party in 1962 due to their support for Britain joining the European Economic Community and founded the Keep Britain Out campaign. No friend of the state-supported BBC, Smedley was keen that the free market should be extended to broadcasting.

Ironically, Major Smedley who was about to challenge the right of the record companies to limit the broadcast of their product was the son of a director of The Gramophone Company who in 1934 had taken that Bristol café owner to the High Court for playing their records without paying for the privilege.

Meanwhile music mogul Allan Crawford, having experienced the success of Australian commercial radio in his work with Southern Music, had followed the ups and downs of the Scandinavian and Dutch pirate stations with interest and had visited both Radio Nord and Radio Veronica. Crawford met the people behind the stations and took careful note of the legal loopholes through which their stations were able to operate.

One of Crawford's acquaintances was prestigious London theatre figure Dorothy 'Kitty' Black who translated plays by Jean Paul Sartre, Cocteau and Anouilh for performance in London. On a business trip to Denmark she had noticed the excitement caused by Radio Mercur and is credited with suggesting to Crawford the idea of forming a company to establish a British station.

It proved difficult to find sufficient and reliable financial backing however. But then, according to Kitty Black: 'Allan met up with a very interesting man called Oliver Smedley. He'd stood for Parliament as a Liberal candidate and had great financial ideas as to how things should be operated, he was very go-ahead, very open to new ideas and he became fired with enthusiasm for the pirate radio ship operation.'[1]

Years later *The People* published a self-justifying series of articles by Oliver Smedley describing him as 'Britain's No. 1 pop radio pirate'. He recalled that first meeting: 'It was at tea-time in the lofty, palm-fringed rotunda of the Waldorf Hotel in London. It was an appointment with two people I had never met. All I knew was that their names were Kitty Black and Allan Crawford, and that they planned to become the first commercial radio operators in Britain.'[2]

He described himself as a dedicated non-conformer: 'I have always had an overwhelming urge to find perfectly legal ways of doing what the law is designed to prevent. Taxation and exchange control offer opportunities. Commercial radio provided another.' Smedley, who immediately saw pirate radio as a way to promote Friedrich Hayek's theories about the freedom of information and market forces, was keen to help and joined a consortium initially based around a company called CBC (Plays) Ltd owned by Crawford and Black.[2]

Thus it emerges that far from being, as I believed at the time, part of the rebellious sixties counterculture, the pirate stations were funded as a right-wing attempt to establish opportunities for capitalists to operate unencumbered by state regulation.

The IEA, co-founded by Smedley, published a booklet in 1965 that made the position clear. *Competition in Radio* discussed the political theory behind the pirate radio stations and concluded with a section entitled Piracy as a Business Force. The new heroes it said were the 'privateers' who were going to open up the system of information flow - so the market could work efficiently.

In 1964 Smedley said that Radio Atlanta was intended to be 'the last bastion of freedom if the country went Communist.' Major Smedley and his old Liberal and new Tory chums regarded a possible future Labour government under Harold Wilson as dangerously left-wing.

Back in 1962 the consortium had raised some funding and, after an abortive attempt to convert a Scottish lightship, made an offer to buy the Radio Nord ship, now re-named the Mi Amigo. After the repairs in Spain the ship moored in the Thames estuary where it seems to have made a number of test transmissions under different names, presumably to impress potential suitors. As a ready-made radio ship, complete with working transmitters and radio mast, studios, radio crew accommodation and even a record library, the American-owned ship was exactly what was needed. The timing was not ideal however, as already mentioned, in the summer of 1962 the Danish parliament along with the governments of other Scandinavian countries passed laws that effectively prohibited all participation in, and support of, their offshore stations. Radio Mercur was raided by Danish police and closed down.

It has never been clear why the British government didn't immediately follow suit. They were aware of the plans to establish at least one similar station off the UK and could have nipped the idea in the bud. It is understandable that later, once the stations had become popular, governments with slender margins were reluctant to risk the electorate's objections to legislation, but with hindsight few people would have been concerned before they had heard Radio Caroline and the other stations. Nevertheless the possibility that the UK government could act in a similar fashion was enough to scare off many of Allan Crawford's initial investors. Finding no other bidders Gordon McLendon and his buddies ordered the Mi Amigo to sail across to Texas where McLendon removed much of the equipment for use in one of his other radio stations.[3]

Even with Oliver Smedley's input Allan Crawford obviously needed more financial muscle than CBC (Plays). could provide and Project Atlanta Limited was formed in July 1963 to take the scheme to a higher level.[4] The new company was chaired by Major Smedley and, in addition to Crawford and Kitty Black, included on its board establishment money-men like Lloyds underwriter and publisher Major Cecil Lomax, prominent city financier Frank Broadribb and accountant William Wells.[5]

'I came into the picture as "someone in the City" who could organise some capital investment in their scheme.' Smedley told *The People*. At the Waldorf meeting Smedley says he asked about sending money to the proposed overseas company which would own the ship: '"Don't worry," Allan Crawford assured me stoutly, "we have applied to the Bank of England for permission." And four months later the permission was granted – after, so it was rumoured, a cabinet decision.'

'With the permit, I was able to raise the sum of £180,000 among my City friends with relatively little trouble. At the same time I agreed to become chairman of a company we three formed, Project Atlanta.'[6]

Over a hundred shareholders were said to have invested in Project Atlanta. The largest shareholder was CBC (Plays) Ltd, with 36,000 of the 150,000 £1 shares. Kitty Black, Allan Crawford and Oliver Smedley each had their own small personal shareholdings and companies of which Smedley was a director held a further 30,000 shares. Various syndicates held most of the balance and these were said to include such unlikely bedfellows as a group of well-known boxing and wrestling promoters, several Conservative MPs, the Port of London Authority Pension Fund and a group of Trinity House Pilots.

Allan Crawford had now found enough financial backing to get his hands on the Mi Amigo, the former Radio Nord ship now back with her original Texas investors. In an interesting and possibly revealing re-write of history in his 1966 article, Major Oliver Smedley said: 'We bought it in America. The Mi Amigo had become redundant when plans for the invasion of Cuba fell through.'

It was estimated that Radio Atlanta would require an initial capital outlay of £250,000 in addition to £2,000 per week running costs, but the Texans pointed out that some of these expenses could be offset if the station would undertake to broadcast programmes supplied by some of their political friends, in particular Herbert W Armstrong's Radio Church of God.

The Radio Atlanta ship was owned by Rosebud Shipping, a company based in Panama controlled by Gordon McLendon, Clint Murchison and their

American friends,. The name 'Rosebud' having its roots in McLendon's interest in the movies and the ending of the classic Orson Welles movie *Citizen Kane*. The ship was then chartered to Rajah Anstalt, a company based in Liechtenstein who in turn leased it to another Liechtenstein company Atlantic Services Anstalt both companies being effectively controlled by Project Atlanta in London.

Project Atlanta was now steaming full-speed ahead but the investors appear to have been completely unaware that they were not the only people planning to launch a well-funded pirate radio operation aimed at the UK.

Unlike the cold political and financial logic driving the Radio Atlanta team the rival plans were built around a young man with a rebellious attitude that could be traced back to Ireland's Easter Rising almost fifty years earlier. At just 23 years old Ronan O'Rahilly had already been involved in running a Soho club, managing several bands and recording artists and operating an acting school.

Since moving to London he had established himself as one of the cool and hip members of the in-crowd who hung around the Chelsea coffee bars. Full of self-confidence with an easy-going charm he seemed to know exactly how to get what he wanted. However he discovered his winning ways did not extend to getting radio airplay for records by the artists he represented – notably Georgie Fame. With limited needle time anyway, the BBC were not interested in playing anything from an independent label and Radio Luxembourg programmes were all stitched-up by the big record companies.

O'Rahilly knew about the Scandinavian and Dutch pirate radio stations and, seeking a way to break the establishment's strangle-hold on new music. he was inspired to find out more about them. Speaking to people associated with Radio Veronica he soon had an idea of how the foreign ships operated and when he went to Sweden to visit Radio Nord he discovered that another British entrepreneur, Allan Crawford, had also been sniffing around.

Upon his return to London Ronan O'Rahilly arranged to meet with Allan Crawford at his music empire offices in Soho's Dean Street, ostensibly with a view to joining forces. According to Crawford, having heard all about the detailed plans O'Rahilly suggested that his father, wealthy Irish businessman Aodogán O'Rahilly, might be interested in investing in Radio Atlanta. Ostensibly to unlock this investment O'Rahilly took away copies of the Atlanta technical plans, research and legal advice.

Obviously not impressed with the Altanta organisation Ronan O'Rahilly was now determined to start his own ship-based station. There were probably insurmountable cultural and political differences between the two models. Atlanta was rooted in ultra-conservative politics, on both sides of the Atlantic, and numbered two British Army majors among its directors. Ronan had a very different heritage.

Ronan was the grandson of Michael O'Rahilly, a prominent Irish Republican revolutionary hero celebrated in the Ireland to this day having been shot dead by British soldiers died while single-handedly charging a British machine gun post during the 1916 Easter Rising in Dublin. Known popularly as 'The O'Rahilly' he was later immortalised under that name in a poem by W B Yeats. A memorial to him stands in a street now called O'Rahilly Parade, the lane where he fell covering the rebels' retreat from the burning Dublin GPO building.

While being no friend of the GPO – who would soon be fighting the establishment of his private offshore radio station – Ronan O'Rahilly could scarcely be expected to have more empathy with the British Army. Neither did he like the tone or content of the American evangelical broadcasts that were being offered as part of the deal with the Texas-based radio operators. He later tried to resist offers to pay for such airtime on his station.

It was now the spring of 1963 and, knowing that the Atlanta project was well ahead of him, O'Rahilly had to move quickly to set up a radio station of his own. Ronan's father agreed that he could use his facilities in the Irish port of Greenore to fit out a ship for broadcasting but, beyond this help in kind, seems to have been reluctant to inject his own cash into the venture. Urgently needing to raise capital Ronan turned to a friend, another member of the Chelsea set, Christopher Moore. They persuaded a mutual friend, Ian Ross to take the idea to his wealthy father.

New Zealand born Charles Ross, then aged 63, had made is fortune in the City and was very well connected. Like so many others he was immediately charmed by Ronan O'Rahilly who, for some reason, always referred to him as 'Jimmy'.

Ross immediately agreed to support the projects and thought some of his friends might also like to invest. All it took was a few telephone calls and soon the project had the financial backing of prominent society magazine publisher Jocelyn Stevens.

Born into a wealthy family, in 1957 Stevens had bought the struggling *Queen* magazine and transformed the staid fortnightly magazine into a radical representation of the 'swinging sixties'. The publication retained its upper class image however. Regular contributors included Anthony

Armstrong-Jones and Robin Douglas-Home, nephew of Sir Alec Douglas Home a senior Conservative politician who was just about to become prime minister.[7]

Robin Douglas-Home was remarkably well connected and claimed to be a friend of soon to be assassinated President John F. Kennedy. He certainly appears to have been given access to secret information and in July 1962, perhaps as a deliberate leak from Home's contacts in MI5, it was *Queen* that published the first piece of gossip linking John Profumo to Christine Keeler and Eugene Ivanov.

So Jocelyn Stevens brought not only much needed cash into the project but also a great deal of social credibility and high-level access. In 1956, the year before buying *Queen*, he had married Janie Sheffield, lady-in-waiting to Princess Margaret. Stevens was therefore able to bring in more finance from his wealthy friend and father-in-law, financier John Sheffield, a descendent of the Duke of Buckingham, the first resident of Buckingham Palace.

Within a few weeks Ronan O'Rahilly's project was fully funded. According to Ian Ross, quoted in Ray Clark's excellent book on Radio Caroline: 'The money was delivered; we got the cash. I think we got it from the bank and we ended up with a suitcase with £150,000, which in those days was a fortune.'[8]

A Dublin lawyer, Herman Good joined the board and, having studied the complex arrangement of holding companies employed by Radio Veronica and the earlier CIA-backed Radio Nord, set up a complex international structure similar to that employed by Project Atlanta.

With funding secured Ronan O'Rahilly set about finding a suitable ship. He made an approach to the Texans for the Mi Amigo but by this time it was presumably already committed to Project Atlanta and his offer was turned down. Using contacts supplied by Ross he and Chris Moore found what they were looking for in Rotterdam, and for £20,000 they had a thirty year old 702 ton former Danish passenger ferry called the MV Fredericia.

Two brand-new 10 kW transmitters were ordered from Continental Electronics in Dallas and new studio equipment was also purchased from the USA. In mid-February 1964 the ship was moved to Ronan O'Rahilly's father's port at Greenore to be kitted out and was renamed MV Caroline.

Why Caroline? If anything best illustrates the way the hype and spin of these clever early sixties entrepreneurs has obscured our understanding of the history of the pirate stations it is the story of the genus of the title Radio Caroline.

The version always told by Ronan O'Rahilly is this: While flying to Texas to buy the transmitters he saw in a US magazine a photo feature about President Kennedy in the White House. One of the photographs showed Kennedy's daughter Caroline and her brother John dancing or playing in the Oval Office while their father looked on. Ronan was modelling his station on the Dutch Radio Veronica and was keen on having another female name. He thought Caroline in the picture came across as fresh, exciting and happy to disrupt the business of government, exactly the image he wanted to promote.

Others believe O'Rahilly was more influenced by the name of the daughter of Tory Chancellor of the Exchequer, Reginald Maudling. Caroline Maudling was a model who Ronan had fallen for after meeting her at a party. A third version is that Jocelyn Stevens' *Queen* magazine had a style guide for the guidance of its writers. It defined the target reader they should keep in mind: Young, trendy, bright and 'with-it'. Writers were told to visualise a woman with long fair hair who was called Caroline.

In the larger scheme of things I don't suppose it really matters where the name Radio Caroline came from, perhaps there is some truth in all the above and the coincidences all pointed in the same direction. It is perhaps more fruitful to speculate on the naming of Caroline's competitor Radio Atlanta.

Most accounts say that Radio Atlanta was named after Atlanta, Texas, where the owner of the Mi Amigo, Gordon McLendon, had grown up and gone to school. The radio ship was owned by McLendon and Clint Murchison of Dallas and, indirectly, leased to the UK company for day to day operations.

I've not heard any other reasonable explanation for the name so this raises an interesting issue. It suggests that Allan Crawford was already committed to working with the Texans prior to the formation of Project Atlanta Limited. Furthermore it means that McLendon was sufficiently influential in the early planning of the operation to dictate, or at least suggest, the name of the radio station. This was not a simple matter of the Texans leasing a ship to the highest bidder.

Both projects now needed a safe harbour where a ship could be fitted out with a tall transmitting mast and where the transmitter could be coupled to the new antenna without attracting unwelcome attention from the authorities. Under the terms of the Wireless Telegraphy Act 1949 this amounted to installing unlicensed wireless telegraphy apparatus and therefore could not be carried out in a UK port. On the other hand previous experience had shown that it wasn't wise to sail the high seas with such a top-heavy mast so a harbour reasonably near to the final anchorage was called for.

Ronan O'Rahilly's father happened to own the ideal port. Greenore was a disused British Railways facility in a discreet sheltered location on Carlingford Lough just on the Irish side of the border with Northern Ireland. When Ronan had met Allan Crawford at his Soho offices he had suggested that Greenore would be the ideal place to complete the work on a radio ship. Aodogán O'Rahilly was able to promise that there would be no trouble from the authorities or anyone else – and as the son of a famous Irish hero with strong Republican connections it was easy to believe him.

The two competitors reached an agreement. Caroline would be allowed time to pre-record programmes in Atlanta's studio on the top floor of the Dean Street offices and in return Atlanta would be allowed to fit out the Mi Amigo in the O'Rahilly family port.

The proposed Radio Atlanta ship was already modified for broadcast use and just needed to have some equipment restored and a new mast fitted. In contrast the Radio Caroline ship needed a lot more work to convert it from its previous life as a ferry. It seemed to Allan Crawford that Radio Atlanta would be ready first and, when Ronan O'Rahilly said that the two stations would not compete for audience – Radio Atlanta covering the prosperous south of England while Caroline broadcast to the north – the deal was done.

The MV Mi Amigo slipped out of its temporary harbour in Galveston Texas at the end of December 1963 and initially sailed to a port in Spain to have work done on her keel to improve her stability. By the time she got to Greenore the Radio Caroline ship was already alongside and having her 165-foot radio mast fitted.

O'Rahilly's family connections in the port ensured that the Fredericia continually got preferential treatment and the Mi Amigo suffered a number of setbacks. In return the Atlanta people tried to delay progress on the Caroline ship. Certainly there were many minor incidents of sabotage against both ships radio facilities, transmitter components and studio equipment went missing and cables were cut.

To the surprise of Project Atlanta, by 23 March 1964 the MV Caroline was ready to set sail from Greenore. The Radio Caroline transmitters had been secretly, and illegally, tested some days before, the initial broadcasting team were aboard and everything was ready to go. As she left the port it was assumed that she was going to take up a position a short way away off the Isle of Man, as agreed with Allan Crawford.

It soon became clear that the Caroline was in fact heading south and, rounding Lizard Point, was rapidly heading up the English Channel towards the North Sea. The Post Office, Royal Navy and coastal stations tracked the unusual looking ship as it carefully sailed just outside territorial waters along the south coast before taking up a position off Felixstowe on the evening of Good Friday.

Test transmissions started almost immediately on 1495 and then 1520 kHz – both described on-air as 199 metres, playing on the rhyme of 'Radio Caroline on 199'. The first trial broadcast had been pre-recorded by Caroline presenter and actor John Junkin in the Radio Atlanta studios in Dean Street, it began with Jimmy McGriff's *Round Midnight*, a jazz standard composed by Thelonious Monk which was to become Caroline's first theme tune, and then the Beatles *Can't Buy Me Love*. To help their friends on land to correctly identify the station Ray Charles records were played repeatedly throughout the Friday night and on Easter Saturday 28 March 1964 the station was officially launched.

Ever the showman and self-publicist, in a picturesque Fleet Street pub Ronan O'Rahilly had assembled a group of reporters to witness the birth of his station. His large transistor radio was tuned to the Ray Charles songs on 199 metres until, at noon, the opening announcement came from Simon Dee: 'Hello everybody this is Radio Caroline on 199, your all day music station'. The first programme, pre-recorded by Chris Moore, followed immediately with the Rolling Stones *Not Fade Away* dedicated to Ronan.

The early broadcasts from Radio Caroline were still very formal with a lot of BBC influences. The presenters were not allowed to 'self-op' – they could not cue up and play in the records themselves. One of the presenters would sit in a small sound booth while a colleague behind a glass screen in the control room played the records or inserted recorded programs from a tape recorder. Initially, with only two radio people on board, Chris Moore and Simon Dee, most programmes were pre-recorded.

There were no jingles, the only concession to a new style of station identification was the now famous pre-recorded Caroline bell, the dong-dong of which would precede advertisements and station identification. The station did however adopt the Fortunes 1964 song *Caroline* the plodding rhythms of which were used as a lengthy musical identification.

Despite the relative amateurishness of the station sound, or perhaps because of it, the novelty of an all-day pop music station was enough to ensure Radio Caroline's instant popularity, within three weeks a Gallup Poll estimated that some 6,840,000 persons had listened to the station, some

36% of the 19 million people living in the claimed transmission area. Statistics like these were seized upon by Caroline's sales staff who had been given the challenging task of educating British companies and their agencies in how radio advertising worked and how it was best bought and scheduled.

Surprisingly it was nearly a month before the American-owned Mi Amigo was ready to leave Greenore.

On board the ship for its journey from Texas had been an experienced radio engineer, Johnny Jackson – who had previously been employed by Gordon McLendon at his flagship Dallas station KLIF – and an experienced American radio engineer and DJ, Bob Scott. A father and son team, they oversaw much of the installation work and sailed with the completed ship to launch the first few weeks of programmes.

The tall transmitter mast had been removed from the Mi Amigo while she was in Texas and it was sensible not to have a new one fitted until after she had crossed the Atlantic. A new 141 foot tall aluminium mast had to be designed, constructed and installed and it was delays in the delivery and rigging the antenna that had given the Caroline, with its heavier 135 foot steel mast, the opportunity to leave the port first.

It seems likely that Ronan O'Rahilly and the Caroline backers now expected the rival ship to head for the nearby anchorage off the Isle of Man to serve the north of England, originally the supposedly agreed location for Radio Caroline to take up. In fact the ship turned right and followed the same route as Caroline.

In view of what had happened to GB-OK's Lady Dixon two years previously it was important to stay outside UK territorial waters. The transmitting equipment had all been installed and tested and therefore might be liable to confiscation if it came into the country. To add to Atlanta's delays and woes the weather was not helpful and as the Mi Amigo was rounding Land's End she met a force eight gale.

In the storm a stay on the mast broke and, when the whole structure started to sway dangerously, the captain had no option but to enter the harbour at Falmouth. Riggers from Portsmouth were summoned and carried out hasty repairs. The government missed yet another opportunity to intervene and, two days later, the ship set sail again, following the Caroline's route round the south coast and up into the North Sea.

While the Mi Amigo took up its position on 27 April 1964, sheltered between sand banks three and a half miles south-east of Frinton-on-Sea, programmes couldn't start until the permanent crew, transmitter technicians and supplies had been transferred to the ship. The two radio ships were now anchored within sight of each other. The first few transmitter tests were carried out in French to avoid drawing too much attention from the authorities before the station was ready. Then, in a cheeky move designed to capitalise on the large audience Radio Caroline had already gathered, the first test transmissions took place on the Caroline frequency, 1520 kHz, after 6 pm – when they had shut down their transmitter for the night.

When the full-time service began on 12 May, Radio Atlanta was broadcasting on 1493 kHz, technically some three channels away from the Caroline signal, but announced on-air as 201 metres and, given the inaccurate tuning knob on the average transistor radio, effectively right next door to Radio Caroline on 199.

At my home in Essex Radio Atlanta sounded noticeably louder than Caroline but, as they were both running around 10 kW this must have been due to the greater amount of American-style audio processing on the Atlanta signal. In a practice then abhorred by the BBC, American AM stations used a great deal of automatic compression – reducing the dynamic range of the signal and bringing up quieter passages of music or speech to sound almost as loud as the loudest moments. In the days before push-button tuning there was a real advantage in standing out on the dial – being louder than your neighbours as a tuning knob was twiddled past your frequency.

Bob Scott introduced the first programme, initially the shows were all pre-recorded and he or Johnnie Jackson had to start the next tape when required. Atlanta was only on the air from 6 am to 8 pm to save generator fuel, to limit the number of programmes that needed to be brought out daily and because night-time interference greatly reduced the station's coverage after dark. However, even with these limited broadcasting hours, avid listeners like me quickly realised that most programmes were pre-recorded when a number of them had to be repeated – presumably because the tender had failed to deliver a fresh supply.

At Allan Crawford's London offices in Dean Street, Soho, a team of presenters used studios, specially constructed on the top floor, to record programmes which were then rushed out to the ship for transmission the next day. The DJ's included Colin Nicol, Richard Harris and, famously, Tony Withers – better known on later stations as Tony Windsor or just 'TW'. Of course cover versions of current hits by little-known artists, released on Allan Crawford's Rocket, Cannon and Sabre record labels featured heavily in the Radio Atlanta programmes. Radio Caroline meanwhile tended towards the cool jazzy end of the pop music spectrum epitomised by artists like Georgie Fame who Ronan O'Rahilly and his team knew from the music clubs of Soho.

The presentation styles of the two stations were distinctly different too. The largely pre-recorded DJs on Radio Atlanta sounded very brash to my British ears while the usually live presentation on Radio Caroline was more casual and relaxed. The live microphones on Caroline frequently picked up sounds of the sea and the clunking of metal whenever another boat came alongside, adding to the romance.

Atlanta and Caroline were now operating independently as commercial rivals, although they were often re-supplied and re-staffed by the same tender boats hired in Harwich.

The list of Caroline's advertisers soon included the *News of the World*, William Hill bookmakers, Harp Lager, Bulgarian Holidays and Kraft cheeses in addition to a host of smaller local Essex businesses. Two advertisers attracted considerable interest, the first was the Duke of Bedford promoting his Woburn Abbey as a tourist destination, the second, more controversial, was the government-appointed Egg Marketing Board booking commercial spots. Ironically the Egg Marketing Board was one of the examples of the government meddling in the free market to which Project Atlanta's Major Oliver Smedley and his Institute of Economic Affairs so objected. Within weeks most of these advertisers, including the Egg Marketing Board, were also to be heard on Radio Atlanta.

Courtesy of founder shareholder Jocelyn Stevens, Radio Caroline had set up its London headquarters on the top floor of the *Queen* magazine offices in Fetter Lane, just off Fleet Street. However once the station had become established and was regularly courting major advertisers, recruiting more staff and having meetings with influential people it became clear to everyone that the radio station needed to have it own premises. Around this time Jocelyn Stevens also became noticeably less keen to be publicly associated with the company.

The Caroline organisation temporarily moved to an address in Regent Street before being offered the use of a large prestigious building in Mayfair. The grand seven-storey house at 6 Chesterfield Gardens had only recently been converted into offices, the previous occupant having died suddenly and mysteriously a few months earlier. Tomás Harris lost his life on the 27 January 1964 in a freak motor accident on the island of Majorca. On a familiar road near his home Harris' new Citroen veered off the road for no apparent reason, he had not been drinking or speeding and the suspicion has always been that someone had tampered with the car.[9]

One of the reasons why conspiracy theories surround Harris' death is that he was a known friend and associate of the former MI5 agent Kim Philby who defected to the Soviet Union the year before. An officer in MI5 during the second world war, Tomás worked to ensure that 'Garbo', an important double agent was regarded as a reliable source of (actually misleading) information by the Germans.

Veteran *Daily Express* defence and espionage correspondent Chapman Pincher thought it posible that Harris had been killed by the KGB: 'The police could find nothing wrong with the car, which hit a tree, but Harris's wife, who survived the crash, could not explain why the vehicle had gone into a sudden slide. It is considered possible, albeit remotely, that the KGB might have wanted to silence Harris before he could talk to the British security authorities, as he was an expansive personality, when in the mood, and was outside British jurisdiction.' [10]

Harris was also an artist and dealer. In his book recalling his own exploits Kim Philby later wrote: 'During my occasional visits to London, I had made a point of calling at Tommy Harris's house in Chesterfield Gardens, where he lived surrounded by his art.'[11]

Tomás shared his love of art with an MI5 contemporary, Sir Anthony Blunt, who was another regular visitor to 6 Chesterfield Gardens. Blunt was a leading British art historian who in 1964 confessed to having been a Soviet spy. This was a very embarrassing revelation for the British establishment as, in addition to being a Professor of the History of Art at the University of London and Director of the Courtauld Institute of Art, he held the post of Surveyor of the Queen's Pictures. His confession was kept secret for 25 years, the truth was not revealed publicly until November 1979 when it was the subject of a statement to the House of Commons by prime minister Margaret Thatcher. It emerged that Blunt had been a member of the so-called 'Cambridge Five', a group of spies working for Russia between the 1930s and the 1950s. Once the truth became public knowledge he was immediately stripped of his knighthood.

Anthony Blunt had joined the British Army in 1939, serving in the Intelligence Corps before being recruited by the Security Service (MI5 as it is now known) the following year. He was instrumental in recruiting Tomás Harris to the Security Service in 1941. What was apparently not known to the Security Service was that Blunt had become a close friend of Guy Burgess at Cambridge University in the 1930s and between them they had identified potential spies for the Soviet Union – including such now infamous names as Kim Philby and Donald Maclean.

This was the group that met regularly at Tomás Harris' home at 6 Chesterfield Gardens. Harris had inherited the magnificent house and contents from his wealthy art-dealer father and it was a favourite haunt for the likes of Philby, Blunt and Burgess. It was handy for work too. Since the war years the secret headquarters of the Security Service had been in Leconfield House on Curzon Street, an anonymous looking office building which stretched along the north side of Curzon Street between South Audley Street and, guess what, Chesterfield Gardens. In fact the entrance to 6 Chesterfield Gardens was opposite the side of Leconfield House. The new home of Radio Caroline was, conveniently, a stone's throw from the headquarters of the organisation tasked with keeping an eye on them, MI5.

Curzon Street was for many years the hub of Britain's internal security service. MI5 was based in Leconfield House and gradually spread into more buildings along Curzon Street until it relocated to premises in Gower Street near Euston in 1972 (MI5 later moved again to its present imposing building on the north bank of the Thames). Neighbouring South Audley Street, which stretched northwards towards the US Embassy was a favourite location for safe-houses. This was the centre of the shady world of George Smiley, indeed author John Le Carre, real name David Cornwell, once worked in Leconfield House.

It is hard to know how much of this was evident to the young people and businessmen who now started frequenting 6 Chesterfield Gardens. The very existence of MI5 was not officially acknowledged until 1989 and any information about it was covered by a 'D' notice – the informal system under which the British media was leant upon to keep sensitive information secret. The locations and activities of the security services were never to be revealed to the British public.

Radio Caroline moved to its new offices in September 1964 re-naming Tomás Harris' family home 'Caroline House'. They submitted an application for 40 new telephone lines. As explained earlier, the General Post Office (GPO) operated all UK telecommunications in the 1960s and was in turn controlled by the government. The telephone infrastructure was creaking under the strain of a chronic lack of funding over many years. For most people telephones were a luxury item, fewer than half of homes had one, and there were long waiting lists due to a shortage of lines. Along with many others I remember our house had a 'party-line' phone, which was not as exciting as it sounds. It meant we had to share our wires to the exchange with our neighbours. We could hear their calls and they, ours. It was common for individuals and businesses to wait several months before they could get a new telephone circuit installed.

The GPO had been given the task of closing down the radio pirates and had refused to permit them to pass messages via the ship-to-shore radio stations - which, of course, the GPO also controlled – other than in life-and-death emergency. The GPO had also refused to allow the Radio Caroline and Radio Atlanta office numbers to be listed in the telephone directory.

So it was rather surprising when a team of Post Office workers almost immediately arrived and started digging up Chesterfield Gardens, installing the required 40 telephone lines within a few days. That would be remarkable service even today, in 1964 it was unheard of. If anyone had looked closely they would have realised that the cable trench led to a large building in Curzon Street.

The direct competition from Caroline had taken its toll on the Radio Atlanta business plan. Allan Crawford's credibility with his initial investors had taken a serious blow when it became clear that he had been out-manoeuvred by Ronan O'Rahilly and their station, despite using a ready-made radio ship, did not gain the benefit of being first on-the-air. Audiences and advertising revenue were way below Crawford's forecasts and Radio Atlanta was losing money with little hope of further investment from the original shareholders.

After less than two months on the air, competing head-to-head for the same market, it became clear that Allan Crawford and Ronan O'Rahilly were going to have to bury the hatchet and reach some kind of commercial agreement. The two teams met to hammer out a deal on neutral ground at the offices of their shared lawyer in Liechtenstein.

On 2 July 1964 it was announced that Radio Caroline and Radio Atlanta were to merge, one ship was to move to a position off the Isle of Man to become Radio Caroline North while the other remained off the Essex coast and would be known as Radio Caroline South.

While Allan Crawford and Ronan O'Rahilly were named as joint managing directors of the new operation their two companies were to remain separate entities. O'Rahilly's Planet Productions would retain ownership of the Radio Caroline ship while the Mi Amigo would still be controlled by Project Atlanta Limited. However the two companies were now to move under one roof and airtime would be sold jointly with a split of 55% going to Planet Productions and 45% to Project Atlanta.

By the next day the two ships had moved close alongside each other and presenters, records and supplies had been exchanged. Caroline DJs Tom

Lodge, Jerry Leighton and Alan Turner chose to move with their ship while others, including Simon Dee and Doug Kerr moved across to the Mi Amigo to stay in the south and bolster the existing Atlanta team which included Colin Nicol.

The MV Caroline being the larger vessel, with a hull designed for a Danish ferry to withstand rough seas and ice, was the natural choice to head north while the Mi Amigo stayed in the relatively calmer waters among sandbanks off the Essex coast.

In the early hours of Saturday 4 July the MV Caroline upped anchor and started to move southwards under her own power. Staying outside the three-mile limit on a lovely summer's day she was able to continue broadcasting as she sailed and I, along with many thousands of others, logged her progress. By 11 on Saturday morning the DJs reported that she was off Beach Head and, by noon, Brighton. For many listeners with their tiny transistor radios this was the first practical demonstration of how far ship-bourne transmissions could be heard. 'Caroline North' continued to be heard through the day as she passed the Needles on the Isle of Wight at 6.45 pm and Portland Bill at 9.45 pm.

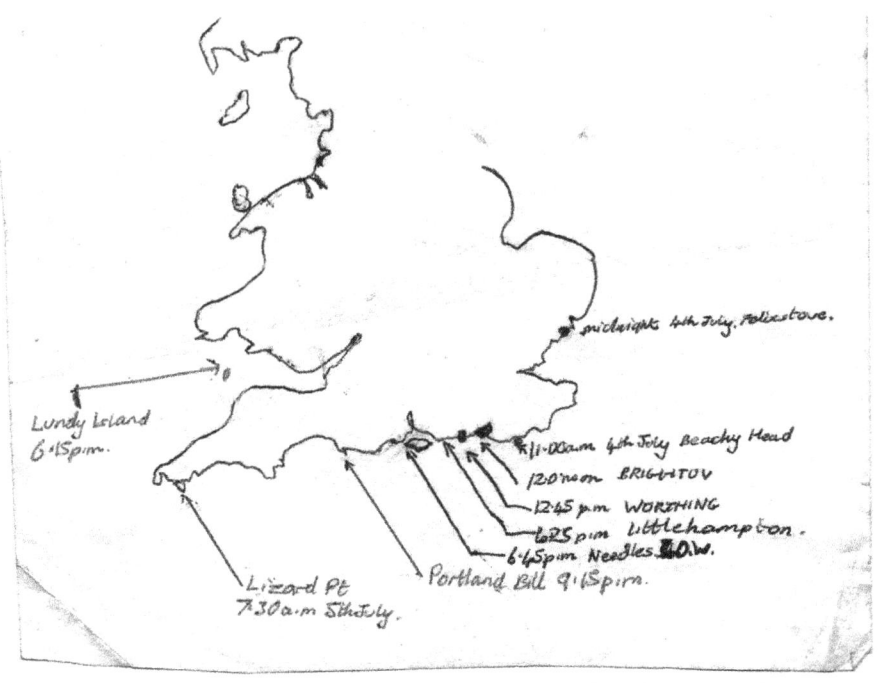

My own map of the exciting progress of the MV Caroline drawn in July 1964.

On Sunday the Radio Caroline ship was still going strong, broadcasting from just off Cornwall's Lizard Point at 7.30 am and Lundy Island just outside the Bristol Channel by 6.15 pm. The ship arrived at its anchorage off the Isle of Man, the one originally intended for the boat under the Crawford – O'Rahilly agreement, on Monday 6 July. A full schedule of regular programmes as Radio Caroline North started a week later, from 6 am to 9 pm on 13 July.

Although the two stations remained on separate frequencies they both identified as being Caroline on the alliterative 199 metres. The joint branding, combined with transmitters in the north and south, allowed Caroline to claim to be the UKs first national offshore station. A few programmes continued to be recorded on land so they could be broadcast simultaneously from both ships.

By the end of 1964 over forty people were employed to work in Caroline House and their number was boosted daily by all the other young, beautiful, famous and trendy people who loved to hang around the offices. The building was far bigger than was needed for a simple radio sales operation and studios were built to record programmes, interviews and advertisements while office space was sub-let to others including The Who manager Kit Lambert and his Track Records label, actor Terence Stamp, the Moody Blues and the Rik Gunnell Agency.[12]

While publicly merged the two rival operations remained distinctly separate within Caroline House. Although there is a school of thought that says Ronan O'Rahilly was just an attractive front-man for big-money interests the fact is that O'Rahilly's Planet Productions and Allan Crawford's Project Atlanta had very different backgrounds and reasons for being on the air. So those working on Radio Caroline North found themselves loyal to a 24 year-old music business maverick who understood and wanted to exploit the new pop-culture scene while the Radio Carline South team were led by relatively dull money-focussed businessmen with their eye on a longer game. The programming reflected these distinctions with the north ship more solidly following a hit-radio format while the southern service continued to include specialist shows featuring music from the musicals, film music and album tracks. And Radio Caroline South continued to pay a lot of material from Allan Crawford's record labels, often favouring his cover versions over the original big-name hits in the top ten charts.[13]

Other entrepreneurs were now starting to see the potential of offshore broadcasting, several smaller stations had now sprung up (discussed in the next chapter) and there were rumours of big American money coming into play.

Many questions were asked, in the press and in parliament, about the government's failure to act against the pirates. Plainly the remedies existed, first the Scandinavian and now the Dutch authorities had passed laws to stop their people from supporting the stations and these had forced many of them to close down.

But in 1964 the government was in no condition to pick an unnecessary fight, particulary not one that would not be universally supported on its own back benches. The Conservatives had been seriously damaged by the Profumo scandal and the resulting fall-out had taken its toll on the credibility and health of prime minister Harold Macmillan who fell ill and resigned as PM in October 1963. His successor Sir Alec Douglas Home was not a popular choice, his aristocratic background and bearing seeming out of tune with a changing Britain. It seemed clear that the Tories were in for a battle at the General Election set for October 1964.

Roy Mason, MP for Barnsley, led the Labour opposition's attack on the government for not acting immediately to stop the new pirate ships. He had repeatedly questioned the postmaster general Reginald Bevins about the issue in the House of Commons and spoke about his frustration at the governments lack of action in an edition of *World in Action* broadcast on the day Radio Atlanta started full broadcasts: 'The vacillation of Her Majesty's government has now allowed Radio Caroline to become established, in now allowing Radio Atlanta to start test transmissions an audience is being built up. They will be to some extent annoyed and so the government are building up trouble for themselves.'

The postmaster general, Reginald Bevins, had told parliament that legislation would have to wait on discussions on pirate radio in the Council of Europe, in the meanwhile, he told *World In Action*, the government was relying on starving the stations of commercial income: 'Some time ago the Post Office put its point of view to the principal advertising associations and they in turn repeated the Post Office point of view to all the principal advertising firms throughout the country. And I certainly hope myself that the principal advertisers will have no truck with these ventures.' His attempts to use the old boy network to thwart the pirates of course failed, the old boys already having been recruited to the pirate cause.

The government's formal position was set out in a statement to the Commons by Bevins in May 1964: 'In order to ensure good reception both here and on the Continent, broadcasting frequencies are agreed by the

PIRATE GOLD

International Telecommunication Union. Pirate radio ships select their own frequencies. This is an infringement of international agreements.

'If no action is taken against pirate radio, such transmissions from ships outside territorial waters may increase, with the result that radio communications with ships and aeroplanes would be interfered with and human life endangered. Also, such transmissions could well lead to massive interference with the reception of existing radio programmes both in Britain and Europe. As it is, protests of interference have already been received from Belgium and France.

'The Council of Europe has been studying this problem and a draft Convention is now in an advanced stage of preparation. What is required to deal with the problem is concerted international action. The Government, therefore, propose to await the conclusion of this Convention and then to consider legislating on lines proposed by the Convention.

'The Government cannot accept the establishment of pirate radio ships as a reason for making precipitate decisions on local sound broadcasting in this country. To legislate for a national service of local sound broadcasting and to establish the necessary machinery for supervision during the remaining months of this Parliament is, clearly, not practicable. In the next Parliament the Government will undertake the review of the situation foreshadowed in the White Paper on Broadcasting published in 1962.'[14]

The government's public statements about the pirates always centred on questions of radio interference and copyright infringement, the very real concerns about who could be behind the stations, what they intended to do with them and the state's lack of control over their output were kept behind closed doors.

As it turned out the Labour Party came to power in October with a very narrow majority of just four MPs. The new prime minister, Harold Wilson, needed to proceed cautiously. Indeed over the next year losses in by-elections reduced the Labour majority to just one seat and there was no appetite for a policy that would upset a lot of voters.

Meanwhile the two main bodies representing music copyright took two somewhat different views of the piracy of their music. For the Performing Right Society, representing those who wrote and composed the music, it was mainly just a question of being able to collect their dues, as they did whenever anyone performed or recorded a song written by one of their members. Talking to *World in Action*, Harold Walters, General Manager of PRS was remarkably sanguine: 'In our daily business we have to deal with a very large number of people whose liability to pay our fees is undoubted but who do their best to evade us. It was therefore very refreshing indeed to find people, business men, whose legal liability was of the slimmest who came forward voluntarily and said they wished to pay our fees. In short from our point of view they are very gentlemanly pirates.'

Phonographic Performance Limited, for the record companies, took a far more aggressive stance, immediately issuing writs against Atlanta and Caroline for breach of copyright. These were not enforceable for as long as the breaches were taking place outside the UK, which technically they were, although it did lead to Radio Atlanta keeping secret the location of the studios in Dean Street where they were recording their record-based programmes onto tape.

Given that some of the leading figures in setting up the stations were, or had been, involved in music publishing it is perhaps not surprising that they felt reasonably well-disposed towards PRS. On the other hand a number of the people behind the early stations had become involved specifically to break the near-monopoly of the big two record companies and had little sympathy for their interests as represented by PPL.

For the pirates what had at first appeared to be a temporary legal stalemate with the authorities had now become the status quo. But, just as offshore radio was beginning to look like a viable investment, the original right-wing business brains behind the scenes felt they had effectively handed control of their baby to a group of free thinking buccaneers.

Ronan O'Rahilly had from the start refused to take money from the American evangelical propagandists and Radio Caroline did not carry the Garner T Armstrong vehicle *The World Tomorrow*. So it was not surprising that the Texans also lost interest in the merged Radio Caroline and started to plan a new station of their own.

CHAPTER FIVE

TOWERS OF POWER

Among the smaller initial investors in Project Atlanta was a consortium of Trinity House pilots and they, unknown to their organisation, offered a great deal of practical advice on the safe and effective location of a radio ship as near as possible to London. Allan Crawford had gone out with them on a chartered launch to identify suitable anchorages for a radio ship. At the same time they took the opportunity to assess the abandoned wartime forts which had been positioned offshore to protect the Thames from enemy aircraft and ships.[1]

Broadcasting from a fixed structure outside territorial waters was a very attractive proposition, quite apart from the stability enabling you to construct a taller, stronger, aerial tower the savings in running costs compared to a ship were very significant. A radio ship required a full-time captain and crew with relevant experience and it needed constant maintenance in order to stay safely afloat. Even with the pirate's casual attitude towards formal rules and what we today call 'health and safety' there were also countless international regulations with which a ship at sea was expected to comply. On a fixed structure, on the other hand, the only permanent personnel required were those needed to operate and maintain the broadcast equipment. In the original Project Atlanta broadcasting model you did not even need the DJs to be at sea, the programmes being pre-recorded on land. Such a station needed no more staff than a maned lighthouse.

Like everything else in this story, the idea of using a fixed tower for broadcasting from the North Sea was not new. In 1963 a Dutch organisation called Reclame Exploitatie Maatschappij (meaning Advertising Exploitation Company and always shortened to REM) started work on building, in another Irish shipyard, an artificial island designed for television transmission. The design reflected plans for the countless oil rigs which were to be dotted around the North Sea from May 1964 onwards. The platform could accommodate 25 workers and the roof included a helipad as well as a 200 foot aerial tower. In the summer of 1964 the legs supporting the rig were fixed to the seabed 10 km off the Dutch coast, the legs were filled with concrete and the rest of the structure was lowered into place.

Radio Noordzee started test transmissions from REM Island, as the platform had become known, in July 1964, with 15 kW on 1400 kHz (214 metres). TV Noordzee joined the radio service on 1 September broadcasting movies and syndicated US shows in the evenings after the radio station shut down. The new stations gained a lot of publicity and, despite the need for new VHF TV antennas many thousands of viewers were immediately attracted to the station.

The project was short-lived however, before programmes even started the Dutch government had started to prepare legislation and had gained support to extend its territorial limit to 11.5 km (about 7 miles).

The Dutch Minister of Justice pointed out in the press that there was a need to make artificial islands located in the Dutch part of the continental plateau legally part of the Netherlands. In parliament he had highlighted the risk of artificial islands being constructed where no law of any kind would apply and where 'murder and theft could be committed without anybody being able to do anything about it.'[2]

The Dutch legislation was based on the Convention on the Continental Shelf, an international treaty agreed in Geneva in 1958 which attempted to establish international law relating to the control of continental shelves, primarily with a view to regulating things like oil exploration. The treaty entered force 10 June 1964 and established the principle of a coastal state being empowered to exercise sovereign rights outside its territorial waters.

By the end of 1964 REM Island was now apparently within Dutch legal jurisdiction. On 17 December in a combined air and sea operation, REM Island was raided by Dutch police and marines who seized the platform and shut down the transmitters.

Despite the savings in operating costs there were plainly two snags with using an offshore platform rather than a ship. Firstly, unlike a ship, a fixed structure could not easily be moved to outwit the authorities and any changing legislation. Secondly, the capital cost of constructing such a station would be considerable compared to the cheap prices at which surplus ships were now available. The construction of REM Island reportedly cost the equivalent of just under a million pounds.

In the UK, however there was an alternative. Just some twenty years earlier the Ministry of War had funded the construction of a chain of offshore forts in and around the Thames estuary. Now abandoned, these seemed ideal for the new purpose.

There were two types of military fort still standing in the waters between Kent and Essex. The naval forts were designed to break up enemy bomber formations, to provide a deterrent to enemy ships and submarines, and to act as early warning stations watching out for airborne or sea-based attack using early radar systems. Separately the Army had wanted to site anti-aircraft batteries within the Thames estuary to make life difficult for heavy bombers heading towards London's important docklands. (Three Army anti-aircraft forts were also built in Mersea Bay to protect Liverpool docks but these were dismantled rapidly following the war.)

The naval forts were further out to sea than the Army anti-aircraft batteries and were designed to simply sit on the sandbanks off the Essex coast. Designed by Guy Maunsell they were based on an original design involving two 24 foot diameter hollow concrete legs resting on a hollow 14 foot deep pontoon. The complete fort could be constructed on land, on the banks of the Thames, and then floated out to sea. Once towed into position the pontoon could be flooded and the whole thing would settle quickly and immovably onto the sea bed. Weighing 4,500 tons each fort was 110 feet high from the sea bed (averaging around 40 feet below sea level) to the top of its radar tower.

Manned by Royal Marines and Royal Navy officers and men, each fort was home to 120 men. Each of the giant hollow concrete legs was internally divided into seven floors with the bulk of the men spending most of their time inside. The forts had large fresh water tanks, electricity generators, radio equipment and of course a full complement of heavy and light naval and anti-aircraft guns.

The four naval forts were strung out beyond the entrance to the Thames estuary: U1 Rough Sands - on a sandbar about 7 miles from the coast of Suffolk; U2 Sunk Head - approximately 11 miles off the north Essex coast; U3 Tongue Sands - six miles to the north of Margate, Kent; and U4 Knock John - ten miles off Foulness Island on the Essex coast.

Meanwhile separate work was underway to build the three Army forts. These were based on the established standard layout of a shore-based anti-aircraft battery. They were constructed in 1942, with each installation consisting of a cluster of six separate towers about 100 feet apart surrounding a central command tower. There were five towers equipped with anti-aircraft guns and, further out, a searchlight tower which was equipped with three 30 kW diesel-powered electric generators. Steel walkways connected the buildings to each other. Four angled 65 foot columns supported each of the octagonal steel buildings which between them could house over 200 men on each fort.

Intended to intercept aircraft traveling up the Thames, the three Army forts were further inland than the Navy ones: U5 Nore - situated close inland just north east of Sheerness on the Isle of Sheppey; U6 Red Sands -

approximately six miles off the Isle of Sheppey to the north of Whitstable; and U7 Shivering Sands - just over nine miles north of Herne Bay, Kent.

The forts were decommissioned after the war ended in 1945 but some were placed under care and maintenance until being completely abandoned in the mid-1950s. The Army's Anti-Aircraft Fort Maintenance Detachment maintained the facilities on the Army forts until 1956, with caretakers staying on board, indeed new searchlights and radar had been installed as late as 1952. It is not clear why they were not then dismantled or destroyed by the British military, you would think they could have offered good training opportunities. One suggestion is that, if not removed thoroughly, they might have posed a greater threat to the safety of shipping than they did standing visibly proud of the surface.

The Nore fort was the closest to the coast, the only one within the three-mile limit, and two of the towers of the Nore fort had been destroyed in 1953 following collision from a Norwegian ship in which four caretakers on the fort were killed. When another collision happened in 1954 the decision was made to dismantle the structure. By 1960 it had been removed. Tongue Sands fort was not sitting comfortably on its sand bank and had started to tilt badly in the 1950s with portions of the fort collapsing into the sea.

In June 1963 Shivering Sands lost one of its gun towers following another ship collision in fog, this also removing walkway access to the important searchlight tower with its generator capacity. However the other towers remained serviceable so, by the start of 1964 there were five possible offshore forts for the pirates to consider.

It is clear that Caroline and Atlanta had considered using the forts, but it was assumed, quite logically, that the offshore bases would still be regarded as Ministry of Defence property and any attempt to squat on them would be met with eviction by armed service personnel. There were also doubts about the legal status of the locations of the Army forts as it was hard to interpret the 'three-mile limit' at the mouth of the Thames, where some authorities argued that a line could be drawn further out - across the mouth of the estuary. Certainly Radio Atlanta's Trinity House shareholders seem to have warned against locating the station near the Thames and Radio Caroline's Ronan O'Rahilly must have received the same advice. When the rival ship housing Radio London started broadcasting from a location near Shivering Sands it was O'Rahilly who contacted them to warn that they were probably within UK waters!

One character though was not daunted by the prospect of being ejected from a wartime fort by the Royal Marines, indeed he would have welcomed the publicity. Reg Calvert was very different to the upper-class men (and apart from Kitty Black they all appear to have been men) behind Atlanta and Caroline. From working class roots he was a serial entrepreneur more in the barrow-boy sense than in the stock-exchange sense. He was a music promoter and manager used to the rough-and-tumble of late fifties and early sixties dance halls. To maintain his string of dance nights around the country he needed a growing roster of singers and groups who would appeal to the new generation of young people now known as 'teenagers'. As described in his daughter's very detailed book, he set up 'The School of Rock'n'Roll' in a run-down mansion in the midlands.[1] In addition to a large number of competent, talented but relatively unknown artists he managed a few who became bigger names, including The Rocking Berries and The Fortunes (who had inadvertently released the song *Caroline*).

Always the showman he encouraged his acts to have a gimmick or over-the-top image. His most famous creation being Screaming Lord Sutch. Accompanied by The Savages, Sutch had a horror-themed stage act, he would appear from a black coffin on stage and, wearing gothic style clothing and heavy makeup, sing songs like *Jack the Ripper* and *The Monster Mash*. The Savages were often to appear in animal skins with other stone age props

As a publicity stunt in August 1963 Reg Calvert had suggested that the screaming lord, real name David Sutch, should stand for parliament in the Stratford-upon-Avon by-election caused by the resignation of John Profumo. Representing the National Teenage Party, with a manifesto that included reducing the UK voting age from 21 to 18, Sutch won just 208 votes but the lost deposit was a small price to pay for the resultant publicity. He was to repeat the stunt some 40 times, later as representative of the Official Monster Raving Loony Party.

In May 1964, mindful of all the press interest in Radio Caroline and Radio Atlanta, Calvert set up another publicity stunt. Hiring a 60 foot fishing trawler called 'Cornucopia' he invited the press to see Screaming Lord Sutch and The Savages – all in full stage costume – set sail from London to launch a new pirate radio station called Radio Sutch. The boat was grossly inadequate for the task and it is doubtful whether it even had any practical transmission equipment aboard, but the doubting reporters were dumbfounded when a radio was produced receiving a strong signal from the new station. Reg Calvert was no stranger to building and operating small transmitters, he had often dabbled with them at his spacious house near Rugby, and on this occasion what the reporters were hearing was in fact coming from a low power transmitter hidden a few yards from where the press had gathered.

The story was that Radio Sutch would broadcast from this small boat for a few hours every day from a position in the Thames estuary about four miles off the coast between Southend-on-Sea and The Isle of Sheppey. However in fact Calvert had previously discussed using the ex-Army forts with local fishermen and had checked them out. The next day Reg Calvert and his small team were seen moving equipment onto the towers at Shivering Sands.

On 27 May 1964 Radio Sutch started broadcasting from the fort with a very weak signal on around 1542 kHz – which they announced as 197 metres - conveniently close to the frequencies of Caroline and Atlanta. Still very much a publicity stunt the first programmes were presented by Reg Calvert, David Sutch and The Savages road manager Brian Paul, who was also in charge of the flimsy makeshift technical arrangements. The first record, repeated regularly, was naturally *Jack the Ripper* by Screaming Lord Sutch.

With supplies now brought out to the towers by a Whitstable-based vessel 'Harvester II', over the next couple of weeks the station gradually became more reliable and I could certainly receive it, although faintly, more than 30 miles away in Upminster, Essex, on the edge of Greater London.

At this stage Radio Sutch was using a war surplus ex-Halifax bomber transmitter which could be bought for £10 on Tottenham Court Road and which, with an inefficient antenna, was probably radiating less than 70 watts. Furthermore, with no access to the generators in the cut-off searchlight tower, the low power transmitter was powered by a bank of lorry batteries which regularly needed to be recharged, requiring the station to go off the air every few hours.

Within 24 hours the Ministry of Defence (then still known as the War Office) issued a statement stating that the broadcasters were trespassing on government property and officials would go out and ask them to leave. A party including an Army land agent and a Kent police officer set out on 28 May, but were mysteriously recalled by the authorities before they could reach the fort.

Maybe it's just the benefit of hindsight, but had the government acted decisively at that time the whole story of UK pirate radio might have changed. While Radios Caroline and Atlanta had built up a wide following, which might cause problems for the government in the coming elections, Radio Sutch had only been heard by a few thousand enthusiasts – and they were listening mainly for the novelty of the experience. Radio Sutch listeners must have found it hard to actually enjoy the erratic and frequently unlistenable signals coming from the fort in those first few days.

Further, while Caroline and Atlanta were operating from ships on the high sea and could hide behind international law, nobody would have been surprised if the government had claimed ownership of the forts it had built expensively only twenty years earlier and had acted decisively to eject any squatters. Whatever the technical legal position, the sight of Army or Navy personnel taking back control over former Army or Navy assets would hardly have seemed shocking. And as the various pirates themselves were to demonstrate a number of times in the next few years it was quite possible to take control of an offshore fort from the incumbents without the use of excessive force. It was just a question of going in sufficient numbers.

Why this did not happen remains a mystery today, as it probably did to Reg Calvert at the time. The government's inaction emboldened other potential station operators and soon many of them were taking a close look at the opportunities offered by the forts.

The Harvester II, skippered by experienced local fisherman Fred Downs, started to supply Radio Sutch three times a week and it became possible to rotate the staff and DJs on the fort. But with limited staff, resources and electricity available, the published broadcasting hours were at lunchtime, 12 noon to 2 pm, with a break until the evening programmes from 5 to 11 pm daily. Often the station failed to appear at the scheduled times.

The transmitter was war-surplus, the antenna a horizontal length of wire strung between scaffold poles on the top of each tower, and the studio consisted of a couple of domestic turntables, a microphone, tape-machine and home-made audio mixer in the corner of a room. The end result was far from professional but then that was half the attraction of the self-styled 'Britain's first teenage radio station'. The music had a consistently harder edge than was current on Radios Caroline and Atlanta with a bias towards rock n'roll, RnB and pop songs aimed at the teen market. In addition to a liberal sprinkling of songs by Screaming Lord Sutch the station featured a great deal of material from the bands and singers managed by Reg Calvert and Terry King at their King Agency in London's 'Tin-Pan Alley', Denmark Street. Famously, late at night the station also featured Reg Calvert reading the naughty bits from *Lady Chatterley's Lover*.

There was little paid advertising on Radio Sutch, what adverts there were came about as 'contra-deals' with local businesses, airtime in return for providing goods or services. Thus regular adverts were heard for a Whitstable record shop and for pleasure cruises from Whitstable harbour. Gigs by Calvert's stable of bands were also promoted.

By mid-summer the novelty of a radio station ostensibly being run by Screaming Lord Sutch was wearing off and the publicity value was waning. Without a decent transmitting aerial and an adequate power supply the station was never going to be a success in its on right. Around this time a new engineer joined the fort. Paul Elvey had been trained as an electrical engineer and heard the station appealing over the air for an electrician who knew how to work with generators. Elvey contacted Reg Calvert and started work on the fort on a one week on, one week off basis, alternating with another engineer

The first priority was to restore some of the suspended walkways linking the towers, once this had been done it was possible to use the other towers to guy a taller antenna mast and to gain access to the fort's generator room in the former searchlight tower. It remained an all hands to the pump operation however and, along with everyone else on the fort, Paul Elvey became a familiar voice on the air.

Denied access to ship-to-shore radio service the station frequently included messages for its land-based suppliers and management in its main programmes. After broadcasting hours the fort could often be heard reading out a shopping-list of requirements and instructions for its supporters in Whitstable. And, intriguingly, someone on land was obviously replying using an illegal transmitter on another frequency - this was a two-way conversation.

In August I heard Radio Sutch, in the middle of the day, asking for listeners to pass on a message that the station urgently needed a rectifier valve for its transmitter. The station gave a phone number for the Punch Inn, a hostelry on Harbour Street in Whitstable (now known as the Quayside) which was known to be co-ordinating supplies to the fort. The message also suggested that if anyone could get their hands on a CV187/U19 rectifier they could take it to one of the station's contacts on land. I called the number they broadcast and I still have my note made on the day - which includes not only the Punch Inn number but also a phone number and address for Paul Elvey's home in Billericay and a number for boatman Fred Downes. Strangely I was also given the address of the Tuskite Works, Marsh Road, Pitsea. Only now I realise this was the location where the lightship 'Lady Dixon' had been taken to be equipped to become Arnold Swanson's ill-fated GB-OK, and, neither before or since has been identified as having any connection with Reg Calvert and Radio Sutch.

Screaming Lord Sutch had never expressed any real interest in running a radio station, this was Reg Calvert's baby and Calvert was spending more and more time on the radio project and less on his music clients. In September 1964 Calvert bought Sutch's interest in the station for a reported £5,000 and set about turning it into a real competitor for Radio Caroline.

Local shop owner Eric Martin, who had been managing the land-based administration of Radio Sutch for several months from The Record Centre at 20a Oxford Street, Whitstable was appointed Manager of the new station – to be known as Radio City. The station's head office was a room shared with the King Agency at 7 Denmark Street in central London, but most day-to-day business was done from shops and pubs in Whitstable.

Reg Calvert now invested more money in the station, although nothing like the amounts that had been spent on the ship-based alternatives. He bought new equipment and fitted it in a new studio, a proper vertical antenna towered over the forts and a more powerful transmitter was installed. Radio City started broadcasting on a new frequency of 1261 kHz (238 metres) on 30 September 1964. Programmes ran fairly regularly from 6 am to midnight and started to build up more of a following than Radio Sutch ever achieved.

The music format of Radio City allowed the presenters a great deal of freedom but the general teenage image was similar to that cultivated by Radio Sutch – without so much of the screaming lord. Some of the programming was very inventive. One innovation was the weekly *Auntie Mabel Hour*, a satirical comedy show which, between the records, lampooned current events. Presented by City DJs Ian McRae and Alan Clark the show was a unique radio equivalent to BBC TV's *That Was The Week That Was* or *Private Eye* magazine. A personal favourite, at 6 pm each evening, was an hour of tracks exclusively from the Beatles and Rolling Stones, alternating between the two groups, each with their own dedicated following. Known as the *Five by Four Show* the programme grasped, in exactly the way the BBC didn't, what young people wanted from their radios and how popular music was changing. And such great music!

Advertising income was still very low compared to Caroline so Reg Calvert agreed to broadcast pre-recorded American religious programmes. With the US evangelical preachers being willing to pay hundreds of pounds per day to communicate their view of the world to the British public the revenue from this source was apparently enough to more than cover City's running costs.

The introduction in December of the more powerful transmitter on a new channel – 1034 kHz, inaccurately described on air as 299 metres – completed the transformation of the station and it now sounded like a real contender right in the middle of the medium wave band. Importantly the daytime signal was also now strong enough to be heard comfortably in central London and Radio City adopted the strapline 'The Tower of Power'.

The new transmitter was still war-surplus equipment, but was a more powerful former US Navy General Electric 3.5 kW transmitter that became known as 'Big Bertha'. When eventually a properly rigged 200 foot vertical antenna was mounted on top of one of the hundred foot high towers the combined height was something unattainable by the ship-based stations and the signal sounded even more impressive. Radio City press releases and advertising rate cards claimed a power of 10 kW in order to seem closer in strength to their competitors. At the same time a war-surplus air force Cossor transmitter was used to air sponsored religious programmes on 1605 kHz (188m) each evening, presumably satisfying the American evangelists who may not have realised that the station's audience was actually listening to pop music on 299 metres.

The original Radio Sutch transmitter was kept for communication on other frequencies with the contacts ashore. Radio links in the other direction were strictly illegal and were cloaked in secret-agent style secrecy. In April 1965 Whitstable shopkeeper Anthony Pine and his wife Susanne were fined a total of £85 by Canterbury magistrates for using an unlicensed radio transmitter to communicate with Shivering Sands.[4] Ever the showman, Reg Calvert responded by telling the press that in future carrier pigeons would be used to send messages between the coast and the station.[5]

In the event of an attack on the fort, or some other emergency which they needed to urgently communicate to shore without alarming listeners, a copy of the Fortunes hit *You've Got Your Troubles* was kept in a sleeve fixed to the studio wall. The song was played on the main frequency as a coded alarm call to management ashore.

As an enthusiastic teenage radio geek I wrote to Paul Elvey in 1965 to ask for more information on the equipment in use at Radio City. I have his pleasant reply in front of me now, handwritten on thin pink Radio City notepaper. In it he says: 'You ask for the technical details of the equipment. Well as you probably realise, so do a great many people, but for reasons not as innocent as yours. However I can tell you that our transmitter is 2 kW with a 1 kW stand-by duplicated system'. He was right to be cagey as the battle for a place on the forts was about to heat up.

Within a week of starting up Radio Sutch had been quietly joined by another station on a neighbouring fort off the north Kent coast. John Thompson, whose Voice of Slough project had never got beyond the drawing board, joined forces with Kent fisherman Harry Featherbee, known to everyone under the more swashbuckling name of Tom Pepper, and the landlord of the 'Oddfellows Arms' pub in Folkestone, Charles Evans.

Encouraged by the fact that Sutch and company had not been immediately ejected from their captured base the new group set up home on the similar Red Sands towers about five miles to the west of the Radio Sutch base, directly to the north of Whitstable. Although it was in much better condition than the damaged Shivering Sands towers, and more easily reached from Whitstable or Faversham, Reg Calvert had ruled out using the Red Sands fort for his station. According to his daughter he had established that it was arguably within territorial waters being too near sandbanks in the Thames estuary.[6] It also seems quite likely that the Kent-based team were already occupying Red Sands before Radio Sutch launched.

Just a few days after all the press attention surrounding Sutch's antics had died down the new team hoisted supplies and equipment onto their fortress. The broadcast facilities were typical of the other stations of the time, just a pair of Garrard 401 turntables, a tape recorder, a microphone and a simple audio mixer. You really did not need much to make non-stop music radio.

Test transmissions from Red Sands started on 3 June 1964 and, as with all the other stations, a number of frequencies were tried out. There was no such thing as a completely unused channel in Europe but, unrestricted by UK transmitter licensing or international agreements, the stations felt able to roam up and down the medium wave band until they settled on a frequency which carried well from their antenna, had a minimum of continental interference and on which, in the case of the cheap fort stations, their modified military transmitter was capable of putting out a signal.

The Kent-based businessmen decided the station should be called Radio Invicta. This was a very well chosen identity, Invicta being the motto of the county of Kent and traceable back to the time of William the Conqueror, meaning unconquered or invincible.

Radio Invicta started regular broadcasting a fortnight later, on 17 June, using a frequency of 985 kHz, referred to on-air as 306 metres. The programmes were deliberately softer-edged than those on Radio Sutch or Caroline and Atlanta, with more easy-listening music and a gentler presentation style.

While, as with Sutch, the transmitter was a government surplus unit, Invicta's choice of an American built RCA ET4336 was much more appropriate. The transmitter, originally designed for short-wave military communications was easily converted for AM broadcast use and was capable of putting out a useful 750 watts. The suitability of this second-hand RCA transmitter was confirmed some years later when details of the government's secret cold-war broadcasting plans started to emerge. When a nuclear bunker in the West Midlands was decommissioned and the contents offered for sale it was found to contain a working RCA ET4336.

The BBC's hidden Wartime Broadcasting Service transmitter network, euphemistically referred to as 'deferred facilities', used a large number of the same ex-military transmitters dotted around the country in secret locations, all pre-tuned and set to go on air on medium wave at very short notice. Several of these same transmitters were pressed into service when BBC local radio stations were allowed onto medium wave in the early 1970s. Other RCA ET4336 transmitters were installed in mobile trailers and stored centrally for rapid deployment around the country.

Although using a fairly decent transmitter, Radio Invicta had an amateurish antenna arrangement using scaffold poles and it is unlikely that it ever radiated much more than 200 watts. Compared to the 10 kw from Radio Caroline and Radio Atlanta the station was not capable of putting a strong signal into London (see note on transmitter power). In Kent and southern Essex, where I was listening, it gave perfectly acceptable reception on a transistor radio however - and was certainly more listenable than Radio Sutch.

After a short-lived experiment with overnight broadcasting the scheduled hours of Radio Invicta settled down to being 5 am until 6 pm, a limiting factor, in addition to a perpetual shortage of generator fuel and staff being the severely coverage-limiting continental interference after dark. Television was also now taking its toll on evening radio audiences, especially for those stations targeting an older audience who, unlike teenagers, were unlikely to huddle under the bed covers with their transistor radio.

Over the next few months Radio Invicta's easy-listening, middle of the road style provided an attractive alternative to the 'pop-pirates' while still providing what the BBC would not: continuous music radio. Promoting itself as 'The Good Music Station' Invicta carried programmes with BBC-style titles like *Lunch Box*, *Memory Lane* and *Date with Romance*.

The show that really sparked my interest in music radio production was a daily listener request programme called *Pot Luck*. With a very limited record library and listener post arriving from shore only sporadically a conventional request show – like the BBC's popular *Housewifes' Choice* –

73

was not really practical. Invicta Programme Controller and DJ Ed Moreno is credited with inventing the original concept that listeners could write in to the programme giving a lucky number, between 1 and 100, and the presenter would then play a song that had previously been allocated that number. It was obvious to me that this gave the DJ the option to play whatever he liked thus being able to read out the listener's dedication without disrupting the consistent station sound.

From the start the staff on Red Sands fort were aware of their precarious position beyond the reach of UK law and that other would-be broadcasters might want to displace them from their perch 100 feet above the Thames estuary. One strategy adopted to discourage such a raid was to consistently overstate the number of persons on the fort. For example when average-height radio ham Eric Davies joined the station he was regularly referred to on-air as 'the six foot three inch Swedish giant Eric Peterson' and also broadcast as a DJ named Ed Laney. DJ John Ross-Barnard also appeared as Larry Pannell, Pete Ross and Peter Barraclough. By giving everyone two or more identities it sounded like Invicta was manned by over a dozen people, although in reality it was frequently fewer than half that number.[7] It worked, as a casual listener I remember having the impression that Invicta was far more labour-intensive than Radio City.

In reality the Red Sands operation was run on a shoe-string just like the nearby Radio City. The fort was serviced on an ad-hoc basis by Tom Pepper from Faversham creek using his 36-foot launch David and by a fishing vessel from Whitstable, the Mallard, owned by Vic Davis. The journey could take over an hour and in bad weather shortages of supplies or delayed crew changes were common.

In competition with Radio Caroline, which could reach into London, Radio Invicta attracted few advertisers other than local companies associated with the station. Invicta advertised a sales office at 110 Fenchurch Street in the City of London but it lacked the on shore infrastructure of the big boys. Although the station gave a postal address in Kent one writer has pointed out that all mail to Radio Invicta in the early days received replies from a department within Polydor records, suggesting that at least one of the major record companies was taking a much bigger interest in the pirate stations than they were willing to acknowledge at the time.[8]

Radio Invicta was later to become King Radio, a station which openly promoted Polydor records. The Polydor label was at that time home to many of the top easy listening artists, including James Last and Bert Kaempfert who figured heavily in the Radio Invicta playlists.

Despite support from the record companies Radio Invicta was not becoming a commercial success and a row developed between Tom Pepper and his partners John Thompson and Charles Evans over the direction the station should take. Over the next few months the situation became more heated, with Pepper taking control of the station and accusations of sabotage and vandalism on both sides.

Matters came to a head when the anarchic rush into offshore radio was to claim its first fatalities.

On 16 December 1964 Tom Pepper set off from Faversham on the David carrying food supplies and the Programme Controller Ed Moreno out to the Red Sands fort. After unloading his cargo and passenger Pepper started back to shore carrying two of the station staff due for a Christmas break, 21 year-old DJ Simon Ashley (real name Barry Hoy) and 18 year-old engineer Martin Shaw. As the boat moved away those remaining on the fort thought they could hear what sounded like engine problems and when the launch met a sudden squall it apparently began to take on water.

The David never reached shore. Late that night Tom Pepper's body was found washed up, hooked to a wooden lift-raft, near Reeves Beach, Whitstable, alongside empty fuel barrels and a water supply tank. It seemed likely that the three men had transferred onto the small raft when the David sank. A helicopter search was started but there was no trace of the two passengers until some months later when one badly decomposed body was found on the Spanish coast, unidentifiable apart from a recording of Radio Invicta on a three-inch tape spool still in its clothing.

The day after the accident disc jockey Ed Moreno, on board the Red Sands towers, told the *Daily Express* that he had been concerned on the trip out to the fort: 'Tom's boat, the David, was leaking when he brought me out here from Faversham on Wednesday. Water was seeping in through the stern and the sea was very rough.' Moreno said that Pepper was not well, but had insisted on making the return journey: 'Tom's last words before he left were "This is the last time I'm taking this boat out to sea. It needs repairs". We noticed he was looking very groggy. He was suffering from a bad attack of flu. But he decided he could make it back.'[9]

At the subsequent inquest into Pepper's death the East Kent coroner recorded an open verdict, saying he was not convinced of the seaworthiness of the launch and pointing out that a communications link should be permitted between the fort and the shore, he said the boat had been leaking on the way out to the fort and the pump was not working properly. While there were suggestions of foul play, and initially the police would not rule out sabotage, nothing was ever proved.

Following the inquest Tom Pepper's widow took over running the station. Newspapers reported that easy-listening pop group the Bachelors were interested in buying the station, not an entirely ridiculous idea as their songs were suspiciously regularly featured on Invicta and other stations. Indeed a year or so later the Bachelors manager Philip Solomon was to invest quite heavily in Radio Caroline after it found itself in trouble so the Bachelors may have just been a front for his radio ambitions. It is not known why the Invicta deal failed to happen, had it gone ahead the shape of UK offshore radio might have changed significantly. It may well be that Soloman, like the bosses of the ship-borne stations, was aware that Red Sands fort could easily be defined as being inside territorial waters.

On 20 December Radio Invicta ran out of fuel. The station's remaining supply boat was preventing from reaching the fort by heavy seas and the people on the towers had no heating, lighting or cooking facilities. Not for the first or last time Southend life boat was called on to supply essentials to the fort and Vic Davis finally managed to reach them with food and fuel aboard the Mallard.

Things continued in this chaotic fashion for a while. In January an SOS broadcasts was made, calling for drinking water and later the same month a doctor had to be taken out by helicopter after DJ Bruce Holland had fallen and injured his head. By February the RNLI and Coastguards were becoming frustrated by the number of emergency calls from the fort and Kent Coastguard claimed that the international distress frequency had been blocked for two hours after the fort's heating system broke down.

When Radio Invicta closed down in mid-February 1965 John Thompson and Charles Evans lost no time in taking back control of the fort. While John Thompson dropped out of the consortium quite quickly Evans was able to bring on board local businessmen like David Lye and Maurice Gothing. The new team also included Oliver Smedley's cousin, Mike Raven (a spectacular personal rebranding from his real name of Austin Churton Fairman) who was part of the original Radio Atlanta but had resigned in protest at the merger with Radio Caroline.

The new station, KING Radio (spelt out on-air in American radio style as K-I-N-G) put out some test transmissions on the old Radio Invicta frequency on 25 February 1965. Thousands of pounds worth of new studio equipment was quickly installed and on 2 March it recommenced test broadcasts on 1259 and 1267 kHz (described as 236 metres).

The format remained calm middle-of-the-road music designed to appeal to 'housewives' rather than screaming teenagers, and former Invicta presenters, including Bruce Holland, Eddie Gerold and John Ross-Barnard continued to broadcast with KING alongside the new programme controller Mike Raven.

Despite the new identity, changed frequency and improved sound KING still suffered from a lack of transmitter power. The signal was still weak beyond Kent and Essex and did not impress the London-based advertising agencies. Unlike Caroline's flamboyant Mayfair presence KING's office address of 'Oxford House, Folkestone, Kent' was not calculated to attract national advertisers either and the station was struggling to survive on local adverts.

As we will see in the next chapter, competition for audiences and listeners had stepped up a notch by 1965 and life was getting more difficult for the bargain-basement stations on the forts. One of KING's directors, David Lye, turned to a former British spy for advice.

A note on transmitter power

The offshore stations fell into three broad categories. Firstly, the semi-professional, often distinctly amateurish, services set up mainly on the former wartime forts off the Essex and Kent coasts which operated with transmitter power levels of, at best, a few hundred watts. Secondly, the first generation of seriously funded pirate ships with power levels around ten kilowatts, Radio Caroline and Radio Atlanta initially fell into this category. And finally the US-backed second-generation operations, starting with Radio London, which boasted transmitters in the 40 to 100 kilowatt range.

The distinction between these categories was more than simply technical. The entry-level stations could be set up for very little cost. In the early 1960s the UK was still awash with war-surplus valve-operated radio gear, aircraft, naval and ex-army equipment could quite easily be converted to work on the medium wave band, often just by replacing or rewinding a couple of coils. The studio required little more than what we would today recognise as a mobile DJ setup. The difficulty came, as we will see later, in maintaining supplies for the station.

While the smaller stations could be powered by a small generator, or during broadcasting hours by a bank of car batteries recharged overnight, the challenges increased considerably when one or more transmitters might be consuming fifty thousand watts of power, requiring big generators to be running for perhaps 18 hours a day. A modern 100 kW diesel generator working at peak efficiency can gobble up seven or eight gallons of fuel every hour, the poorly maintained units on the ships needed much more. Quite apart from the need to keep the DJs and crew supplied with food and water (on average the Radio Caroline North ship required some 11 tons of fresh water each week) this required regular visits from a tender boat bringing barrels of diesel oil.[10]

The Mallard, supplying the Red Sands fort could handle ten 45 gallon barrels of diesel on each tendering trip, at the above rate this might have kept a bigger station on-air for just a few days.

According to a list supplied to the *Daily Express* in January 1965, a normal requirement for weekly provisions for the 17 men aboard the Caroline North ship included: 'One pig, one hindquarter of beef, 5lb of lamb, 5lb of sausages, 15lb of bacon, 10lb of fish, six chickens, 18 dozen eggs, 48 tins of baked beans, 3lb of lettuce, 12lb of tomatoes, 1 or 2 cwt of potatoes, 12lb of bananas, 28lb of butter, 24 tins of orange juice, 5lb of cheese and packets of breakfast cereal.' In addition bags of flour, apples, tea and coffee were taken out periodically and large supplies of tinned beer and cigarettes were brought, duty free, from the Netherlands by the Dutch tender.[10]

Although one of the Radio Caroline ships had moved quite quickly to a position off the north-west of England and other ships were later stationed off the coasts of Yorkshire and Scotland, the bulk of the stations were inevitably clustered around the affluent and highly-populated south east of England. The aim had to be to reach the population and commercial hub that was, and remains, central London.

Unfortunately for the smaller stations the distance covered by a radio signal is governed, among other factors, by something called the inverse square law. Doubling the transmitter power does not double the range, the area covered may have doubled but this is not the same thing. As I was just learning at school, the area of a circle is given by the formula πr^2 where r is the radius – or in our case range from the antenna. Because the signal spreads out in all directions from a simple aerial it requires four times the total radiated power to just double the range of a signal (for the same received signal strength). Some of the first stations could barely be heard on the coast five or six miles away. Significant parts of London were more than 60 miles distant from some of the forts. To increase the transmission radius by ten times would require one hundred times greater transmitter power – corresponding to an increase from, say, 100 watts to 10 kilowatts.

By the end of 1964 it was clear that any serious commercial proposition required a power of at least 10 kW, preferably far more, to overcome night-time interference, and required space for a large vertical antenna. It was this thinking which informed the planning of the second-generation stations starting with Radio London based on a former US minesweeper.

PIRATE GOLD

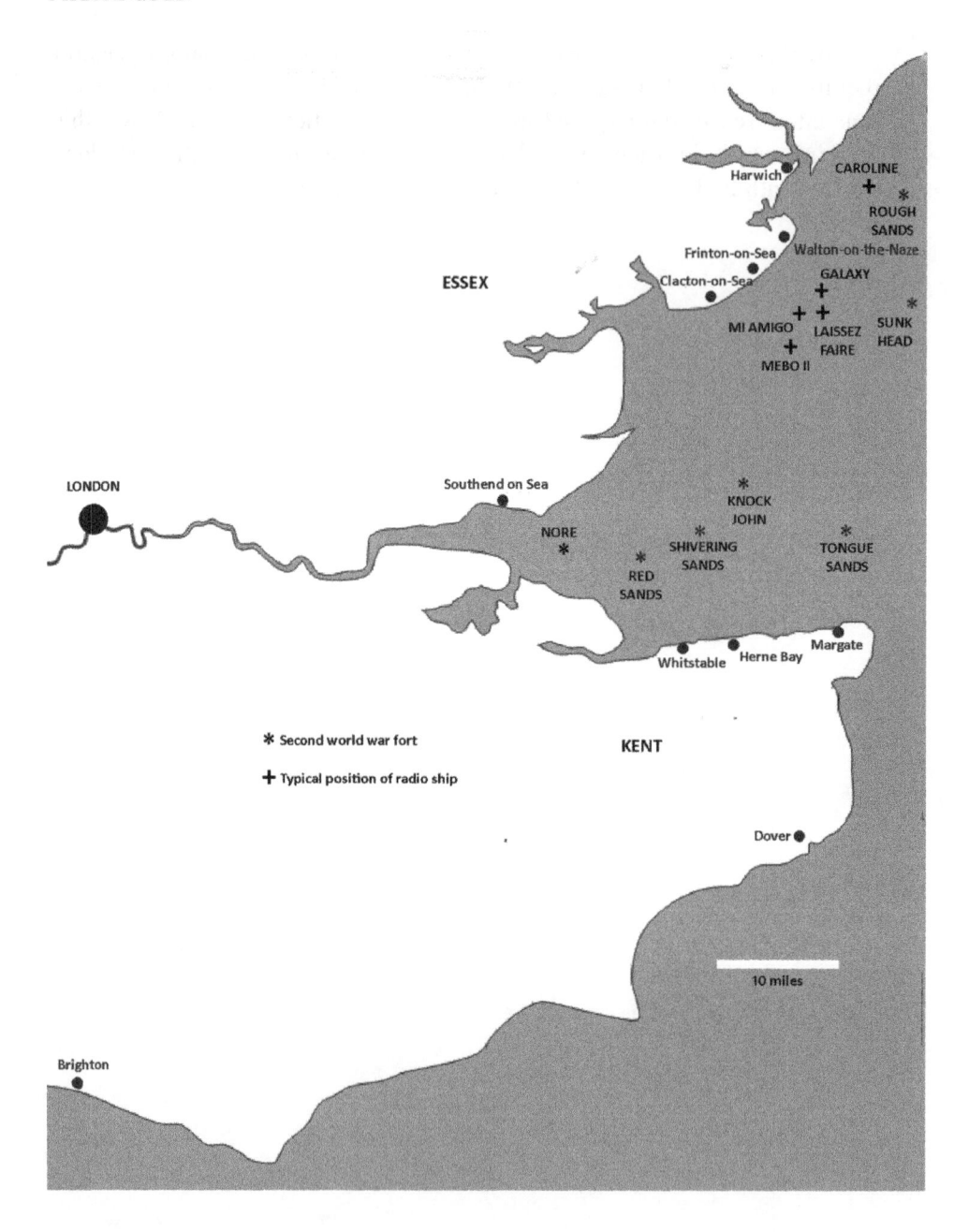

Approximate locations of the ships and forts in south-east England

CHAPTER SIX

OIL ON THE WATER

Caroline had been on the air for a year and still there were no significant changes on BBC radio and the government had not acted against the pirates. The levers of power were still in the hands of the establishment old boy network and they had little to gain by challenging this new broadcasting status quo, some of them even hoped to make a nice profit from the offshore stations. And if a novelist wanted to invent a name to evoke that sixties old boy network it would be hard to beat Theodore Edward le Bouthillier Allbeury.

Born in Stockport in 1917, 'Ted' Allbeury had been a fully-fledged Britsh secret agent. While working in industry he had learnt French and German at night school and at the start of the second world war he responded to an advertisement in *The Times* personal columns for linguists to work with the Army. He was instructed to attend a secret interview in the back-room of a barber's shop in Trafalgar Square and the job turned out to be with army intelligence. After serving in Africa, Italy and Germany he left the Inteligence Corps in 1947 as a Lieutenant Colonel

Ted Allbeury was later to make his name as a best-selling spy fiction writer. Like his contemporaries – Ian Fleming, Graham Greene, and John le Carré – he knew the real world of espionage from the inside and still had his contacts in that world. He was thought to have continued to work for the secret services, MI5 and MI6, into the fifties and sixties. During the cold war, according to his friend and fellow spy writer Len Deighton, Allbeury was running agents across the border between communist East Germany and the west. His first novel, *A Choice of Enemies*, published in 1973, was partly autobiographical, detailing the recruitment of the hero into the wartime secret service and his being dragged back into the spy business many years later. His 1981 book *The Other Side of Silence* was a fictional exploration of the story of Kim Philby.

After the war Ted Allbeury had found work in advertising and sales management before running his own advertising agency. In 1964 he had founded a public relations and marketing consultancy with a colleague: Allbeury Coombs and Partners.[1]

Following the tragic loss of life at Radio Invicta the remaining original investors had pinned their hopes on KING Radio on 236 metres. However the station was not a great success and was said to have attracted a peak audience of only around 20,000 listeners. That's when KING director David Lye turned to his friend Ted Allbeury's consultancy company for advice.

Allbeury Coombes and Partners presented a report to the KING Radio board proposing a radically different programme format for the ailing station, an 'audio magazine' targeted at the daytime housewife audience. In the early sixties much of the nation's advertising spend was aimed at this group of supposedly house-proud women who were in the home for much of the day while their husbands were out at work. They were thought to control most of the household's routine day-to-day spending. Allbeury's consultancy suggested a gentle easy-listening style of presentation with 'sweet music' contrasting with the harder edged mid-Atlantic rock n'roll style being adopted by the other pirate stations in 1965.

The proposal was to launch something called 'Eve - the Woman's Magazine of the Air' playing similar middle-of-the-road music to the BBC Light Programme but more of it, more consistently. Ted Allbeury also pointed out that, in order to take on the BBC and win, the station needed to be received strongly and in high quality (as high quality as possible via Medium Wave AM on a transistor radio anyway). It was clear that the Red Sands fort needed a big injection of cash to pay for a new transmitter and better studios. Allbeury Coombes and Partners drafted a business plan and used it to raise around £150,000 in capital for a new company, Estuary Radio Limited, which was to operate the improved station. Ted Allbeury was the Managing Director.

During the summer of 1965, while KING Radio continued to broadcast on 236 metres using its old facilities, a 10.5 kW RCA BTA 10J transmitter was installed and a 150 foot tall aerial mast was built on top of the central control tower, guyed to three of the outer towers. With the fort standing some 80 feet above mean high water the station was able to claim an aerial height of 230 feet. Two well-equipped modern studios were built, each including two turntables, two tape recorders, two Spotmaster cartridge players for commercials, a microphone and a seven channel audio mixer. Adding to the relative luxury the studios were even air conditioned.

Two of the wartime 30 kW generators on the fort were renovated and restored to use and, together with two new ones, they could produce up to 160 kW of electricity, more than enough to run everything on Red Sands. Nobody had spent such sums of money on a fort-based station before.

Test transmissions started at 4 pm on Thursday 23 September 1965, on a new frequency of 773 kHz, defined on-air as 390 metres. Setting the tone the first record was the 1939 hit *Moonlight Serenade* by Glen Miller and his Orchestra.

Regular programmes started the following Saturday. The large antenna permitted the station to efficiently use a lower frequency (longer wavelength) than any of the other pirates to date and this gave the station impressively solid coverage across most of south-east England. In publicity materials the station claimed to be using 35 kW and this was believable where I was listening in Essex. In practice the effective radiated power must always have been less than 10 kW.

KING Radio had closed down on 22 September but stayed on air for a few days broadcasting a tape loop with an announcement inviting listeners to the new frequency: 'If you have enjoyed the programmes on K-I-N-G we invite you now to retune your radio to 390 metres in the medium wave band.'

Being carefully targeted at a closely defined audience, and one that advertisers wanted to reach, the new service was an instant success. One marketing mistake became evident early on however. During daytime the announcers (the station would not let them be referred to as DJs) and recorded station identification messages told me I was tuned to 'Eve the Woman's Magazine of the Air' while at other times the station was Radio 390. I never liked the woman's magazine idea at the time, there seemed little 'magazine' content other than the 'sweet music', but then I was not a member of the target market. To clarify the situation, and to ensure the press would have to promote the wavelength every time they mentioned the station, the emphasis soon moved to calling it 'Radio three-nine-oh' with 'Eve' being more like a daytime programme title.

Radio 390 broadcast from Red Sands from 6.30 am until midnight daily and Estuary Radio Limited ran the station from its offices at 35a Bessborough Place, London SW1. On-air the address given was PO Box 390, BCM 390, London WC1.

The programme schedule was comforting and traditional, largely following the convention of 15 minute to one hour long programme slots, each with a theme which would not have been out of place on the staid BBC Light Programme. Highlights included *Masters of the Organ*, *Keyboard Cavalcade*, *Music from the Shows*, an Australian radio soap opera *Dr. Paul* and even a mid-morning *Pause for Prayer*. There were also children's programmes and family health advice from the *390 Radio Doctor*, plus a daily edition of the American evangelist Garner T Armstrong's *The World Tomorrow* bringing in the Texas dollars.

There were specialist programmes in the evenings and weekends. Mike Raven presented a regular rhythm'n'blues show and on Sunday nights Ted Allbeury even had his own programme: *Red Sands Rendezvous*.

Discussing postmaster general Tony Benn's proposed legislation against the pirates in early 1966, the *Financial Times* cautioned that 'seizure of the stations may be legally commendable but it will certainly prove unpopular with a large section of the electorate. Radio 390 broadcasts middle-brow popular tunes rather than straight pop music and achieves its strongest following among London's suburban housewives. Several hundred of them have already written to Mr. Benn, in response to an appeal from 390's managing director Mr. Ted Allbeury, to express their support for the station.' Estimates of the number of letters received ran as high as 10,000, but an indication of their real impact was given when Benn decided to reply to all of them with a printed sheet explaining the government's position.[2]

It's generally understood that the arrival of the pirate stations revolutionised UK radio but this wasn't only a result of the different kind of music that was being played and the different people playing it. For example Radio 390 was the first real attempt to aim a whole UK radio station at a specific target audience other than teenagers and young adults. The *Financial Times* later concluded: 'While the pop ships have fought hard to retain the mass audiences they need, Mr. Allbeury and his backers have easily recouped their investment (probably around £100,000) by catering for less fickle tastes.'[3]

The big leap forward actually came with the introduction of programming rather than programmes. Until now British radio stations had broadcast a sequence of distinctly separate programmes, each seldom more than one or two hours long. Each programme had its own remit, might start with its own signature tune and end with the presenter telling you goodbye. This was true of the BBC and stations like Radio Luxembourg and inevitably was the model for all the early pirates. Throughout its existence the top Dutch pirate Radio Veronica broadcast pre-recorded programmes sent out on tape from land-based studios.

The duration of a programme was dictated by the need to give each a memorable start-time on the schedule, typically on the hour or half-hour, and by technical considerations – a reel of tape could hold an hour-long programme in decent quality, anything more would require a cinema-style reel change.

When US programmers started to take control over the output of the new pirate ships the emphasis changed. Programmes were less important than the consistency of the station sound, the programme schedule no longer listed sequences titled *Lunch-Box* or *Sweet and Lively* but was simply a list of times and presenter's names. A presenter would typically be on-air for three or four hours and, when they handed over to their colleague, the music content, presentation style and programme features hardly changed at all.

The relationship between the listener and the radio station was now different, far more personal and individually tailored. You chose a radio station and expected it to be talking to you no matter what time you might tune-in.

It would be nice to think that the desire of American entrepreneurs to become involved in European commercial radio was driven by an evangelical zeal to promote this new concept in radio programming. In reality their interest was driven by other interests, including those of more conventional evangelists.

Gordon McLendon and his Texan chums were undoubtedly very competent and shrewd business operators, but, despite the threat of imminent government legislation and the losses incurred previously, for some reason they could not stop themselves from putting money into yet another European radio venture. As 1964 drew to a close the battle for UK listeners suddenly got hotter with the arrival of Radio London.

You did not have to be a broadcasting expert to recognise that Radio London was a quantum leap ahead of Caroline and the other pirates in many ways. With a powerful 50 kW transmitter on a frequency in the middle of the medium wave dial the station sounded big and strong. The programmes were punctuated with amazing American-style jingles made by the world's top jingle singers at PAMS of Dallas and the presenters sounded slick and professional.

When the UK offshore station Gordon McLendon had backed, Radio Atlanta, was effectively taken over by Radio Caroline, his plans to control a radio ship in the North Sea had suffered a serious setback. Companies McLendon controlled still owned the Mi Amigo but the ship was now leased to the Caroline organisation which was not convinced that the overt Americanisation of UK radio would work and was not keen on selling airtime for religious propaganda broadcasts.

Gordon McLendon shared his frustrations with a millionaire friend Don Pierson who owned a number car dealerships and the Abilene National Bank and was the conservative mayor of Eastland Texas. McLendon pointed out that there was a lot of money available to support a new radio ship from the people behind the Radio Church of God, the Texas-based right-wing evangelist broadcaster headed by Herbert W Armstrong and his son Garner T Armstrong.

Herbert W Armstrong, who had been a major US radio evangelist since the 1930s, believed that the white citizens of the US and the UK were the descendants of the lost tribes of Israel and were therefore destined to inherit the Earth. His reading of the Bible also suggested that Armageddon would be a nuclear war caused by a 'United States of Europe'. Therefore the unification of Europe was to be avoided at all costs. This conclusion was then, as now, shared by many others including Major Oliver Smedley. It also coincided with a world view being promoted secretly by the CIA through 'grey' and 'black' publishing activities and radio outlets on mainland Europe. Armstrong's close ties with the US propaganda machine were frequently evident in his choice of subject material and advance knowledge of American foreign policy strategies, for example his controversial revelation that General Franco wanted Britain to relinquish control over Gibraltar in return for the US being able to keep its air force bases in Spain. Armstrong's Radio Church of God was officially funded by heavy tithes payed by his followers but, for as long as he stayed on message, the broadcast fees were almost certainly underwritten by the CIA.

Pierson immediately grasped the opportunity, even travelling to England to investigate the existing stations and hiring a light aircraft to fly over the ships taking photographs. On his return Don Pierson wasted no time in pulling together a group of initial investors using readily-available Texan oil money. They included wealthy car dealer and airport owner Tom Danaher, another car dealer Mal McIlwain, and Jack McGlothlin, a Texan oil mogul.

From the start this was an efficient businesslike operation. Each of the original investors had an executive role, with McGlothlin in charge of the financial and legal matters, McIlwain planning the sales organisation, and Danaher responsible for fitting out a radio ship. Gordon McLendon remained involved, but only in a consultative capacity. The four originally raised around half a million dollars for the project, but after they started attracting other friends and like-minded individuals to the project they soon had a total investment measured in millions of dollars. Among those said to have invested – through trust funds – was 'Ladybird' Johnson, the wife of then US President's Lyndon B Johnson, who already owned a number of Texas radio and television stations.

This was to be the best funded and most professional of the UK offshore stations and it was run by people with shrewd business sense. The station would be owned by Marine Investment Inc., P.O. Box 456, Freeport, Grand Bahama while advertising sales would be controlled by a UK company Radlon (Sales) Limited.

The ship chosen by Tom Danaher was built in 1944, a substantial second world war US minesweeper, USS Density, which after the war had been bought by a Greek shipping company and operated as the Manoula. The 940-ton, 185 foot ship was bought by Pierson's consortium for a reported $70,000 and renamed the MV Galaxy.

Registered in Honduras the ship was taken to Miami, Florida, to be fitted out. Designed for live broadcasting from the start, a self-operated studio was built in the hold while a 50 kW RCA transmitter was installed in a large specially-built steel structure on the deck at a cost of some $250,000. Unusually for a pirate station at that time there was also a second smaller studio which was to be used for the hourly news bulletins, audio production and for backup purposes.

While the planning of the technical aspects of the operation went ahead efficiently and relatively without controversy the intended programming was to cause division among the backers. Don Pierson's original idea was for the station to be heavily based on Gordon McLendon's flagship Dallas station KLIF, even to the extent of using recorded programmes from the Texas station and calling the station KLIF London.

A 37 year old Englishman was appointed to head up the UK advertising operation and to take charge of the day-to-day management of the radio station. After doing post-war national service Philip Birch left the UK to work in advertising in the USA. At 23 he joined the giant J Walter Thompson advertising agency in Detroit where he was handed the huge Ford motors account, dealing with advertising and sponsorship of thousands of radio and TV stations across the states. Birch, who had made a point of befriending the rich and influential Texas motor dealers and was reputed to have visited the Johnson's Texas ranch, had impressed Mal McIlwain and was given the role of Managing Director. Resigning from JWT after almost 15 years Philip Birch moved to London to set up Radlon (Sales) Limited.[4]

Philip Birch was less sure that an overtly American sound would play well with the British public. In particular he pointed out that, only a year after the fatal shooting of President Kennedy, the word 'Dallas' had unpleasant connotations in the UK. A split started to form among the founding investors. While McIlwain had appointed Birch, Pierson had chosen as his Programme Director an experienced American programmer Ben Toney. A former programme director of the top Fort Worth stations

KCUL and KJIM, Toney was also involved in conservative Texas politics. Ben Toney campaigned for the right-wing Barry Goldwater in the 1964 primaries where Goldwater sought the Republican nomination for President to challenge the incumbent, Lyndon B Johnson.

Pierson persisted in his insistence that the station should be called KLIF London and be referred to on-air, like the original KLIF, as 'The Big K' broadcasting to 'The Big D'. But under pressure of time – Philip Birch urgently needed to distribute advertising rate cards and Ben Toney needed to get jingles recorded – Birch and Toney agreed to call the station Radio London. One concession to the original plan was that it would also be referred to as 'Big L'.

It was also decided that most programmes would be broadcast live by presenters on board the ship, Gordon McLendon himself had never been convinced by the plan to rebroadcast KLIF shows. This dilution of his original vision caused Don Pierson to lose interest in the project and, a few weeks before Radio London appeared on the air, he left the consortium to start planning an even bigger rival UK offshore station. He did however keep a shareholding in the MV Galaxy itself.

On 22 October 1964 the ship crossed the Atlantic to the Azores where a 165 foot tall tubular steel transmitting mast was fitted. Arriving in the Thames estuary on 19 November 1964 the Galaxy dropped anchor South West of the Shivering Sands Fort occupied by Radio City. Following what had now become standard pirate procedure short test transmissions were made on a variety of potentially suitable frequencies, including 725 kHz (412 metres) and 926 kHz (324 metres).

Revealing some of the homework that had gone into the siting of the previous pirate ships and their understanding of the limits of territorial waters in the Thames estuary, Radio Caroline boss Ronan O'Rahilly contacted the Galaxy's captain and warned him that they were probably anchored within British jurisdiction. O'Rahilly sent maps and legal opinions to Radio London to demonstrate the risk they were taking.[5]

The Radio London ship moved up the Essex coast to a position four miles off Frinton-on-Sea within sight of Radio Caroline and test transmissions continued on 1125 kHz (266 metres), 1133 kHz (265 metres) and 1079 kHz (277 metres). The 50 kW transmitter was far more powerful than Caroline's in central London but they were also concerned to maximise coverage after dark where the signal was limited by continental interference which varied from frequency to frequency.

Settling on 266 metres Radio London started regular programmes on 23 December 1964, the first show presented by Paul Kaye. Although not running full power – most of the time it was radiating 17 kW – Radio London's modern 50 kW Ampliphase transmitter permitted the efficient production of a punchy and crisp fully-modulated AM signal. The audio was highly compressed and over much of southern England Radio London sounded like the loudest thing on the band.

On air daily from 6 am to 9 pm (later from 5.30 am to 2.00 am) Radio London's slick professional sound exuded confidence. The high quality beautifully recorded jingles projected a consistent station sound with messages like: 'It's smooth sailing with the highy successful sound of Wonderful Radio London'. Big L presenters were schooled in presentation techniques never before heard in the UK. The station was referred to as 'Wonderful' Radio London and their top 40 chart was always 'the Fab Forty'.

And, although far more tightly formatted than the other pirates up to that point, Radio London had the knack of selecting talented broadcasters who made their mark not only on the station but on British radio for decades afterwards. Great names, many on board from the early days, included Kenny Everett, John Peel, Dave Cash, Tony Blackburn, Tony Windsor, Ed Stewart and Tommy Vance.

For the first time in the UK the music followed the principles developed by Todd Storz in the fifties and wholeheartedly adopted by Gordon McLendon at KLIF. Six Beatles records had achieved the number one position in the 'hit-parade' by the time Radio London came on-air but the BBC Light Programme was still struggling along within its traditional format. A few times a week auntie BBC might lift her skirts long enough for us to hear an actual Beatles recording but on more occasions we would suffer one of the BBC house bands - or worse, house orchestras – giving their jaunty rendition of a song like *A Hard Day's Night*.

By 1965 the Beatles, and other bands such as the Beach Boys, were starting to produce music on record that they would themselves be unable to reproduce live on stage. Inviting the Fab Four to perform live on Saturday Club once a year just did not work anymore. This was a new phenomenon which the BBC had not anticipated. Arguably, even had the pirate stations not existed, the position taken by the BBC and Musicians Union in relation to recorded music on the radio would have become unsustainable by the time of *Sgt. Pepper's Lonely Hearts Club Band*.

The presence of Radio Caroline and the other smaller offshore stations had done little to satisfy the demand for non-stop pop music on the radio, if anything it had highlighted the BBCs shortcomings. Radio London addressed this head-on using the Top 40 formula perfected on Gordon McLendon's KLIF in Dallas.

Radio London DJs were not allowed to choose their own music, all the records broadcast were scheduled according to a rigid formula and initially had to be drawn from a universe of fewer than a hundred discs. The station was the first in the UK to introduce a system of interlocking playlists. Each hour consisted of two or three tracks from a A List which contained Radio London's weekly top ten, a few from a B List which consisted of the remainder of the Fab Forty, a couple from the C List of new releases and individual records from small approved lists of 'golden oldies' and album tracks. The sequence of music was carefully designed to spread the big hits and less familiar new material evenly through the hour. Each presenter also had a Fab 40 climber (selected for them by Radio London management on shore) which featured in all their shows for a week.

As well as giving the London-based management a great deal of control over what the presenters could get up to on the ship this arrangement shifted any opportunity for 'payola' from the individual DJs to the centre of the organisation. It was easy to spot that certain artists and record labels entered the Fab 40 more often, and climbed with greater speed, than others who seemed equally popular in the real world.

To the evident delight of Philip Birch, when word got round that he wanted to set up a new pirate radio headquarters in London, he was offered a prestigious address in Mayfair for what was described as a very reasonable rent. The office was at 17 Curzon Street, just round the corner from Caroline House in Chesterfield Gardens and similarly only a few doors down Curzon Street from Leconfield House, the then secret home of MI5.

The landlords of Curzon Street appear to have been very well disposed towards offshore radio operators. When Don Pierson launched his rival to Radio London the following year he too was offered prime premises at an affordable price, Radio England and Britain Radio moving in to number 32 Curzon Street just across the road from Radio London and even nearer to the MI5 building. From the windows of Leconfield House (some of them converted to be machine-gun ports during the war) it was possible to watch the comings and goings at the front doors of all three pirate ship offices!

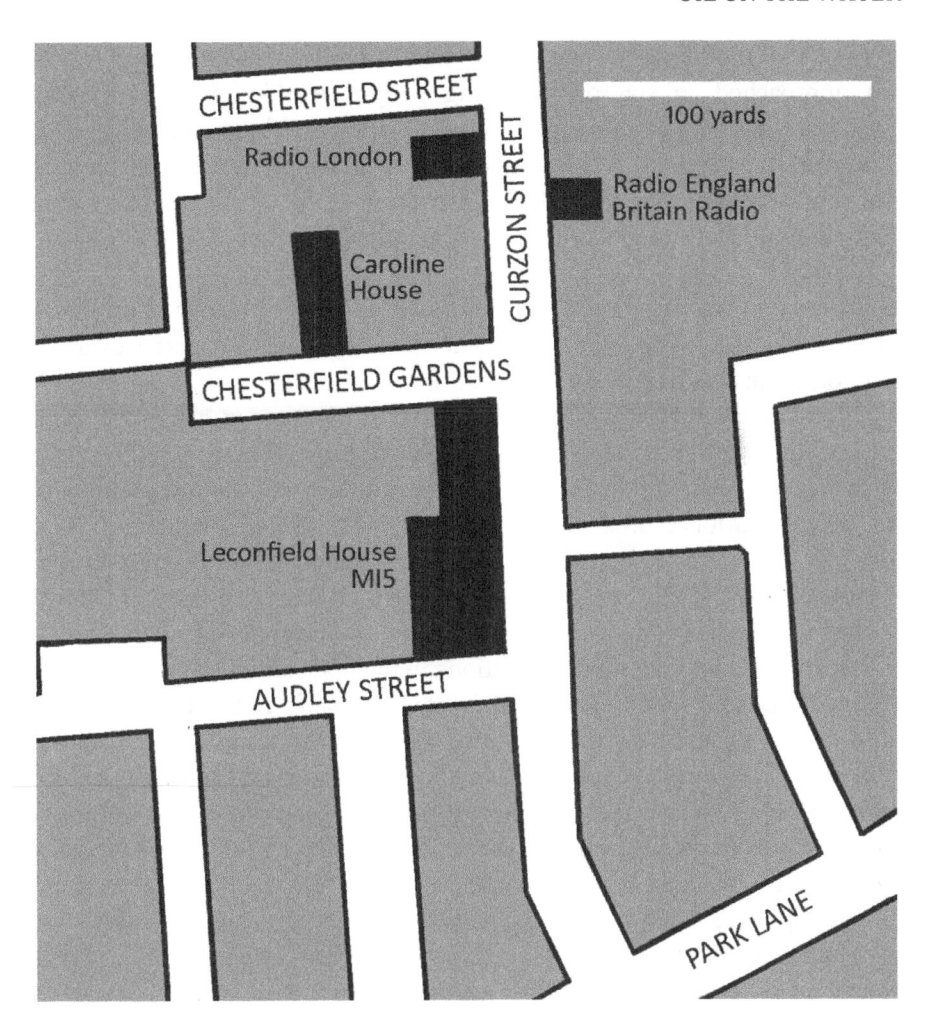

Sketch map of the main pirate ship offices in Mayfair, all within 100 yards of the MI5 headquarters.

As more and more unregulated radio broadcasters started to spring up the response of the Security Service was to ensure that it had someone inside each organisation to act as its eyes and ears. It was generally understood that every station included someone who was secretly making regular reports to 'the authorities'. A number of people associated with the pirate stations (who declined the invitations) tell of approaches from the security services (presumably those who said yes find it better to maintain their silence). In his autobiography *Shooting History*, Channel 4 News presenter Jon Snow revealed that, in the 1970s, as a young journalist working for LBC and ITN he was approached to spy on 'left-wing people' working in broadcasting. Presumably his background as the son of a Bishop of Whitby marked him out as one of the 'right sort of people'. He says he attended a meeting in Whitehall where he was offered a regular tax-free sum matching his normal salary in return for his services. He declined the offer.

Radio London was the first of the pirates to include a regular hourly news bulletin and this added to the British establishment's concerns over the potential misuse of unpoliced airwaves.

The Texans were well aware of the value of news on a popular radio station, albeit presented in a punchier more upbeat style than would be heard on the somewhat pompous BBC. Thanks to its network arrangements, and the lack of national broadcasters at the event, KLIF monopolised radio coverage of the Kennedy assassination and became famous for its fleet of innovative live mobile news units (in fact it only had two but in a typical display of showmanship it called them units four and six).

KLIF was one of the first US stations to include editorial opinions within its newscasts, often from Gordon McLendon himself. In the UK we take an editorial line for granted in our printed media but it seems strange coming from a broadcaster. The Texans thought it would be good if their London station could be heard to take a different editorial position from the BBC. To this end it was originally intended that Radio London's hourly news would be independently sourced from one of the wire services, AP, UPI or Reuters. Technically these could be supplied to a teleprinter on a ship by short-wave radio but the GPO were not going to permit this and none of the agencies wanted to risk their reputations by doing anything that might possibly be construed as illegal.

In the end the use of a wire service was ruled out on the grounds of cost anyway and the newsreaders had to rewrite material pirated from the BBC.[6]

The Radio London news bulletins were aired on the half hour to allow a hasty rewrite of the hourly BBC bulletins. (BBC Radio One was later follow the pattern of news on the half-hour in order that it could be presented by the same person who read it on the hour on Radio Two.)

While the Big L programme format was much stricter than anything we had heard previously in the UK, the station managed to get the balance right – while maintaining a consistent overall station sound they still allowed the presenter's personality and individuality to shine through (something that eludes many commercial radio 'content directors' today). The comedy antics of Kenny Everett, especially when teamed with Dave Cash in the *Kenny and Cash Show*, were among the radio highlights of the sixties. And the Radio London management knew enough about the young audience to allow John Peel to wander far from the station playlist and standard hourly format in his late night programme *The Perfumed Garden*.

More than anything else Big L brought professional and polished business and marketing skills to the radio business. Indeed it was arguably the first time the UK had seen a proper 'radio business'. The attractive programming had been designed to appeal to the largest possible audience and in this they were successful. Within a short while it was clear that the newcomer had overtaken Radio Caroline. By 1966 a survey showed that Radio London could boast an audience of almost ten million while Radio Caroline North and South combined had 9 million listeners. Phillip Birch told the press: 'The pirate stations have given radio a new image. For the man in the car, driving alone, and the lonely housewife, they provide instant companionship. To the teenage audience they mean instant "beat" presented in a "happy" package of pops, plugs and pleasantries.'[7]

In media advertising, all other things being equal, the money follows the audience and soon revenue was flowing towards Radio London and away from the other stations. The lucrative deal with Garner T Armstrong's Radio Church of God meant that their fee for the daily broadcast covered all the basic overheads of running the ship (Armstrong was later quoted as saying it was the most expensive airtime they had ever purchased) and as a result any advertising revenue flowed straight to the bottom line.

In its peak months, which were in mid-1966, Big L was probably attracting around £100,000 in advertising revenue each month while running expenses are believed to have been around £30,000. According to the *Financial Times* 'a more likely average for the whole of the 31 months of London's operation is something like £50,000 in monthly revenue and £25,000–£30,000 in expenses.' Some time in 1966 the station started to break even.[8]

The profits came despite Radio London having to meet all the overheads of a ship at sea. It required a full crew of captain, engineering officers, cooks, stewards and deck hands in addition to the broadcasting team. The Galaxy had been brought across from Florida by a Haitian and American crew but once the ship was on-station a Dutch crew took over. The ship was initially supplied by a tender from Ipswich but this was soon replaced by a Dutch vessel based in Harwich which transferred crews to and from the mainland

and, every three weeks, made the longer journey to Holland to pick up fuel, provisions and duty-free goods.

Radio Caroline faced the same fixed overheads and, while Radio London appears to have been profitable from the outset, Caroline had spent all its original capital and, facing an unexpected downturn in advertising income, was now running short of cash. Prior to the arrival of Radio London, Caroline's income from advertising for one month to December 1964 had reached £47,952. By January 1965 this had fallen to £28,721 and in February recovered only slightly to £32,558. At these levels the Radio Caroline companies were barely covering their costs.[9]

Caroline shareholders Jimmy Ross and John Sheffield were concerned at what they saw as Ronan O'Rahilly's profligate spending on flashy offices and unnecessary distractions and forced the appointment of a general manager to bring the costs under control. Educated at the Sorbonne, Madrid University and the London School of Economics, merchant banker Barry Ainley was attracted to the job by a promise from John Sheffield that, when the inevitable end came, he would be guaranteed a position in Sheffield's own organisation. While Ainley was able to instil some management and financial discipline in the bohemian world of the Radio Caroline headquarters the real problem lay elsewhere – the relatively unfocussed programming just wasn't attractive enough.

Radio Caroline, particularly from the south ship, needed to sound more like a pop music station. The station soon adopted its own version of a top 40 format, with a *Sounds of 65* pop chart, hourly news bulletins and a pre-recorded programme every evening from famous New York DJ Jack Spector. In an attempt to copy a marketing ploy of Spector's station, WMCA, the Caroline presenters became known as 'the Good Guys'. They were given sharp matching outfits to be worn at all public appearances, including a blue blazer, blue and white check shirt and grey trousers. On-air jingles told us that Radio Caroline was 'where the Good Guys are'. I didn't understand the point of it at the time and I still don't.[10]

By the end of the 1965 Project Atlanta had run out of money. In December Ronan O'Rahilly's Planet Productions, which had been sharing the management of the Radio Caroline brand with Project Atlanta, bought out Allan Crawford's group. It appears that, in the end, Atlanta's shareholders got their money back but little if anything more. Writing in 1966 Oliver Smedley explained: 'By then we had realised that our original aims for commercial radio were unattainable – at least until legal circumstances changed.' Indicating that his aims had never been purely commercial he went on: 'We had not managed to use our pirate platform for any useful purpose. And we had not made money. In fact we had lost it in thousands.'[11]

Ronan O'Rahilly was now in control of both ships and Allan Crawford, Oliver Smedley and Kitty Black were, separately, looking for new outlets for their piratical ambitions. General Manager Barry Ainley, replaced Allan Crawford as joint managing director. Ronan O'Rahilly taking responsibility for programming and sales while Ainley was responsible for the administration and finance of the business

The shore-based Programme Director, Bill Hearne, found it hard to instil similar discipline into a team of presenters producing programmes on ships anchored miles out to sea. Developing, guiding and controlling creative individuals by memos which could take days to reach them was never going to work. It was generally agreed that the north ship had a more attractive sound than the southern offering which had been diluted by Allan Crawford's musical tastes and commercial interests. The senior DJ on the north ship, Tom Lodge, was moved south to overhaul the output of Caroline South, the station in direct competition with Radio London. New DJs were recruited, including future big names like Tommy Vance, and some of the old guard left, some in protest at the enforced changes.

In the fallout from the Profumo scandal a Labour government had been elected in October 1964 and Anthony Wedgwood Benn – Tony Benn – became the postmaster general. The pirate radio stations were one of the big issues in his in-tray. In his diary of the time he wrote: 'The outgoing Conservative government, realising that pirate radio was popular and having some sympathy with piratical entrepreneurs of that kind, decided to do nothing about it and the problem landed on my plate when Labour came to power. A narrow majority and the likelihood of another election made it a sensitive and difficult subject.'[12]

Within two months the arrival of the American-funded and highly professional Radio London made it clear that offshore pirate radio was not just a passing fad but, barring a change in the law, had come to stay. A couple of rusty ships and a few buccaneers perched on decaying old forts could be ignored for a while but the coolly calculated foreign investment behind Radio London forced the government's hand.

For example, determined to shed itself of the 'pirate' image, and to rob the PMG of one of his arguments against them, Radio London announced that in future it would pay composers of the songs they used a share of the station's income from advertising. According to the *Daily Telegraph* Radio London had agreed to start by paying the Performing Right Society 1.6 per cent of their advertising revenue during the first year, rising to 3.25 per cent in the third year. Philip Birch told the Telegraph: 'We have always said it was right to make these payments. We do not like the pirates tag. At present we are broadcasting for 15 hours a day to an audience of 10 million people.'

The press reported that Radio Caroline had also started paying royalties to PRS and that the other station with 'establishment' backing, Radio 390, intended to start shortly. Royce Whale, general manager of PRS said: 'We have agreed to accept the money tendered to us under a moral obligation by the offshore radio stations. But we shall continue to press the government to take action against them. It may be that the stations are wanting to buy respectability.'[13] There was however no mention of the stations making any payments to Phonographic Performance Limited, representing the record industry, for the use of their recordings of the songs. The stations always argued that the record companies were benefitting from their promotion of the latest releases, as witnessed by the labels eager supply of new discs to the broadcasters.

At the end of 1994 Tony Benn confirmed that, while he could not control what happened on the high sea outside British waters, he would be introducing legislation making it an offence for a UK citizen or business to supply an offshore radio station with advertising, food, fuel or any kind of support

Progress remained very slow and in May 1965 Benn could only repeat the same government position in a House of Commons debate: 'Whatever future there might be for local sound broadcasting in this country the pirate stations have no part of it. These stations, which started last year, were designed to force the hand of Parliament on the future development of sound radio. That has been made crystal clear many times. As I have said time and time again in the House the stealing of copyright, the endangering of the livelihood of musicians, the appropriation of wavelengths, the interference with foreign stations, the danger to shipping and ship to shore radio make the pirates a menace'.

Unlike many of his contemporaries Tony Benn was a politician who understood the legal issues surrounding pirate radio and the political risks attached to broadcasting policy. He was more technically proficient than most MPs, had at one time worked for the BBC, and had a surprising family history. In chapter three I outlined how in 1922 the General Post Office had forced the radio set manufacturers to form a single broadcasting entity, the British Broadcasting Company Limited. One of the most strident critics of this policy was a Scottish Liberal Party MP who challenged the powers of the postmaster general under the Wireless Telegraphy Act of 1904, stating that they were being improperly interpreted and that he would attempt to deprive him of these powers altogether. That MP was none other than the father of the postmaster general now attempting to defend the BBC's monopoly. Captain William Wedgwood Benn, the first Viscount Stansgate, was Tony Benn's father.[14]

The pirates were sensibly starting to make plans to face future legislation – although in the event more than two years would pass before it came into force. They looked at ways the stations could be supplied from other countries and supported by international advertisers while Radio Caroline North, recognising that any legislation would need the support of Tynwald, the ancient Isle of Man parliament, started giving a lot of free promotion to the Isle of Man Tourist Board.

A note on the shortage of frequencies

Throughout this tale, indeed running throught any account of the history of the regulation of British broadcasting, there is a common thread. Since the 1920s successive UK governments have always pointed to an unfortunate 'shortage of frequencies' as the main reason why, regrettably, access to the airwaves had to be tightly regulated. Intelligent readers, recognising that none of the relevant laws of physics have been repealed during the intervening century, might wonder why, if there was no room for even one more national radio service beyond the three BBC offerings in the early 1960s, there are now literally hundreds of stations broadcasting within the UK using the same traditional AM and FM bands. The answer lies in politics rather than electronics. Politicians, of whatever political colour, found it easier to point to a supposed technical limitation rather than admit that they wished, for other reasons, to keep a tight rein on who could broadcast to the British public. While the more recent huge explosion in media choice has been driven by developments in new digital devices, the introduction of dozens of BBC local radio stations, hundreds of local and regional commercial radio stations, over 240 community radio services and three national commercial radio channels during the seventies, eighties and nineties was achived using the same technology and frequencies available in the sixties. The only relevant change was the removal of the Home Office emergency services from the upper half of the internationally-recognised VHF FM broadcast band from 1968 onwards, but this, of course, could have been achieved far earlier had there been the political will.

As with present-day attempts to regulate the internet, politicians have frequently displayed a sad lack of understanding of how media technology works, believing their own officials' self-justifying explanations, passing laws and approving impractical or unenforceable regulations which fail to reflect how the same spectrum is being used elsewhwere, or how it could be better used in the future.

The common lack of technical literacy among our lawmakers and journalists was also exploited by the government in pronouncements about interference caused by the offshore pirates. On many occasions the stations were alleged to be 'blocking emergency frequencies' or 'interfering with air traffic control' without any evidence being produced. To a public unschooled in the magic of radio these charges seemed entirely plausible, and presumably, this is why they kept recurring.

While any transmitter is capable of causing interference to other users of the same frequency, and a poorly adjusted transmitter (as many of them were) may cause interference on neighbouring or related frequencies, some of the claims were plainly ridiculous. For example, when it was stated that the medium-wave stations were causing interference to fire brigade and ambulance communications in the VHF band. The only emergency channel near to the medium-wave frequencies used by the pirates was the international maritime distress and calling frequency of 2182 kHz and I have never come across any evidence of this being blocked.

In this age where virtually everyone carries a miniature two-way radio with them wherever they go (in their mobile phone) it is important to remember that, in post war Britain, licences for all radio links were strictly regulated by the General Post Office. While the USA and many other countries permitted the free use of 'citizens band' walkie talkies the devices, while widely imported, remained illegal in the UK. Few people could afford to have radio telephones in their cars (and those that could were only permitted to connect via a GPO operator). Businesses had to justify why they needed the facility before they could be granted two-way radio licences and radio hams like me (G8DDV if you're interested) had to pass a stringent technical exam. Even radio-controlled models required the operator to obtain a licence from their local Post Office.

When, as late as 1978, the House of Lords was debating whether citizens band radio should be permitted in the UK, the government spokesman, Lord Wells-Pestell alluded to the real reason for the ban: 'I think we have to seriously consider the enormous disadvantages of having a vast army of people who can communicate with each other very easily...'

CHAPTER SEVEN

CASH CASINO

In the early weeks of 1966 it was not the British government but the severe winter elements that caused the most concern to the pirate ships. On 12 January the Galaxy carrying Radio London dragged her anchor in a force eight gale overnight, ending up inside territorial waters close to the shore at Clacton. Her transmitter had to be shut down and the Clacton lifeboat was launched to attend her. In the end the captain managed to regain control using the ships own engines and the station returned to the air the next day.

On the night of 19 January the decision was finally made that the Swedish pirate Radio Syd, already struggling under the new Scandinavian broadcasting laws, should close down for good. Severe pack ice in the Baltic Sea threatened to damage her hull and the ship, the Cheetah II, sailed into the port of Esbjerg the next day.

Later the same evening in the North Sea, just after Radio Caroline South closed down at 10 pm, unnoticed by the crew the Mi Amigo had broken her anchor chain in heavy seas during another force eight storm and began to drift towards the shore. Nearby Walton-on-the-Naze Coastguard spotted that the ship was at risk and they vainly attempted to warn her by radio and flashing light messages from the shore. While those on board were oblivious to their fate the Walton-on-the-Naze lifeboat was launched and their tender and a tug were hastily despatched from Harwich.

Once the crew on board the Mi Amigo became aware of the situation it was too late to get the ships engine started and at about midnight the ship ran aground in freezing conditions fifty yards off Holland Haven beach near Frinton. Miraculously the ship had beached between some concrete groynes which, if they had hit the hull, would almost certainly have meant disaster.

The coastguard Life Saving Apparatus team shot a line onto the deck of the Mi Amigo from the snow-covered beach and a breeches buoy was rigged up. The broadcasters were quickly taken off the ship by breeches buoy, including Tom Lodge, Tony Blackburn, Graham Webb, Norman St. John and Dave Lee Travis, and two of the engineers. They were all briefly questioned by customs officials and given new clothes and temporary overnight accommodation in Walton-on-the-Naze.

The story made front page news for the next couple of days, with large photographs of the Radio Caroline ship lying at a spectacular angle on the Frinton beach.

In daylight at high tide the tug from the tendering company Wijsmuller made several unsuccessful attempts to pull the Mi Amigo off the beach and it was not until two days later that the captain managed to get the ship to float clear. The hull was now leaking and the tug towed the ship across to Zaandam in Holland for inspection of the damage and repairs.

It transpired that the Mi Amigo was going to be out of action in dry dock for quite a while. In the midst of revamping its programmes to regain listeners from Radio London this was not a good time for Radio Caroline South to be forced off the air. Fortunately the Scandinavian radio ship Cheetah II had now become surplus to requirements and its owner, Britt Wadner, offered to loan it to Caroline while the Mi Amigo was being repaired.

It was not a cheap solution, work needed to be done to convert the Cheetah and, contrary to naive reports at the time, it was not a free loan. Wadner was charging around £750 a week for the use of her boat. But it was better than being off the air.

The Cheetah II had been designed to broadcast only on FM, first as the Danish station Radio Mercur and then later as the Swedish Radio Syd. The Cheetah was also the first European pirate ship to have been equipped for TV broadcasting and had a UHF TV transmitter and television studio in the hold. Before it could take the place of the Mi Amigo Caroline's engineers had to install an AM transmitter and rig up some kind of medium wave antenna using the Cheetah's much shorter masts. One of the Mi Amigo's two 10 kW transmitters had to be dismantled and shipped across from the dry dock in Holland together with a 75 kV diesel generator salvaged from the ship.

From mid-February until the end of April Radio Caroline South was able to return to the airwaves on '199 metres'. The transmissions were unreliable and sporadic, the signal was weaker and night-time reception was particularly poor but at least it meant the station could still collect some advertising revenue. In March, having weathered several days of North Sea storms, the Cheetah II started to leak and had to be towed in to a Lowestoft shipyard for repairs, resuming transmissions at the start of April just as the Mi Amigo was declared fit to return to service.

While the Mi Amigo had been in the Dutch harbour Ronan O'Rahilly had seized the opportunity to make all the changes he wanted to make to the ship he had just inherited from Project Atlanta. A new 50 kW Continental Electronics transmitter had been installed and, learning from the coverage of

Radio's London and 390, the antenna was modified to operate on a longer wavelength. When the original ship anchored near the Cheetah II and the Radio London ship the MV Galaxy she started to test the new powerful transmitter on the professed wavelength of 259 metres, using the full 50 kW first on 1169 kHz and later 1187 kHz.

The Mi Amigo took over the origination of Radio Caroline South from the Cheeta II on 27 April, for a few days the programmes being rebroadcast on 199 metres by the neighbouring Cheetah II with some fascinating two-way broadcast conversations between presenters on the two ships. Shortly afterwards Radio Caroline North also moved down the medium wave band to 1169 kHz – again described as 259 metres. The GPO quickly pointed out that the new Caroline South frequency was allegedly causing interference with the signal of a station authorised to use the channel in Hungary while the new Caroline North frequency belonged to a station in Russia.

It wasn't only the technical arrangements that were overhauled during this time. The former Caroline North Senior DJ Tom Lodge had taken the opportunity to galvanise his new presenters into a coherent team and by the time they were all back on the Mi Amigo the station sounded much more exciting, modern and spontaneous.

Radio Caroline's finances had also been transformed during these first months of 1966. When Ronan O'Rahilly's Planet Productions had taken over Project Atlanta in December Allan Crawford's company was virtually bankrupt. The loss of revenue due to the break in transmission from the southern ship combined with the continued growth of Radio London and the new Radio 390 now put Caroline's cash position under even greater pressure. Enter music industry mogul Philip Solomon.

Philip Solomon had a great deal of experience at the top of the British music industry, as a manager and agent and in tour promotion. In February 1966, while the Mi Amigo was still undergoing repairs, Solomon invested £30,000 of his own money and became an executive director of Planet Productions. His most successful act, the three piece middle-of-the-road singing group the Bachelors, previously associated with a bid to buy Radio Invicta, each put up an additional £5,000, giving Solomon a significant stake in the company.

Unlike the romantic figure of Ronan O'Rahily, Philip Solomon was a no-nonsense businessman. Although his role was supposed to be restricted to growing the revenue of the stations in return for his investment he demanded changes at Caroline House and on board the ships to reduce costs. This was not popular with the DJs - who faced reduced fees and less time ashore - and several left.

The presenters were not keen on the new shareholder's other major innovation either. To Solomon radio was all about making money from the music. He launched his own independent label, Major Minor Records, and expected to be guaranteed a specific number of plays each day for his material. He also insisted that any other record companies would have to pay £100 per week to get their new releases broadcast on the stations (until and unless a track got into the Top 50 when all plays were free)[1].

While the DJs had a great deal of freedom on air they objected to the restricted lists of songs, many of which were simply unsuitable for their supposed new hit-radio format. Solomon's artists had received more than their share of Caroline airplay for some time, songs by acts including Twinkle, Them and the Bachelors featuring regularly. Demonstrating the value of pirate radio exposure Twinkle's record *Terry* – about the death of a boyfriend in a motorcycle accident – reached number four in the official charts in November 1964 despite receiving no plays on the BBC on the grounds, they said, of bad taste.

As had happened previously with Allan Crawford's cover versions, broadcast from the same ship when it housed Radio Atlanta, the problem for the DJs was that many of the Major Minor artists did not fit the hot hits image they were being asked to project. The label's material included a disproportionate number of Irish middle-of-the-road singers and bands and easy listening material from the Raymond LeFevre Orchestra which was not that different from the sound of a BBC staff orchestra.

Among the DJs who rebelled against the music policy openly on the air were some who went on to be big names in UK radio - like 'the Emperor' Rosko (real name Michael Pasternak) and Johnnie Walker. On several such occasions, and indicating the fault line that now ran through the troubled Caroline organisation, Rosko was sacked by Philip Solomon only to be re-hired by Ronan O'Rahilly.

With all the main pirates now having a music policy dictated by their business allegiances or pay-for-play arrangements (some more openly admitted than others) it was now quite possible to identify a station just by listening to two or three consecutive tracks.

On a hot mid-summer's day in 1965 at Herne Bay on the north Kent coast it was impossible to ignore the impact of pirate radio. In addition to the ubiquitous tiny, and tinny, pocket transistor radio most households now had a somewhat larger portable radio capable of reproducing punchy audio at a volume more than adequate for group listening. Then, as now, rows of colourful beach huts lined the shore and I remember walking the length of the beach without ever being out of earshot of a radio. It would seem criminally unsociable today but in the mid-sixties the transistor radio provided a shared soundtrack to our lives and every hut and cluster of deckchairs seemed to be accompanied by its owner's choice of tunes.

As a young teenage boy my quest had started as an attempt to find the bikini-clad girl from my Essex school who I had unexpectedly met earlier and who had invited me to join her family further along the beach. To my eternal regret my inner geek must have won the battle for my soul because, although I did eventually reach Annemarie, I wasted a lot of time carrying out my own ad-hoc listening survey. Herne Bay was uniquely well positioned to receive strong signals from all the offshore pirates in the south of England. Facing north just outside the Thames estuary the town had a line-of-sight path across the water from the ships off the Essex coast and you could clearly see the former Army forts from the beach.

While a few radios were tuned to the BBC (I recall one receiving the lengthy shipping forecast) most were tuned to Radio London and almost as many to Radio Caroline. Several others were carrying the distinctively distorted sound of Radio City and a few the melodic tunes from Radio 390.

On board Radio Caroline it was the popularity of the station with listeners lining the Essex coast which was later to inspire Johnnie Walker to one of the most original pieces of popular radio programming. After dark, from their vantage point some four miles off Frinton-on-Sea, the DJs could see the coast for miles in each direction, picked out in thousands of lights. Car headlights could be seen moving along the clifftop roads, some of them obviously swinging round and parking facing out to sea, towards the radio ships.

Johnnie Walker's shows from 9 pm until midnight on Radio Caroline were very popular, not least for his *Kiss in the Car* feature. Nightly at 11 pm he would invite couples to snuggle up together in the car while he played smooth romantic soul songs like *When a Man Loves a Woman* by Percy Sledge. The success of *Kiss in the Car* led to another regular segment which became known as the *Frinton Flashers*.

Yes children, this is what we did in the days before mobile telephones and social media. In one of the first truly real-time interactive radio features Walker and other DJs would stand on deck asking questions with the parked motorists responding with one flash for 'yes' and two for 'no'. Apparently the sight of the coast lighting up with hundreds of headlights was spectacular and, for presenters cut off from their friends and listeners for weeks at a time, very good for morale.

The process could take all evening but, starting with general questions about names, makes of car, birthdays, and so on Johnnie Walker became adept at reducing the field of flashing lights down to one or two individual cars. By the end we would know an indecent amount about the occupants. On one occasion I remember him identifying a car in Clacton full of boys and directing it towards a car at Walton-on-the-Naze occupied by a similar number of girls.

Johnnie Walker summed up the difference between Radio London and Radio Caroline in a piece he wrote some years later for a book on the pirates: 'Radio London had a much more professional approach and format, style and jingles and the rest of it... Radio Caroline was a pirate station, first and foremost. It did crazy things, it said crazy things.'[2]

Walker explained that, while the Radio London DJs were professional radio broadcasters doing a job, the Caroline jocks were: 'there for the challenge of the whole thing because they believed they could do something with that freedom'. Certainly talented broadcasters like Walker must have been motivated by something more than money as, by 1966, the average weekly pay for a Radio Caroline DJ was around £25 while on Radio London they could have made about twice that.

Despite the shortage of cash in early 1965 Philip Solomon expensively recruited two highly recommended commercial radio men from Canada to give the stations' revenue a much needed boost. Terry Bate, who went on to set up one of the UKs first commercial radio sales houses, was a radio sales expert while Alan Slaight had programmed Canada's biggest Top 40 station CHUM.

Not only did Terry Bate overhaul the entire Radio Caroline sales operation, he also introduced some, to English ears, incredibly innovative sales promotions. The biggest was *Caroline Cash Casino*.

On five occasions every weekday both the north and south ships broadcast identical inserts pre-recorded on land by Bill Hearne. Each day he gave a new clue, in the form of a rhyming couplet cryptically describing a person or thing. Listeners entered the contest by sending their guesses to Radio Caroline together with a proof of purchase from one of the game's sponsors, with the product's name on the outside of the envelope. Hourly three randomly chosen letters naming the particular sponsor for that hour were opened. With every wrong answer read out the cash prize, which started at £100, was increased by £10. Within a week or two, helped I suppose by the delay in getting the audience response through the post and onto the ship, and perhaps due to a creative interpretation of 'randomly', the prize fund would snowball into the thousands of pounds – an unheard of sum in those days.

As a promotion it won on four levels: Firstly it increased listener loyalty, you talked to your friends about it and you had to keep listening to get the next clue; secondly it generated a huge mail response with tens of thousands of entries arriving daily, these sacks full of mail – with proofs of purchase - were shown to the relevant sponsors; thirdly it worked for the advertisers, generating noticeable increases in sales of the featured products; finally, and most importantly, it generated a phenomenal amount of income for the station, even after the total £30,000 prize fund was deducted. Major consumer brands using the promotion included Shredded Wheat, Weetabix, Libbys tinned fruit, Findus frozen food, Galaxy chocolate and Alberto VO5 shampoo.

Cash Casino illustrated how the stations were now thinking big and becoming established as serious media companies. As all the stations became more professional and cost-conscious pragmatic solutions to efficiently improve their operations were adopted. For example on each trip out from Harwich the same tender serviced Radio Caroline and Radio London (and later Radio England and Britain Radio) calling at each to drop off supplies and pick up or drop off staff in turn. In total three tenders were operated by a Dutch supply company owned by the Wijsmuller brothers. The vessels 'Offshore I' and 'Offshore II' supplied the ships on the east coast from Harwich while the larger 'Offshore III' was capable of making the run to supply Radio Caroline North on the west coast and could bring larger items across the North Sea from Holland.

Even the authorities' procedures for personnel coming and going to the ships had become standardised. Because technically this involved leaving the UK, every trip out involved being seen by HM Customs and Excise, HM Immigration and HM Waterguard (then responsible for the control of vessels, aircraft, vehicles and persons arriving into and departing from the UK), and there was always a man from Special Branch in attendance. Once the bureaucrats had caught up with the situation there was a pile of paperwork to be completed too, for the Board of Trade, Ministry of Transport, Port Health Authority, the local Harbour board and even British Railways.[3]

So, just as we have found with the internet and social media, such innovations in popular technology start in an atmosphere of idealistic, inventive, creative fervour but soon the idealism and euphoria is lost to commercial practicality as the cool hands and minds of big money start to take over the controls. In January 1966 the *Financial Times* concluded: 'Advertisers, including some of the best-known companies in Britain, spent a total of £1¾ million (with the pirate stations) last year, which, though miserly beside television's millions, is evidence – if any were needed – that the old-style piracy of Screaming Lord Sutch and his generation has been unobtrusively replaced by the strict commercialism of accountants and admen.'[4] However there were still some exciting developments elsewhere in the UK and from newcomers seeking a slice of the action.

Towards the end of 1965 a new fort-based station, Radio Essex, emerged, Radio Scotland started broadcasting from the Firth of Forth, a further fort-based station, Radio Tower started test transmissions and Radio 270 took up position in a boat off Scarborough, serving Yorkshire and the north-east of England.

Meanwhile the Texans, having lost effective control of their previous projects Radio Atlanta and Radio London to their British partners. were to return with an even bigger and better ship broadcasting two separate stations.

Radio Essex was the idea of Roy Bates, a tall well-built man described at the time as having 'a ruddy face and the kind of high, hectoring voice which afflicted so many of his generation who had been to private schools.' Yet another former senior military man, Roy Bates had been a Major in the British Army fighting in North Africa and Italy. After the war he built up a personal fortune through his wheeler-dealer investments in various businesses including a fishing fleet.

The reported buccaneering adventures of the fort-based radio entrepreneurs were attractive Roy Bates, who was by this stage no stranger to exploiting dodgy business opportunities. He visited the remaining unoccupied forts off Essex and the Thames estuary and set his sights on the former naval base at Knock John.

Separately Radio City boss Reg Calvert had been in discussions with Project Atlanta's Major Oliver Smedley, who was losing his hold on Radio Caroline, to jointly set up a new fort-based station. In reality Calvert, who did not like or trust Smedley, had been considering completely selling the Radio City operation to Smedley and then setting up his own new station on the nearby Knock John fort. In preparation for this in September 1965, unknown to Roy Bates, Calvert had moved some £3,000 worth of equipment onto Knock John, including the redundant Cossor transmitter previously used by Radio City on 188 metres and a small diesel generator. He left a couple of people on board to guard his equipment and establish his claim to the fort.

With the former military offshore bases thought to be outside the UK, and indeed outside the reach of any country's domestic legal system, the territory was literally lawless. This was the very British equivalent of the wild west, fought over by retired Majors rather than cowboys. With the government reluctant to claim any ownership rights the only way for a pirate station to take or keep control of a fort was to occupy it and defend it by force. As had previously been pointed out in the Dutch parliament it seemed possible that someone could even commit murder out there and it would have been hard to prosecute. This was not a situation the UK government could stomach for much longer, it was no longer simply a question of a few DJs playing pop tunes, they were aware that organised crime was starting to wake up to the possibilities.

In East London Ronnie and Reggie Kray were now making very good money from their investments in nightclubs and gambling joints in addition to their widespread extortion rackets and were looking for places to put their cash. Money laundering became a major issue for the twins who set about purchasing property and businesses particularly in their old stomping grounds along the Thames estuary. Indeed the Krays bought a lot of properties on the north coast of Kent, a region which they knew from family holidays. These included a number of pubs in the Whitstable area, some of which were associated with the supply runs to Radio City and Radio Invicta. Distant relatives still run hostelries in the area.

The Kray twins were also trying to restyle themselves as part of the swinging sixties culture. Through people they met at Esmerelda's Barn and other clubs they owned in East London the Krays started to flirt with the idea of pop music management. They signed a band from Yorkshire called The Shots but had no idea how to promote them and, faced with a lack of bookings, the band tried to leave the Krays management, only to be slapped with an injunction preventing them from recording or performing for anyone else. Eventually the band changed their name and bravely continued under other management. (Later, in early 1967, it was only pirate radio airplay that brought the band, by then called The Smoke, to the attention of a wider audience. Their minor hit My Friend Jack having been banned by the BBC

PIRATE GOLD

for drug references. A *News Of The World* headline called it 'This Disgraceful Disc').

The lawless nature of the offshore projects, together with the financial potential of using the forts for other activities beyond the reach of the law, made the pirate enterprises seem a very attractive investment opportunity for the Kray twins. While the radio ships were now in the hands of companies striving for, or at least trying to give the impression of, commercial respectability, the Krays made contact through intermediaries with the more independent-minded individuals who were showing interest in the remaining forts, including Roy Bates, Oliver Smedley and Reg Calvert. Whether the pirates knew who was behind the approaches or not they were left in no doubt that there was money available to support future development of the forts.

While several people have told me that they are certain Kray money and influence had supported at least one of the fort projects, many of the individuals who might have hard evidence are still very reluctant to talk about the details. Perhaps we will never know for certain.

When Roy Bates tried to go back onto the Knock John tower he found it had been occupied by two of Calvert's people. Using 'I saw it first' as his moral justification, Bates returned later with a raiding party of nine burly men who forced their way on board and ejected the Radio City staff who were ferried back to Whitstable. Bates left two teenage fishermen on board.

Reg Calvert was concerned not only about the lost business opportunity but also to regain the transmitter, generator and other equipment he had placed on the fort. So, getting together his own gang of ten heavies on the Radio City supply boat some days later, he retook the fort, allowing the two teenagers to return to land and leaving his own people on board. The battle for the fort continued like this for several weeks without any serious violence – the outnumbered side always realising that they had to surrender.

In the end Reg Calvert became aware that widespread press coverage of the raids and evictions was damaging his chances of attracting serious investors and when Roy Bates set out yet again from Southend with another band of heavies the Radio City DJs and engineers didn't put up a fight and were transported back to their base on Shivering Sands. Radio City was careful to distance itself from any suggestion of violence, a spokesman telling the press: 'We are a respectable organisation and we do not go in for punch-ups.'

With control of the Knock John fort Radio Essex started test transmissions on 25 October 1965. Initially using the Cossor transmitter and generator left behind by Radio City the Essex engineers eventually got two of the wartime fort's big generators running and installed their own transmitter, modified from a former US Airforce 1 kW radio beacon transmitter. They got the fort's original electrics and lighting working again and converted an old store room into a studio with the typical pirate facilities: two Garrard 401 turntables, a Vortexion tape recorder, a spare turntable for things like jingles, a microphone, headphones and home-made mixer.

I was strangely attracted to the amateurish sound of the early Radio Essex transmissions. Their frequency drifted around 1351 kHz, promoted on-air as 222 metres. The former navy forts did not lend themselves to the installation of a tall transmitting mast and Essex had to content itself with a zig-zag of wire held up on scaffold poles. It is unlikely that they ever effectively radiated more than about 100 watts, and the quality and range of the signal was severely limited. The station really could only cover Essex and northern Kent and could have no pretentions to serve London, a fact acknowledged in their mailing address of 33 Avenue Road, Southend-on-Sea, Essex.

We would now recognise, as the Americans already had, that the popularity of Radio Essex was also restricted by the sheer range of programming it tried to offer. Roy Bates was proud of the breadth of music and the amount of locally-relevant speech (read from local newspapers) he encouraged his presenters to include, but this variety was in fact a self-inflicted injury. From its launch of 7 November Radio Essex played easy listening and middle of the road music during the day and top 40 pop in the evenings - but also featured big bands, R'n'B and jazz. A tiny team of two or three presenters bravely kept the schedule going from 7 am until 9 pm or later and soon the station was to be able to claim to be the UK's first 24-hour station, although it could never have made any money.

All this pirate activity had not gone unnoticed by entrepreneurs elsewhere in Britain. North of the border it stirred an advertising executive into action. Thomas Vernon Shields – known as Tommy Shields - had been a journalist, PR man and advertising executive. When working for ITV contractor STV he had written a biography of their wealthy proprietor Roy Thompson and noted that his wealth had originally been built on a local commercial radio station in Canada.

Now running his own advertising agency, TVS Publicity, Tommy Shields decided to launch Scotland's own offshore radio station.

Together with such luminaries as Dundee theatre manager James Donald, London financier Stanley Jackson, Glasgow casino operator Alan Carr and Sir Andrew Murray, a former Lord Provost of Edinburgh, Tommy Shields formed City & County Commercial Radio (Scotland) Limited to handle the advertising sales and programming. Following a now familiar pattern the ship and transmitter were to be owned by a separate company registered in the Bahamas, Antilles Associated Company. While the station's headquarters would be in Cranworth Street, Glasgow the company's letterhead also gave a London office address as Royalty House, Dean Street, London W1 (familiar as the address of the early pirate radio operation CNBC in 1961).

The chosen vessel was the LV Comet, a 90ft 500 ton former Irish lightship built on the Clyde way back in 1904. A lightship seemed the ideal platform for an offshore transmitting mast, as Arnold Swanson had recognised with his ill-fated 1961 plans for GB-OK. It was built to sit at anchor in a fixed location and its central mast was built to carry the weight of a substantial light housing. The downside was that she had no engine and a tug had to be hired whenever she needed to be moved.

With an initial investment of £200,000, the Comet was specially fitted out in Guernsey with twin RCA transmitters and a 145 foot aerial mast. The RCA BTA-10J 10 kW Ampliphase-modulated transmitters were intended to be connected in parallel to provide 20 kW to the antenna. In practice, as was discovered by other stations using them at sea, the advanced Ampliphase technology, difficult enough to set up on land, was hard to keep correctly tuned when the antenna was being being buffeted by salt water. For much of the time the station was to use only one unit at a time.

The Scottish ship had the standard pirate DJ studio arrangement centred on two Garrard 401 turntables but with a greater emphasis on tape recorders. Three Ferrograph machines and a Brenell tape deck were provided as many of the programmes were to be pre-recorded on land in a fully-equipped sound studio at the Glasgow offices.

In December 1965 the MV Comet arrived at her anchorage between Fife Ness and Dunbar at the mouth of the Firth of Forth, just in time for Radio Scotland to start regular programmes on that most important of Scottish dates, New Year's Eve.

The music generally comprised around 60% commercial pop with 40% being more traditionally Scottish, including a dedicated Ceilidh show. Radio

Scotland was the only clearly audible station playing continuous music, added to which it was targeted specifically at Scotland, so it soon won a substantial audience away from the BBC.

Sadly Tommy Shields had not done his homework in assessing the viability of different anchorages and the propagation of radio waves. Initially located just 25 miles to the east of Edinburgh Radio Scotland put a wonderfully strong signal into the Scottish capital city but the station was much weaker in the commercially important city of Glasgow. Although the station was still announced as broadcasting on 242 metres the frequency, initially 1241 kHz, had to be changed to 1259 kHz as a result of heavy incoming continental interference after dark.

To solve the Glasgow problem, in April 1966 the Comet was towed all the way round the north of Scotland to a new anchorage, a hazardous journey of almost a thousand miles during which the ship was almost lost on a couple of occasions. Tommy Shields insisted that the station should stay on the air throughout the trip and as a result she could not shelter from the worst of the storms. Radio Scotland was soon broadcasting from positions between Troon and the Isle of Arran. The signal into Glasgow and Scotland's heavily populated central belt was vastly improved but the new anchorages were clearly within territorial waters and, following an £80 fine for operating a transmitter without a licence, the Comet was forced to move closer to the coast of Northern Ireland. For a time the station operated as 'Radio Scotland and Ireland' but reception was no so poor in the east of Scotland that the ship was eventually towed back to the Firth of Forth.

Meanwhile in Yorkshire a similar group of businessmen were putting together a plan for their own pirate radio ship. Their vessel was to be a Dutch fishing lugger, traditionally a small sailing vessel with two masts, called the Oceaan VII. With the ship anchored off Scarborough the plan was to serve the whole of the north east of England.

The consortium was brought together by 28 year old north-east wrestling and entertainment promoter Don Robinson. Their Ellambar Investments Limited included Bill Pashby, a well-known Scarborough fishing boat skipper; Roland Hill, a poultry farmer based just outside Scarborough; and Leonard Dale, the owner of an electrical business in nearby Grisethorpe specialising in generators.

The founders were joined by Scarborough supermarket owner, and former Conservative MP for Cleveland, Wilf Proudfoot after he read about the project in a local newspaper. Leaving the RAF in 1946 Proudfoot had set up a grocery shop in the village of Seamer on the outskirts of Scarborough. This was in the days before self-service shopping was common in the UK and his supermarket model, selling a high volume of goods at low prices was very successful. By the end of the 1960s he had twenty shops in the region and some still exist today bearing the family name.

Bringing credibility and business expertise to the board Wilf Proudfoot was appointed as Managing Director and set about attracting further investors. By the time of the station's launch the company had attracted some two hundred shareholders, the vast majority of them being drawn from Scarborough and North Yorkshire. Leonard Dale was elected Chairman of the company, Bill Pashby was the station's Maritime Director and Don Robinson planned the programmes - which were to include a mixture of light music and lifestyle speech features, like the BBC's Light Programme but with a local angle.

The choice of vessel fell to Bill Pashby, and the 27 year old 137 foot, 150 tonne fishing vessel was purchased in the Netherlands for £2,500 and towed across the North Sea by a local trawler to be overhauled and fitted out in Scarborough. Renamed the Ocean 7 and registered in Honduras in the name of the station's first programme director, an Australian, Noel Miller, the boat's former fish hold was converted into a radio station and living space for three DJ's and three engineers. A self-operated DJ studio was built together with a second smaller studio for news and a 154 foot tall aluminium antenna mast was fitted. Twenty tons of ballast was added to the hull to compensate for the tall mast. The vessel's main four-cylinder 240 hp diesel engine was overhauled and two 50 kVa Dale Marine generators installed by Leonard Dale's company.

As was the case with the Radio Scotland ship MV Comet, the Ocean 7 had to be taken all the way to the Channel Islands to have its 10 kW BTA 10J1 transmitter fitted by RCA. Apparently this was because the American company had a tax-free facility in the harbour on Guernsey, it may have also sidestepped the provision in the 1949 Wireless Telegraphy Act making it illegal to install an unlicensed radio transmitter in the UK. The total cost of setting up the radio ship has been estimated at £75,000. The directors had done their homework on the legal position and announced that the station would be owned by an offshore company, Progressiva Compania Commercial SA of Panama while the ship was separately owned by Marmado Cia Naviera SA in the Honduras. Ellambar Investments Limited simply represented these companies in the UK but, following the model of Radlon Sales for Radio London, would take the advertising revenue and pay the bills.

The original plan had been to call the station Radio Yorkshire but it emerged that the name had already been registered by another group and it was thought that it might also be too geographically restrictive. Indeed, when the station started transmitting as Radio 270 from a commanding position off Scarborough, it put a good signal into much of the east coast of England from the east Midlands up to Northumberland.

The station launch, originally scheduled for April 1966, was delayed due to problems with the mast and regular transmissions did not begin until June by which time the middle of the road programme format had been ditched in favour of the Top 40 style proving so popular on the other pirates. Following another offshore tradition the frequency of 1115 kHz was described - inaccurately, not that it mattered - as 270 metres.

'Radio two seven oh' neatly filled in a gap on the east coast of England between the pirates clustered around the Thames and the Scottish border. Estimates suggested that between 10 and 25 per cent of the 15 million people in this region listened to the station.

Although all the directors played significant roles in setting up the station, once it was on the air the day-to-day management was centred on the offices of Wilf Proudfoot's supermarket business on Scalby Road in Scarborough. Radio 270's rate card suggested a basic rate of £30 for a standard 30 second commercial and the company was successful in selling spots to local businesses and for Scarborough Borough Council events. However the north-east station found it difficult to attract the lucrative national clients who could be heard on the likes of Radio London and Caroline and its largest advertiser was in fact Proudfoot's supermarkets. Although the station featured many adverts for the supermarkets and for Leonard Dale's electrical business these were partly funded as contra-deals, free airtime in exchange for services rendered, and did not contribute to the company's cash flow. It will come as no surprise to discover that the station could not have survived financially had it not been for the substantial revenue generated by nightly transmissions of Garner T Armstrong's *The World Tomorrow*. As with all the other stations the Radio Church of God magically paid a sum which almost exactly covered the station's day-to-day running expenses.

Proudfoot's effective control over the station started to concern his original partners. For example it was Proudfoot who brought in Noel Miller from Australian commercial radio to be the programme director and together they had thrown out Don Robinson's easy listening format. Relationships with another founder, the Chairman Leonard Dale, came under pressure due to persistent problems with the electricity supply on the Ocean 7 which had been installed by his company Dales Electric. One of the issues was in maintaining the exact 50 Hz frequency of the mains supply – vital to keeping the turntables turning at the right speed – as the ship rocked from side to side.

As with most of the radio ships Radio 270 originally intended that its programmes would be pre-recorded on land, this requiring a smaller ship with just room for the transmitter, simple payback facilities and a couple of technicians. No thought had been given to accommodating disc jockeys and a full studio on the tiny Ocean 7.

Original chief engineer Peter Duncan set up a studio in Newcastle-upon-Tyne to produce all the 270 programmes. Although more than 70 miles away from the chosen anchorage off Scarborough this wasn't an entirely daft location. The advertising business in the north was then centred on a handful of agencies based in Newcastle and Leeds and either city would have made a good headquarters.

However, although the practice was commonplace elsewhere in the world, all the UK offshore stations were quick to drop a reliance on pre-recorded programmes and the reasons why go to the heart of the pirates' popularity. The stations were not simply offering an alternative of non-stop popular music, although this was a crucial part of their attraction. They were also reflecting a new attitude towards authority and traditional values which in television this had manifest itself in programmes like *That Was The Week That Was*.

The public now wanted their music radio programmes to be spontaneous and irreverent. On the BBC programmes were still largely scripted, with an announcer sat at a desk while in a separate room a producer and panel operator were in control and a 'grams operator' played in music and other items off discs or tapes on cue. The BBC schedules were largely constructed from what were known internally as 'built programmes' researched and prepared to within an inch of their lives.

So the listeners were not looking to the pirates for the professionalism and control implicit in carefully pre-recorded shows in which every error or indiscretion could be edited out. In a live programme from a ship it was not unusual for the stylus to be sent skipping off a record in a rough sea or when a visiting boat banged up against the hull. The sounds of seagulls could be heard through an open porthole or studio door on a hot summer's day, even the sound of a seasick disc jockey throwing up while reading a live advertisement for Wilf Proudfoot's bacon (as happened to Paul Burnett on

Radio 270). These all added to the romantic notion of a different kind of broadcasting, coming from outside the established order, an excitement that fitted the mood of a new young generation and the music they were playing.

Once Radio 270 had taken the decision to present programmes live from the Ocean 7 the ship became very cramped. Conditions on board were very basic at the best of times but in rough weather the ship became intolerable. The problem was that the former fishing boat was too small to operate comfortably in an exposed part of the North Sea. In November 1966 one storm was so severe that the crew and broadcasting staff threatened to mutiny. The Ocean 7 continued to broadcast as waves broke high over the deck but listeners could hear that the DJ's were frightened for their lives as water started to enter the studio and living quarters in the hold. Radio 270 stayed off the air for a week while the damage was repaired.

After the storm the DJs gave Wilf Proudfoot an ultimatum: either the ship should move to a more sheltered anchorage in Bridlington Bay (although that would mean a reduced transmission area) or it had to put into port during any heavy storms. The Radio 270 ship was in fact no stranger to the local harbours. While the other pirate ships had to rely on small tender boats to bring their supplies and staff to and from the shore the small size of the Ocean 7 meant it could easily dock at Scarborough or Bridlington to take on supplies and exchange DJs and crew. The original plans called for the crew to work on a one month on, one month off, basis for this reason. It emerged that there was nothing illegal about the ship entering British waters once it had switched off its transmitter for the night and it regularly pulled into Bridlington in the early hours of the morning to transfer people and supplies, usually under the watchful gaze of a local police constable.

Wilf Proudfoot finally agreed to moving the ship's regular anchorage to Bridlington Bay and moved to a one-week rotation for most crew and DJs. But Proudfoot's management style was commanding and confrontational and he reacted to the DJs concerns about health and safety on the ship by immediately sacking all three.

Even before the storm the staff turnover at Radio 270 was unusually high and Wilf Proudfoot's dictatorial behaviour was raised as an issue at equally stormy shareholders' meetings. On two occasions an attempt was made to remove Proudfoot from the board. He had already crossed Don Robinson and Leonard Dale and now the other founding shareholder Bill Pashby resigned to protest at the continuous sackings of the crew and the use of an unsuitable traditional 26 foot coble fishing boat to supply the ship.

While his other partners were first concerned at the extent to which Radio 270 was now becoming entangled with Wilf Proudfoot's supermarket business, it was increasingly hard to see where the income and costs of one stopped and the other began, there were also growing concerns about how the station was becoming linked to his political interests. Despite happily taking dollars from a bigoted right-wing pseudo-Christian organisation supported by the CIA the other offshore stations had, largely, up to this point avoided being used as a propaganda platform in UK politics. Given the tiny majorities held by each party in power in the early sixties this made pragmatic sense, nobody was really sure who would form the next government.

Wilf Proudfoot saw no problem with giving airtime on Radio 270 to promote political causes with which he happened to agree, including support for the increasingly unpopular white minority regimes ruling South Africa and Rhodesia. Proudfoot's friend, Conservative MP Patrick Wall. chaired several party committees on Africa and was convinced of the benefits of white rule on the continent. Despite being a Top 40 pop music pirate Radio 270 found time for a programme pre-recorded by the York University branch of the right-wing Tory Monday Club, in which Patrick Wall was outspoken in defence of Ian Smith's white government in Rhodesia. And Harvey Proctor, then chairman of the University of York Conservative Society, made regular half hour current affairs broadcasts. When, ahead of the May 1967 local council elections, the station broadcast airtime on behalf of Conservative candidates the then Labour postmaster general Edward Short told the House of Commons 'It is the first time in peacetime that this country has been subjected to a stream of misleading propaganda from outside our territorial waters.'

Another prominent Conservative Member of Parliament Roger Gale, now Sir Roger Gale, served as a DJ on board the Ocean 7 before he ran for parliament. He had been with Radio Caroline North from August 1964 before joining Radio 270 in 1965. The only former offshore radio DJ to become an MP he has represented North Thanet in Kent since 1983. Strangely the official biography on his personal web site, at the time of writing, makes no mention of his time as a pirate in Yorkshire!

Although I lived in Essex, at the epicentre of most pirate radio developments, the chance of hearing stations like Radio Scotland, Radio 270, Radio Caroline North and a new commercial radio station legalised by the Isle of Man parliament, Manx Radio, encouraged me to become proficient at listening to more distant medium wave broadcasters. Indeed at that time, when most European stations closed down overnight it was often possible, using my ex-Army communications receiver, to receive signals from some of the larger commercial stations in the eastern USA, like WKBW Buffalo and WNEW New York.

So it was that, in October 1965, I received a weak and wobbly signal on around 236 metres from a station announcing itself as Tower Radio. The presenter said they were testing from the Sunk Head fort. Although the former Navy tower was only some 35 miles away from me the weak signal was comparable with the ones I would receive from Scotland or the Isle of Man, it certainly was not a commercial proposition.

It emerged that the project had been stumbling along for some months. An Essex businessman Reg Torr, who traded as TD Radio & Television with TV sales and rental shops in Colchester and Clacton, had the idea of setting up a pirate television station on one of the offshore forts and calling it Tower Television. More as a publicity stunt than as a serious venture, he had been broadcasting sporadically since May at low power, on Sundays daytimes only, allegedly from his service manager's 18-foot day-boat the Pamela. Each Sunday, weather permitting, the little boat with its outboard motor chugging would set off from Brightlingsea towards the Gunfleet lighthouse three miles off the Essex coast.

The service manager, George Short had assembled a very basic radio station using a war surplus transmitter and car batteries but it was not possible to broadcast live, talking into a microphone and playing records, from such a small craft, so the Sunday programme would have to be kept short, pre-recorded and played out from a small tape recorder. In practice the transmitter was on dry land, often broadcasting illegally from the TD Television Shop at St Osyth near Clacton or from the back of the shop's van on St Osyth Marshes with a wire antenna supported by a helium-filled balloon. The subterfuge worked, the GPO being convinced that the broadcasts were coming from the boat in international waters. The Pamela of course didn't really have to go that far, usually being content to vanish from view round the nearby Point Clear.

Reg Torr's involvement with pirate radio did not go down well with his business partners and, also realising just how much time, effort and money it would take to run a full-time operation, Torr dropped out of the project.

George Short wanted to continue and formed a new consortium, known as Vision Projects, with Essex businessman Eric Sullivan. Their company set up a small office at 15 Trinity Street in Colchester Essex, and started looking for more backers and a fort to base the station on permanently. They spoke to people like Reg Calvert and Roy Bates but they already had their own plans for the towers and were not interested, or were not keen to encourage further competition.

At this time three of the forts were known to be occupied, Shivering Sands had Radio City on board, Red Sands had Radio 390 and Knock John was being fought over by Radio City and Roy Bates of Radio Essex. As far as the public was concerned that left three of them available for use: Tongue Sands to the north of Margate; Rough Sands, a few miles off the coast of Suffolk; and Sunk Head the furthest off shore some 11 miles off the north Essex coast.

In fact, on the basis that possession was the only law that mattered on fixed structures in international waters, the other forts had already attracted squatters, as Eric Sullivan and his colleagues were to discover when they visited them in a hired boat.

The closest inland was the Roughs tower but they found this had already been occupied by 'caretakers' operating on behalf of Radio Caroline. The Tongue Sands fort was badly damaged and tilting alarmingly and was of little use except perhaps as a supply base, and Sunk Head was known to have been occupied by people acting on behalf of Radio Caroline.

Sunk Head was the furthest of the forts from land and stood in deeper water than the other navy towers. As a result it was subject to rougher seas and stronger tidal currents than the other offshore structures and was more difficult to get alongside by boat. A ship had collided with the fort in the 1950s and both the cylindrical concrete legs were flooded with water rising and falling inside with the changing tides.

Seizing an opportunity after Sunk Head was left unmanned by the Caroline squatters following a series of severe storms, Eric Sullivan hired a local boat and on 13 October 1965 his friend John Waters managed to get aboard the fort and claim it for Vision Projects. He left two young labourers from Southend on board to clean and tidy the place as best they could and to act as fort guards to repel any other boarders.

After a week the deck area of the fort was more or less habitable although the accommodation was always going to be spartan and primitive. The basic broadcasting equipment that had been used for the Pamela test transmissions, with two cheap domestic turntables a crystal microphone and a tape machine, was brought out to the fort and assembled into a makeshift studio.

Eric Sullivan had bought a war-surplus Canadian Army Wireless 52 set, a transmitter and receiver unit which could easily be modified to tune down to medium wave frequencies. It was designed for relatively low-power point-to-point communication but had a powerful 813 output valve and could be operated off 12 volt batteries.

Using an antenna wire held aloft by a helium-filled barrage balloon, which broke free in the winds of the exposed North Sea, and then, equally unsuccessfully a kite, the station started making test transmissions from 22 October. The radio set was not crystal controlled and Tower Radio appeared on various frequencies broadly equating to 236 metres, between 1258 kHz and 1293 kHz. The rather dodgy slogan 'Get a fix on 236' was adopted.

Using a makeshift aerial array constructed on top of the fort's former radar house the low power transmissions struggled to reach the Essex coast, some eleven miles away, and you had to be an enthusiast, like me, to listen to them further inland. The amateurish nature of the broadcasts was hypnotic though, almost like watching a car crash in slow motion. The microphone sound was terrible and such records as they played were not cued in neatly, they openly described the technical difficulties they were facing, including only being able to transmit for a few hours at a time before taking a break to recharge their bank of lorry batteries with a noisy generator (just like Radio Sutch in its early days). Most of the time they spent talking about their ambitious future plans for Tower Radio and, surprisingly given how very poorly-funded they appeared to be, Tower Television.

Initially Tower Radio was run from an office at the Martello Holiday Park in Walton-on-the-Naze and then from the rented premises in Trinity Street, Colchester. Robin Garton ran Martello Studios from his family's caravan park and the studios were to be used to record programmes and adverts and jingles for the station.

Sporadic test transmissions continued with those stranded on the fort regularly appealing over the air for fresh supplies. In November Tower Radio agreed a deal with the Wijsmuller company for the Dutch boat Offshore I to supply Sunk Head, which was quite near to the anchorages of the Radio London and Caroline ships which they already serviced. However the agreement was abandoned after the tender was damaged trying to come alongside the concrete legs of the tower in difficult conditions. On 2 December following a frantic on-air appeal a local tug delivered emergency stocks of water, food and oil to the fort but all transmissions ceased on 20 December.

Nothing more was heard until March 1966 when occasional test transmissions on around 236 metres recommenced with the station now calling itself Radio Tower. Vision Projects had raised some more cash from new shareholders and a better generator and more powerful transmitter were reportedly installed at Sunk Head. Hoping to overcome the tendering problems they bought a former Icelandic fishing vessel Maarje which was to become the fort's own regular supply ship. On 24 March the station broadcast that Radio Tower would start regular programmes, from 7 am to 7 pm daily, on 21 April.

Among those putting more money into Vision Projects were Irish millionaire Steve O'Flaherty, American Country Music fan and DJ Dave Simser and businessman Peter Jeeves, who invested £10,000 on the understanding that he would become joint Managing Director. Tommy Shields, who went on to launch Radio Scotland, also was reported to have shown some interest.

However the station was still woefully underfunded. While Vision Projects claimed that it had agreed a contract for twelve months of advertising with the *News of the World* there was little sign of interest from other advertisers, the only adverts heard during the new broadcasts being for a couple of small shops in Colchester and Clacton. The costs were starting to mount up and the company seemed to have no means to meet them. Things came to a head when that newly acquired tender boat, the Maarje, was impounded by HM Customs & Excise in Ipswich and sold off to meet unpaid bills.

Despite all the press hype conditions on Sunk Head had never really improved, the staff effectively camping in filthy, cold and wet conditions with no proper cooking or toilet facilities, those on board often existing for weeks on end without any visit from a supply boat and the clandestine ship-to-shore radio link being ignored. Each time fresh water and food supplies ran low the station had to resort to SOS messages.

On 28 April Vision Projects was declared bankrupt. Radio Tower continued to broadcast for a few days but finally left the air at the start of May 1966.

While Tower Radio had never really achieved anything resembling a viable regular broadcast service from the start they constantly promoted their intention to launch Tower TV. The pirate TV station was to broadcast syndicated American series, movies, music programmes and local news for three hours every night using the old VHF 405-line channel five, which was vacant on the east coast as it was reserved for radio astronomy at Cambridge.

There had been press reports that the service was to start on 9 November 1965 but there were no confirmed reception reports other than a photograph of a blurry test card. It's thought that, as with the Radio Pamela radio broadcasts, the test signals actually came from a very low power home-built transmitter based on land.

Photographs of Sunk Head tower do show what appears to be an array of homemade TV transmitting aerials on top of the old wooden radar house at the top of the fort, but there is no evidence that a TV transmitter was ever installed there. While the idea generated considerable press interest the proposed television station would have faced insurmountable difficulties anyway, as we shall see shortly.

So while Tower Radio is probably the most famous pirate radio station to have never actually broadcast, the project having been mismanaged from the start with little understanding of the technical, financial and practical issues involved, it also served to alert the authorities and others to the potential uses of an offshore platform well outside any territorial waters where no laws appeared to apply.

Indeed, 'others' were quick to occupy the damp and dirty conditions vacated by the Tower Radio enthusiasts. The offshore wartime bases were widely considered to be of great use as staging posts for smugglers and the Kray twins were associated with attempts to gain control of several of the platforms.

In November the press reported that Walton-on-the-Naze lifeboat had rescued two squatters, weak from lack of food and water, from Sunk Head. The two men, identified as Dexter Stoneham of London and C T Payne of Bexley, Kent, refused to divulge why they were on the fort but a millionaire avant-garde film director David Hart later admitted that he had paid the men to guard the fort in order to enable him to lay claim to it and exploit it 'for commercial purposes'. He said his plans did not have any connections with broadcasting.[5]

David Hart, then in his early twenties, was an interesting character. Eton educated and with a wealthy father, he made a fortune in property during the 1960s and spent it all in the early 1970s. Hart became known as a controversial figure during the 1984 – 1985 miners' strike. He was an unpaid advisor to prime minister Margaret Thatcher, the National Coal Board, and its chair Ian MacGregor, and personally helped to organise and fund the anti-strike campaign in the coalfields.

During the strike David Hart was able to call on the resources of MI5 to discover the National Union of Mineworkers future plans, via a Special

121

Branch informant at the heart of the NUM, and was able to employ former members of the SAS to protect working miners and their families.[6]

In 1987 David Hart formed the Committee for a Free Britain with Lord Harris and others (in 1955 Lord Harris worked with Major Oliver Smedley to form the Institute of Economic Affairs and was the think-tank's first Director General). The very right-wing Committee for a Free Britain opposed the Labour Party in the 1987 General Election campaign, supporting the abolition of the National Health Service and the privatisation of all education. The pressure group also took what they thought to be a very moralistic position in strongly opposing homosexual and lesbian rights.[7]

David Hart went on to be a senior adviser to successive Tory defence ministers and in the 2000s became a defence industry lobbyist for BAE and Boeing. In 2004 an arrest warrant for Hart was issued concerning his alleged involvement in that year's coup attempt in Equatorial Guinea and in 2007 the *Guardian* newspaper alleged Hart had received £13 million in secret payments from BAE Systems via Defence Consultancy Ltd, an anonymously registered company based in the British Virgin Islands.[8]

Upon his death in January 2011 his *Daily Telegraph* obituary concluded 'There were many, however, notably in the Tory party, who detected a whiff of sulphur about Hart. His enemies likened him to Rasputin and accused him of being an agent of the CIA, the KGB, Mossad, or of all three — charges which had the great merit of being impossible to disprove.'[9]

None of the above helps with this story, except in speculating why such a man should want to occupy and hold on to a concrete and iron ruin eleven miles off Clacton-on-Sea.

Certainly the government had an idea why Sunk Head fort held special significance. While none of the other forts were touched by the authorities, within days of the Act outlawing support for pirate radio coming into force in 1967 a Royal Navy tug set out with a team of twenty Royal Engineers to demolish the structure. The metal platform was cut away with oxyacetylene torches and over two thousand pounds of explosive charges were set.

At 4.15 pm on 21 August 1967 people on the Essex shoreline saw and felt an enormous explosion. Large sections of the concrete legs flew up to half a mile away leaving only short stumps of the two giant legs protruding above the sea.

A note on offshore television

Tower Television was not the first broadcaster to propose a pirate television station but it was surely the first to so hugely underestimate the scale of the technical challenges involved.

The idea was not new, until it was forcibly closed down by the Dutch government TV Noordzee had broadcast to the Netherlands for a few months in late 1964 from the artificial REM island planted in the North Sea off Noordwijk. It used 625 lines on the VHF channel 11. And, as mentioned earlier, the Cheetah II had a television studio on board feeding a UHF TV transmitter which was used to broadcast TV Syd programmes to Sweden for a little over a year from December 1965.

However television broadcasting posed huge challenges which simply did not exist for the radio pirates.

Firstly, although BBC2 TV launched in April 1964 using 625 lines in the present UHF TV band, in 1965, the great majority of television viewing in the UK was on VHF frequencies using the original 405 line standard. Many TV sets were still unable to tune to the new UHF channels. With radio there was now a ready supply of cheap portable transistor radios with easy tuning, listeners would twiddle the knob until they heard something they liked, perhaps re-orienting the receiver to get the best reception. Television reception was more complex, most homes still had only one television set and it had to be specifically re-tuned to receive a signal on any channel other than those already used by the BBC and ITV services. Many older sets had rotary 'turret' tuners which had to be clicked round to the required channel – numbered 1 to 12. Fine tuning was generally by way of a ring outside the big clunky knob. Inside the works each channel had its own pre-set 'biscuit', a small circuit board with tunable coils and a set of switch contacts. Often only the biscuits required for the BBC and ITV frequencies in a particular region were fitted, different models being sold around the country. In Essex ours only had Channel 1 (BBC1) and Channel 9 (ITV London), any attempt to receive on any other channel was doomed to failure.

A second issue was the limited range of TV signals. VHF and UHF transmissions are far more dependent upon a line-of-sight between the transmitter and receiver than medium wave radio signals. The BBC and later the Independent Television Authority spent millions on building very high transmitter masts in order to achieve decent population coverage and still each mast might only cover around 40 miles. A typical TV mast built in the 1950s and 1960s – many of them still in use today – would be placed on high ground and be 500 to 1000 foot tall, giving a much higher antenna than anything that could be placed on a small ship or navy fort.

Thirdly, good analogue TV reception, particularly of a weaker signal, required a proper outdoor antenna designed for the correct channel(s) and pointed in the right direction. For example, due to an accident of geography and broadcast history the majority of the TV aerials in populous south-east England were pointed roughly towards south London rather than towards the North Sea.

Finally, quality programme origination was also a much bigger challenge for TV than for radio. This was a time before the availability of cheap videotape recorders. Even major broadcasters had few of the bulky, expensive and often troublesome two-inch VTR machines. Most imported programmes, repeats and advertisements were distributed on film and played on large telecine machines. Colour TV was only at an experimental stage (regular colour programmes did not start on BBC2 until July 1967) and even black-and-white studio equipment was quite complex and difficult to set up and maintain.

Despite the seemingly insurmountable problems rumours persisted of pirate TV launches. Before the days of music videos it was thought that such a station might mainly carry imported syndicated programmes and movies. Many people also expected to see pirated copies of top US entertainment shows not then screened in the UK.

In a similar vein to the ill-fated Tower Television, in May 1965 Radio City's owner, Reg Calvert, made plans to launch City TV, to be broadcast from a former US minesweeper off the Essex coast. The capital costs of the venture, estimated to be in the region of £30,000 were to be met by mysterious American investors (we can probably guess) and it was hoped the running costs would be met by revenue from cigarette advertising, which was to be banned on ITV from the start of August, and religious advertising, which had not been permitted on TV in the UK.

Calvert promised top movies and news bulletins were to be broadcast on 405-line VHF channel 3, a frequency mainly used by the BBC in other regions. However it is unlikely that a ship-based transmitter could have reached London and, even if it had, few sets and aerials would have easily received it. Nothing more was heard of the project.

Also in 1965 a proposed project called 'Radex TV' was announced to the British press by a 49 year old New Zealander James De Grey. He said the station would broadcast recorded television programmes for 18 hours a day.

Using a ship moored 14 miles off Whitstable coverage would extend to Greater London and most of south-east England.

Around the same time separate reports in the Dutch press suggested that Radex TV would be based on a 1250 ton ship registered in Panama which would anchor near the Noordhinder, close to Ostend. They claimed that the station would be seen in London, the West of the Netherlands including Amsterdam, the north of France and the coast of Belgium using relay transmitters on two or three other ships. While the UK broadcasts would be on the old 405-line system still used by most viewers the continental transmissions would be on the new 625-line system.

Six minutes of advertising an hour was planned, including cigarette adverts, and programme material would largely consist of imported American shows, most of which would not have been seen on BBC TV or ITV. Forty crew and broadcasting staff were to be recruited to work on the ships.

According to the press report the UK ship would use a 35 or 50 kW transmitter on VHF channel 6, using an antenna atop a 125 foot mast. A BBC spokesman was sceptical of the claim that this would mean a potential audience of 5 million viewers in south-east England, pointing out that the receiving aerials would have to be pointed into the direction of the ship and that the picture would be disturbed by the transmitting ship moving on the waves. The laws of physics were certainly against the project: due to the curvature of the earth the distance to the horizon for an antenna only 125 feet above sea level is less than 14 miles, nothing like far enough to reach London from the Thames estuary.[10]

In August 1965 the British press reported that due to problems in finding a suitable frequency the Radex TV project was being postponed and would not start until the spring of 1966. In September the American financial backers suddenly withdrew their support and the ill-conceived and over-hyped service never materialised.[11]

Similar technical coverage issues prevented the proposed use of the Cheeta II for a Caroline TV service after she was no longer needed as a temporary base for Radio Caroline South when the repaired and re-equipped Mi Amigo returned to service in May 1966. It had originally been reported that Caroline TV would broadcast to London and south east England from 10 am to 3 pm and from 10 pm to 3 am daily, other reports suggested that the Cheeta II would be anchored off Lundy Island in the Bristol Channel to serve Wales and the west of England.

While in a small but well populated country like Britain it was a practical strategy to build a network of tall terrestrial transmission towers to cover most of the country in the USA it was much harder to supply a basic television service to people living in vast sparsely populated rural areas. A solution had been demonstrated by the Westinghouse Electric Corporation and the Glenn L Martin Company as early as 1948, initially using a twin-engine aircraft carrying a TV transmitter at an altitude of 25,000 feet. The TV test signals were received over a wide area using a UHF channel on 514 MHz and this quickly led to a second test using a B29 Superfortress flying at 30,000 feet. The aircraft was fitted out to receive programmes from the Westinghouse television station WMAR-TV in Baltimore, using aerials on the vertical tail fin and to rebroadcast them via a retractable antenna hanging below the plane using a 5 kW video transmitter on the US VHF TV channel 6.

Key to the success of the system was the fact that a transmitting antenna 30,000 feet above the Earth's surface has a line of sight distance of around 212 miles. The transmissions were watched by viewers in nine neighbouring states. A receiver was set up for the press in a hall on the outskirts of the expected coverage area in Zanesville, Ohio, to demonstrate that the system, now known as Stratovision, would be able to reach remote small towns and farms. The tests proved that it would be possible to provide coast-to-coast coverage of the USA using just eight aircraft.

While the big networks, who had already invested heavily in terrestrial infrastructure in all the major population centres, found it hard to justify the enormous costs involved in reaching the smaller numbers of viewers scattered across the central states, and the Federal Communications Commission struggled with how it could licence stations using scarce channels across such a wide area, Stratovision did seem to have its uses. The first was in education.

The Ford Foundation funded a three year experiment, starting in 1961, in which a DC-6AB aircraft flying at 23,000 feet above Indiana from the airfield of Purdue University broadcast educational programmes to 13,000 schools and colleges. The aircraft, operated by a non-profit organisation, the Midwest Program on Airborne Television Instruction, used two UHF TV channels to transmit recorded lectures from two massive two inch videotape machines.

The CIA soon found a second application for the Stratovision technology. In the aftermath of the Cuban missile crisis, it was proposed that the propaganda war against Castro using Radio Swan should be expanded to include television broadcasts into Cuba. In a secret memo to US President Kennedy the famous television journalist Edward R. Murrow had suggested that the Stratovision system could be used to target the Cuban population.

The secret memo, now released by the Kennedy Presidential Library, described how recorded TV programmes could be transmitted from two specially equipped DC-6 aircraft flying at 18,000 feet just outside Cuban airspace. The full plan was not put into action against Cuba in the sixties, although President Reagan later launched something similar as TV Marti.[12]

It is known that the US Navy equipped at least two aircraft for TV broadcasting in 1965 to carry out what were known as 'psychological operations' or PSYOPS. The project was known as Blue Eagle and involved Navy electronics experts at Andrews Air Force Base stripping-out NC-121 Lockheed Super Constellation aircraft and installing AM, FM, short wave and TV transmission equipment supplied by RCA. The planes each carried two large RCA TR-22 videotape recorders, telecine machines and a 100 kW diesel generator.

It is thought the aircraft were used to transmit propaganda into Cuba on a few occasions and remained on standby for use if the Cuban situation were to flare up again. During the 1965 Dominican Republic crisis one of the planes was used to broadcast pre-recorded TV programmes to the local population in Spanish

Shortly afterwards the aircraft were sent to South Vietnam where, circling between 10,000 and 20,000 feet above the Saigon area, they broadcast two VHF television channels, one a Saigon government service for the Vietnamese on channel 9, and an Armed Forces Vietnam Network channel for US servicemen on channel 11. Reports at the time suggested the aircraft could also present their own live programmes from a small on-board studio.

While now largely overtaken by developments in satellite broadcasting and social media, the US still finds it useful to retain at least one aircraft capable of broadcasting to foreign places of interest. The EC-130 Commando Solo has been used to broadcast information and propaganda for the United States over a wide variety of television and radio frequencies around the world. Other modified C-130 Hercules aircraft have been used relatively recently to broadcast in several areas of operation, including Bosnia, Haiti and Iraq. Equipped to broadcast at high power on AM, FM, short wave, TV and military communication channels the planes can generate VHF and UHF colour television signals in worldwide formats and have equally well been used to disrupt or jam enemy broadcasts or communications. They can be refuelled in the air and stay on-air for protracted periods.

It wasn't until after the Marine Broadcasting Offences Act had outlawed support for offshore broadcasting in the UK that Ronan O'Rahilly announced his plans for Caroline Television. In 1968 he claimed that the service would be ready to start in the spring of the next year broadcasting on a UHF channel in 625-line colour from 6 pm to 3 am nightly.

Unlike the technically implausible earlier proposals for UK pirate TV broadcasts Ronan O'Rahily had learned from the American experience. Indeed his plans appear to have been guided by someone close to the US military PSYOPS projects. Using an aircraft to beam the signal from 20,000 feet above the international waters of the North Sea Caroline Television would overcome any signal coverage problems and the plane could land overseas to be refuelled and take on new programmes for the next day's transmission. The programmes from 6 pm to midnight daily were to be mainly pre-recorded shows bought from foreign television stations and – a novelty at that time - short music videos.

Backing for the project was said to have come from American companies interested in the advertising potential of the station. To get round the UK's new Marine Broadcasting Offences Act, offices in Canada and the United States would sell airtime and cigarette advertising was expected to loom large.

Caroline Television's start-up cost using two large aircraft, one in service and one as a stand-by, was estimated at a million pounds, but against this the short-lived Dutch pirate station TV Noordzee was said to have taken £300,000 of advertising revenue in a little over three months. Ronan O'Rahilly claimed to have got his hands on two aircraft already fitted-out and ready to operate the service from the spring of 1969.

The programmes from Caroline Television were to have been beamed to the ground using Stratovision-type technology from two Lockheed Super Constellation aircraft – suspiciously the same as the US had been using in Cuba and Vietnam. How Caroline would be able to get the use of two such expensively equipped four-engine aircraft was never made public.

While it was perhaps plausible that the kind of businessmen who found the initial funding to convert ships into radio stations might have identified rich backers to meet the costs of setting up such a TV project, the ongoing cost of maintaining a service from an aircraft circling off the coast for several hours every evening would have been considerable.

Most press reports remained sceptical and, in an attempt to silence the doubters, Ronan O'Rahily organised a demonstration for the press one evening in central London. The press were gathered around a specially set-up television but at the appointed hour absolutely nothing appeared. Some speculated that the project, and the aircraft, never really existed and the story was just an elaborate publicity stunt. However I think it seems unlikely that a serial entrepreneur like Ronan O'Reilly would have risked such damage to his reputation without believing that something was really going to happen.

Publicly Ronan O'Rahilly later said that the project folded on the withdrawal of support from his American backers and advertisers in the face of British Government pressure. It is possible that following the defeat of Labour in the 1969 General Election some of his backers were no longer so motivated to make life difficult for the UK government (see Radio North Sea International later in this book). Privately O'Rahilly told friends and colleagues that the two aircraft he was to charter had been destroyed overseas before he could use them, but he did not know by whom.

CHAPTER EIGHT

LAISSEZ FAIRE

By 1966 there were nine radio stations broadcasting from ships and abandoned wartime forts dotted around the British coast. The broadcast spectrum, which government ministers had once claimed was too crowded to permit any more radio channels, suddenly seemed a lot more elastic. And not one offshore station had been closed down by the UK authorities.

But was there really room in the market for another two commercial stations? The Texans thought so.

At the start of May 1966 Radio London's MV Galaxy and Radio Caroline's Mi Amigo and were joined some four miles off Walton-on-the-Naze by the MV Olga Patricia. The new ship was lavishly equipped and housed two separate radio stations. Each station had its own studio built into a prefabricated module lowered into one hold of the former cargo vessel while a pair of brand-new Continental Electronics 317C 50 kW transmitters was expertly installed in another prefabricated unit lowered into the other hold.

This was not a cheap and cheerful, make-do-and-mend, operation like the recently established Radio Scotland or Radio 270. This was a very well-funded project which had learned lessons, at least in terms of technical matters, from the previous American offshore radio ships.

The Olga Patricia had been built for the US Army in 1944 as the USS Deal, a substantial landing craft 177 feet long and displacing 550 tons. After the second world war she was sold and converted into a tramp freighter, plying the Caribbean. She conveniently flew the Panamanian flag. Procured for the new radio project in March 1966 she was moved in great secrecy from Panama to the Dodge Island shipyard at Biscayne Bay, Miami, to be fitted out for radio broadcasting. The shipyard was close to the CIA's giant JM WAVE base secretly located a few miles away in a heavily wooded 1,571 acre area that is now home to Miami zoo.

JM WAVE was the Central Intelligence Agency station in Florida. Being, among other things, the operational headquarters for Operation Mongoose, the CIA's project to overthrow Cuba's President Castro, the base employed more than 200 CIA officers and controlled the USA's clandestine broadcasting activities in the region.

The Olga Patricia was painted black and white and quietly and expensively fitted out with broadcasting equipment, a 160-foot transmitting mast and powerful generators. The transmitter and antenna work was done by the LTV-Continental Electronics company (CEMCO) of Dallas as a complete turn-key installation. Outsiders were not allowed anywhere near the ship and queries from the local press were met with a story that the ship was being fitted out for oceanographic research.

In April 1966 a press conference in London had been told of the plan to launch, at the end of the month, two new pirate radio stations operating from a single ship. 'Swinging Radio England' would be an American style Top 40 station while 'Britain Radio, your hallmark of quality' would play easy listening 'good music'. Both were to be operated and presented by experienced American broadcasters.

The man behind these two stations was the Texan who had just sixteen months earlier launched Radio London, the well-connected millionaire car dealer Don Pierson. Pierson had lost control of the Radio London project to his English partners and some of the less idealistically committed American investors but this time he was determined to stay in the saddle. Going back to his tight network of Texas millionaires he raised the equivalent of well over a million pounds to start his new European radio venture.

While the project was still driven by Don Pierson, financial control was plainly in the hands of Pierce Langford III and his Wichita Falls, Texas, group of investors for whom Pierson was the banker. Langford had a lot of contacts in high places and was a key supporter and close ally of Republican Senator John Tower who served in the US Senate for Texas between 1961 and 1985. Senator Tower was no stranger to ships and radio stations, he had served on a similar vessel in the Pacific in the second world war and had been involved in radio during his time at college in Texas. He had been a political science instructor at Midwestern University in Wichita Falls before coming to the London School of Economics in the UK in 1952 to study the organisation of the Conservative Party, leading to his masters thesis on *The Conservative Worker in Britain*.

Senator John Tower devoted much of his time in the Senate to the oversight of US military spending and intelligence affairs. He served on the Joint Committee on Defense Production and became chairman of the Senate Armed Services Committee. In the mid-1980s Tower retired from the Senate to become a highly-paid defence consultant. (In November 1986, President Reagan appointed Tower to chair the President's Special Review Board to study the actions of the National Security Council and its staff during the

Iran-Contra affair. However when President George Bush selected Tower to become his Secretary of Defence in 1989 the Senate refused to confirm his nomination because of alleged excessive drinking and womanising. He went on to chair the White House Foreign Intelligence Advisory Board.[1]

It is widely known that Senator John Tower paid a secret visit to the Curzon Street offices of Radio England and Britain Radio in 1966 but those involved have always declined to explain why.

The mystery, then as now, is why, especially given pending UK government legislation, a group of astute and busy American businessmen should think that a third attempt at operating a floating radio station in the waters of northern Europe constituted a worthwhile commercial investment of their time and money? Were these men (yet again they were all men) just playing at radio stations like their contemporaries at Tower Radio (no relation) – but with budgets a hundred times larger – or did they have ulterior motives? Or was it not their money at all?

These questions were being asked at the time and were giving the UK government and their secret services some concern. In his 1966 book *Billion Dollar Brain* spy novelist Len Deighton has as his key bad man an oil magnate from Texas who is working with and for the CIA: 'Look, the guy's a multi-millionaire, a multi-billionaire maybe. This is his toy. Why should I spoil his fun? He made his money from canned food and insurance; that's a dull way to make a billion, so he needs a little fun. The CIA syphon a little money to him... He has two radio stations on ships that beam into the Baltic states.'

The financial model for Radio England/Britain Radio was very similar to that used for all the previous US-funded radio ships, including of course the Texan investors' first European venture Radio Nord in the Baltic Sea. The initial capital cost of setting up the station largely appeared to come from individuals with considerable oil wealth at their disposal and what they would call a patriotic desire to spread the American way of life around the globe. Then the ongoing running costs were underwritten by income from the Radio Church of God and other conservative religious groups.

This time it was slightly different though, the hard-hitting fast-paced Top 40 station would not have to disrupt its format to include the religious sermons from Garner T Armstrong because these would only appear, twice daily, on the more sedate and traditional Britain Radio. This mirrored the Radio City technique of putting God on 188 metres while Mammon continued uninterrupted on 299 metres.

Don Pierson surrounded himself with talented and experienced US radio professionals. For example his technical plans were overseen by Bill Carr, an experienced consulting radio engineer of Fort Worth, Texas, and he brought in experienced American programme director Ron O'Quinn from WFUN in Miami, Florida. William E Vick of Amarillo, Texas, whose wealthy family were also investors in the venture, was given an exclusive contract to handle the advertising sales. Vick formed a British company called Peir Vick Limited to run the UK end of the business and it was he who found the surprisingly affordable offices at 32 Curzon Street, directly across the road from Radio London, round the corner from Radio Caroline and, of course, less than a hundred yards down from MI5's Leconfield House on the other side of the street.

Having no radio sales experience himself, William Vick entered into a contract with a company called Radiovision Broadcasts International (RBI) to sell airtime on the two stations. RBI had been formed at the start of the year to act as European agents for the ABC radio and television networks in the USA and was a subsidiary of Pearl & Dean, famous for their business of selling advertising on British cinema screens. Their strident theme music lives on in multiplexes today. He also contracted Peter Rendall and Associates to handle public relations and organise parties to launch the stations.

Writing some years later DJ Johnnie Walker recalled meeting William Vick and Don Pearson: 'They were supposedly very wealthy. One looked the part, with ten gallon hat and cowboy boots, JR and everything. But I am not sure. I think it was maybe all pretty much of a scam.'[2]

Despite the use of experienced contractors and their lavish budgets, or perhaps because of it, the project was beset by technical difficulties. Firstly the Continental Electronics people handling the installation at the Miami facility were used to working on defence contracts where cost overruns and missed deadlines were the norm and as a result the ship had to set sail before it was fully kitted out. Secondly some basic mistakes were made in choosing the frequencies and transmitter configurations. As supplied in the USA the transmitters were set to operate on 850 kHz and 640 kHz. These frequencies did not correspond to the European medium wave band channels. While in the North America AM stations were spaced 10 kHz apart – all frequencies ending in zero – to fit more stations in the crowded European airwaves the channels were spaced at just 9 kHz. Broadcasting on a nearby frequency on top of an interfering signal creates an audible whistle, a 'heterodyne' which can be annoying to listeners to both services.

It seems that nobody had properly researched the frequencies chosen as the 640 kHz transmission would have been hopelessly close to the powerful BBC national transmitter carrying the BBC Third Programme (now Radio 3) on 647 kHz. New crystals had to be obtained and the transmitters and antennas were re-tuned to operate on 1322 kHz and 845 kHz before test transmissions could begin.

A third technical issue arose from Don Pierson's desire to make use of state-of-the-art automation systems just being introduced on music stations across the USA. Each station was equipped with an elaborate mechanical device that could run the station on its own, complete with pre-recorded time-checks and commercials, without the need for intervention. We take such technology for granted today but in those days before digital audio and cheap computers the system depended on pre-recorded music on reels of tape with spoken links, commercials and jingles inserted on pre-recorded cues from tape cartridges. The automation could mean a considerable reduction in the number of live DJs required, off-peak and overnight programmes being completely automatic.

When Ron O'Quinn joined the station he told Don Pierson that, while the clunky automation might work for the easy listening format of Britain Radio, he was not convinced it could handle the tight, high-energy, format he had in mind for the Top 40 Swinging Radio England. A full sized Collins Radio studio mixer was hastily purchased and installed in the Radio England studio together with the traditional pair of record turntables and manually fired cartridge machines for jingles, adverts and sound effects. The addition of more DJs also meant the construction of more sleeping accommodation, which was in fact not completed until the station was already on the air off the Essex coast.

Fourthly, in Miami Bill Carr had overseen the erection of a 160 foot mast to support two separate transmitting antennas. To accommodate the second antenna CEMCO installed an additional mast and boom complete with a heavy cable and electrical insulators. Following the experience of the earlier radio ships crossing the Atlantic, Don Pierson was concerned that the mast was not up to the job and, sure enough, it collapsed in rough seas within a couple of hours of leaving port and fell overboard. The ship dragged the toppled mast all the way across the Atlantic to the Azores. The mast was eventually refitted in Lisbon and the Olga Patricia was able to continue her journey to the North Sea.[3]

As a result of all these delays the ship was not ready for the original 30 April launch date, but test transmissions did commence on 3 May 1966.

Initially Britain Radio appeared on 1320 kHz, publicised as 227 metres, and Swinging Radio England on 845 kHz, promoted as 355 metres. The station quickly received complaints from Italy of interference to the Italian station Roma II on 845 kHz and so a number of other options were tried, eventually settling on Swinging Radio England being on 1322 kHz (227 metres) while Britain Radio was on 854 kHz (still promoted as 355 metres). To further minimise interference Britain Radio operated on reduced power during the hours of darkness when medium wave interference would become an issue.

With test transmissions complete Swinging Radio England and Britain Radio were launched with a very expensive star-studded party organised by Peter Rendall and Associates at the Park Lane Hilton Hotel. The extravagant celebration created a great deal of press attention, it was dubbed 'the party of the year' and separately RBI hosted some 250 potential advertisers at the Savoy. It was as though money was no object, although in reality it was running out rapidly (the project later collapsed without paying the huge Hilton Hotel bill for the party and three months accommodation for Pierson and Vick).

The message that came across loud and clear was that this was a serious incursion into British radio by a very rich and powerful American organisation. To make sure everyone got the point Swinging Radio England launched by playing *The Yellow Rose of Texas*. Although Swinging Radio England was to launch UK radio careers of Brits Roger Day and Johnnie Walker, it was dominated by American voices and high-pressure US-style presentation the like of which had never before been heard in Britain. While the BBC and Radio 390 had 'presenters' behind the microphone and Radio London had 'disc jockeys', Swinging Radio England had 'Boss Jocks'.

The 'Boss Radio' format put in place by Ron O'Quinn was an amalgam of what was currently happening on a number of US Top 40 radio stations ranging from KHJ on the west coast to KLIF in Dallas and WABC in New York. Everything was delivered in strong American accents in fast-paced, high-energy, shouted links with full use of echo and recorded effects. The station jingles were, like those commissioned for Radio London, recorded by the then world leaders in radio jingles, PAMS of Dallas (the fresh and powerful jingles, based on the Jet Set series 27 originally composed for WABC in New York, were broadcast extensively during the test transmissions without anyone talking over them - with the result that all the other pirates were able to record them off-air and edit them for their own purposes).

It is hard to imagine in today's world dominated by instantaneous social media, but in the sixties it could take months for a song, movie, or hit TV show to cross the Atlantic from the United States. Media companies could wait to put out their product in other markets or licence them to other companies in foreign territories. Swinging Radio England with its carefully cultivated American image was able to exploit this gap in the market by broadcasting US hits before they reached our shores.

This was what Don Pierson had wanted his Wonderful Radio London to sound like, an undiluted example of contemporary American culture not softened for the possibly more refined English market. To my ears the most blatant example of Swinging Radio England's disregard for UK broadcasting traditions was its news bulletins at 15 minutes past each hour. Ron O'Quinn brought the news format directly from his previous station, WFUN in Florida. It involved rapid-fire headlines delivered with echo and punctuated with electronic effects. Originally the ship apparently used a teleprinter to collect the news but the teletype radio link could not cope with the proximity of two high power transmitters and in the end the news presenters were reduced to copying the news headlines from the BBC just like the other pirates.

In comparison to SRE the second service from the Olga Patricia, Britain Radio, sounded far more relaxed and, in that sense, British. However the station's continuous middle-of-the-road music was introduced by silky American voices to which the stations older more conservative target listeners found it hard to relate. The syrupy smooth delivery of the 'Hallmark of Quality' did not sound like the sincere conversation of a friend - a key attribute for any radio presentation - it didn't have a human touch. As much of the programming was in fact automated this was, I now recognise, not surprising.[4]

The brash new station Swinging Radio England initially created a great deal of excitement among teenagers, although I remember that the expression 'swinging' already seemed rather dated in mid-1966. It was the sort of thing an uncle said when they were trying to sound 'with-it'. It had already been done to death in the catchphrase of comedian Norman Vaughan as host of the very popular ITV show *Sunday Night at the London Palladium*, where 'swinging!' or 'dodgy!' were illustrated with a thumbs-up or thumbs-down gesture.

Where Wonderful Radio London DJs had balanced the professionalism and polish of American radio with the personality, warmth and humour of presenters like Dave Cash and Kenny Everett, and the originality and talent of John Peel, listening to Swinging Radio England was just like voluntarily subjecting yourself to non-stop high pressure salesmanship, and it didn't work in the UK. Crucially for Don Pierson's dreams the harsh American sound did not attract many advertisers either, while Britain Radio's softer American sound failed to tempt its potential audience away from Radio 390 and the BBC.

Don Pierson's attempt to launch two new all-American radio stations to compete with what he saw as the watered-down sound of Radio London suffered from an almost complete lack of understanding of the radio landscape in the UK. A well-funded and professionally conceived project in Texas had failed to do any research on this side of the pond. From the frequencies used to the state of the advertising market, from the branding of Radio England to the music policy of Britain Radio they obviously thought they knew best.

The stations were never as powerful as they should have been, frequently sounding weaker than Radios London, Caroline or 390 in central London. While the station was fond of claiming that the Olga Patricia, now renamed the SS Laissez Faire, was the most powerful UK radio ship - and indeed it would have been if both 50 kW transmitters had ever operated together at their full potential - in practice both transmitters had to be backed-off to prevent serious issues with the antenna tuning. Having two high-power transmitters feeding the same mast created immense technical problems in the damp, salty, unstable environment of the North Sea. Most of the time the stations were radiating less than half their potential power with Swinging Radio England being allowed a slight advantage due to its poorer frequency.

In July 1966 Radio Caroline commissioned National Opinion Polls (NOP) to survey one weeks radio listening among adults aged 15-54 across the UK.[5] The headline was that 45% of the population said they had listened to a commercial radio station (a pirate or Radio Luxembourg) during the previous seven days, a figure rising to a massive 78% of the 16-24 age group.

The seven-day reach of each station among all adults was given as:

Radio Caroline	8,818,000
Radio Luxembourg	8,818,000
Radio London	8,140,000
Radio 390	2,633,000
Radio England	2,274,000
Radio Scotland	2,195,000
Britain Radio	718,000

With such poor audience figures and little advertising support the only thing making Britain Radio viable was its twice-daily broadcasts of *The World Tomorrow,* the revenue from the mysterious Radio Church of God keeping the station in the black. Without the religious income the more popular Radio England was struggling financially, the RBI advertising operation only able to forecast sales at 15% of the originally projected levels.

By the beginning of October 1966 the Texan investors were growing restless. The shareholders fell into two main camps, Pierce Langford's group based in Abilene and Wichita Falls and a second group of smaller investors from western Texas who were beginning to suspect that they had not understood the real purpose of the radio ship. At a heated board meeting in Abilene, Texas on 7 October 1966 Pierce Langford III won a vote to have Don Pierson removed as Project Manager, a replay of his dismissal from Radio London two years previously.

William Vick was now CEO of the operation and he chose Britain Radio's programme director, Jack Curtiss, to become general manager of the two stations. Faced with the British governments intention to legislate against the pirates it was decided that Radio England should be replaced by a Dutch station with its offices based in Amsterdam. Radio Dolfijn, with a new team of Dutch-speaking DJs, took over the 227 metres transmitter in November. Supported by its 'religious' sponsors Britain Radio continued to struggle along for another three months

By early 1967 Ted Allebury had resigned from Radio 390 and was brought in as managing director to breathe new life into the easy-listening Britain Radio. Modelling the station on Radio 390, Allebury renamed the station Radio 355 and brought in the experienced and respected DJ Tony Windsor as programme director. Allebury's company Carstead Advertising took over the sales operation from the hopeless RBI. Peir Vick Limited, the operating company formed a year earlier by William Vick to run the two stations from the plush offices in Curzon Street had now spent all those Texan dollars and went into liquidation on March 1967 with debts of over £100,000. With control of both stations in Allebury's hands Radio Dolfijn became the Dutch Radio 227 ('Radio Twee Twee Zeven') and sat alongside the new Radio 355 as a popular Dutch-language equivalent of the original Swinging Radio England.

Unfortunately it was all too little too late for the stations on the Laissez Faire (the ship named after the French expression meaning a system or point of view that opposes regulation or interference by the government in economic affairs beyond the minimum necessary to allow the free enterprise system to operate according to its own principles). The government was now finally determined to enact legislation which would make it an offence for anyone in the UK to supply or support an offshore radio station. Once the law was in place an Englishman like Allebury would be arrested entering the country even if he attempted to run a pirate station from offices abroad.

In a last-ditch attempt to recoup at least some of the original Texan investment Ted Allebury looked into ways to offload the station or stations onto a completely foreign owner. Herbert W Armstrong's *The World Tomorrow* was still broadcast twice daily and paying the bills for Radio 355 so one idea was to sell him the whole operation. Allebury befriended the American millionaire evangelist and even visited him at his home near the Church's headquarters in Pasadena California. However neither Armstrong or his financial backers were interested in being seen to directly control a radio station in northern Europe with a blatantly controversial political agenda.[6]

With no alternative plan Radio 227 closed down at the end of July and Radio 355 followed on 6 August 1967.

CHAPTER NINE

SHIVERING SANDS

Radio City was, and had always been, a very different operation from any of the other stations. Owner Reg Calvert appears to have been in exclusive control of the station. There was always a feeling, usually well-founded, that the managers of the other stations were merely front-men for the big money interests lurking some way behind them.

With Reg Calvert you got what you saw. He was motivated by a simple desire to make money while having fun, this theme ran through all his previous exploits and business ventures. As a result he was seen by other pirate operators as a loose cannon, he was also an easy target for those who wanted to expand their empires.

Until 1964 the rusty, decaying, abandoned sea forts, although visible on the horizon from the beaches of Kent and Essex, had been largely forgotten. In the space of a year they had become valuable real-estate for the radio operators and their backers and were like the squares on a pirate radio game of Monopoly.

Back in early 1965, with advertising revenue suffering after the launch of Radio London, and running out of cash, Project Atlanta shareholders Allan Crawford, Major Oliver Smedley and Kitty Black had to find a way to reduce the cost of operating Radio Caroline South. They had realised that newcomers like Reg Calvert appeared able to operate profitably from ex-military forts even with relatively small audiences. The forts offered free accommodation for low-budget radio stations, whereas ships required substantial investment and expensive maintenance to keep them seaworthy. And they were labour-intensive, in addition to the broadcasting staff the Caroline ships each had a Dutch crew of around ten, including the captain, first officer, engineering officer, deck hands and a cook.

Many of the fort-based radio stations were estimated to have total weekly costs of just £600, compared with more than ten times that for the ships. For Radio City, it was said the entire operating costs were met by a single contract for the evening religious broadcasts for £125 per hour.

Initially the ship-based broadcasters had assumed that the government would move fairly quickly to evict their rivals from the wartime forts in the Thames estuary. While the forts appeared to be just outside territorial waters they were undoubtedly owned by the Ministry of Defence and, although they had been largely abandoned for many years, it would be a simple matter for the MoD to reassert its ownership. When it became clear that this was not going to happen the option of occupying a fort started to become attractive to operators like Radio Caroline and Radio London.

And it wasn't just a question of cost. The former Army forts in the Thames estuary were ideally placed to send a strong signal into central London. For a while Caroline and London had tried anchoring near Shivering Sands fort but, faced with strong currents, rough water and heavy passing traffic both had retreated to their regular position off Frinton-on-Sea. Looking out on a seemingly empty sea from the Essex beaches it was easy for a landlubber to underestimate the problem of finding a safe and secure home for a stationary ship surrounded by busy sea lanes, shifting sand banks and some of the most challenging sea conditions.

The forts offered other advantages too, the widely spaced towers of the Army forts made it possible to erect a full size quarter-wavelength long vertical transmitting antenna and guy it solidly to the other towers. Combined with the excellent electrical earth provided by miles of salt water a decent transmitter could cover most of southern England. The stable platform also solved a recurrent problem for the DJs, quite apart from issue of sea-sickness the rough North Sea was not the ideal environment for paying seven-inch single vinyl records. The usual trick was to stick one or more pennies on top of the turntable pickup to keep the needle in the groove but this could only go so far.

So Allan Crawford started talks with Reg Calvert, owner of Radio City. Calvert was aware that, in order for his station to compete seriously with the better resourced Radio Caroline and Radio London, he needed a major injection of capital and a more powerful, better quality, transmitter and antenna. They reached an agreement that Radio Caroline South would transfer onto the Shivering Sands fort and a joint company would be set up to run the combined operation. Project Atlanta would sell advertising and take all the revenue but would meet all of the station's running expenses. In return for managing the station Calvert would be paid £1,500 per month and would receive half of the profits. Meanwhile the Mi Amigo ship would be moved away from the south east to provide a Radio Caroline service for a less well-served stretch of the English coastline – perhaps the south west or north east.

Further negotiations between Oliver Smedley and Calvert led to Smedley arranging for a powerful American transmitter to be shipped out from Texas to Shivering Sands. Calvert was doubtless eagerly awaiting the arrival of a shiny new 50 kW Continental Electronics or RCA transmitter like those recently installed on the other ships. However when the Caroline tender, Offshore I, brought the transmitter out to the fort the reality turned out to be rather different. When the beast arrived, accompanied by two engineers from Project Atlanta, it was packed in three very heavy crates each larger than a telephone box. Winching the first crate up to the tower from the deck of the tender proved too much for the fort's old crane and it crashed back down onto the deck of the boat, on the second attempt the weight was too much for the two-inch rope being used and, when the crate caught on the edge of the platform some seventy feet above the sea, the rope parted and the crate fell into the sea, coming to rest in about twenty feet of salty water at the foot of the tower.

The remaining cases were slightly lighter and were successfully transferred onto the fort and, eager to rescue a transmitter which he had been told was worth £10,000, Reg Calvert arranged for divers to retrieve the submerged crate. When everything was unpacked and the first unit, containing the heavy power supplies, had been washed with fresh water and dried out, the fort-based engineers were disappointed to find that this was not a state-of-the-art American import but second-hand equipment bought from a country music station in Fort Worth Texas, KCUL. The 25 year-old 10 kW transmitter, recently pensioned off and replaced by the Texas station, was in fact older than some of the war-surplus gear that it joined in the transmitter room on Shivering Sands. Indeed it was older than the abandoned fort in which it was now housed.

Whether Oliver Smedley knew what he was doing or whether the non-technical Major had been sold a pup by one of his Texan friends is not clear, but the transmitter was not what Calvert needed to lift his station onto a higher level of broadcasting. Despite many attempts to commission it the pre-war design was incredibly power-hungry and it demanded more current that all the generators on the fort could provide. It was put to one side and Radio City continued to broadcast using its existing lower power kit.[1]

Although Smedley and Crawford had made little progress with the arrangements, the deal with Project Atlanta to merge with Radio Caroline South was supposed to start from October 1965 and Radio City started to re-broadcast some Radio Caroline news bulletins and promoted some programmes for their erstwhile rival. Things were not going well for Reg Calvert however, while Radio City was no longer collecting any revenue the promised payments for his time and station costs from Project Atlanta were not arriving. The final straw was when Project Atlanta sent Radio City the

£600 invoice for shipping the useless transmitter from Texas. Calvert refused to pay the bill, which he had always assumed would be met by Smedley as part of their deal, adding that the equipment did not work, was Atlanta's property and that they could come and collect it any time they wanted.

Of course we now know that Project Atlanta was broke and within weeks had to sell-up and hand over control of Radio Caroline South to Ronan O'Rahilly and his Planet Productions. While the original Radio Caroline company took over all the assets and liabilities of the old Atlanta these did not seem to extend to the outstanding deal with Reg Calvert. Radio City claimed that it was owed some £8,000 in operating costs and as its share of revenue, but this was not forthcoming. It is not clear whether O'Rahilly or his fellow directors had ever been aware, much less approved of, the side deal with the transmitter and the fort set up by Crawford and Smedley.

With Project Atlanta apparently gone Radio City became independent again and from the beginning of 1966 started meeting its own operating costs and selling its own advertising airtime. Allan Crawford had resigned but Major Oliver Smedley was not finished, he still wanted to run his own pirate radio station and was particularly keen to make use of the cheap and well-positioned Shivering Sands fort as the base for a new high-power station. Smedley offered Calvert £10,000 to buy the station but Calvert declined the offer, believing the station and its squatters rights on the useful Shivering Sands fort were worth far more.

Meanwhile, Radio City's chief engineer Paul Elvey pushed for the proposed better antenna to be installed on the fort anyway and, realising that this would enhance the value of the station to new investors, particularly to compensate for the lower power of the transmitter, Reg Calvert agreed. Without the new capital required to pay for an expensive professional antenna mast Calvert struck a deal with an aerial engineer called Alan Arnold to rent one. Arnold and his men soon installed a 200-foot mast which, when added to the height of the tower on which it was mounted, meant Radio City could now boast the tallest antenna of any of the pirate stations. It was ready for the next step.

Oliver Smedley tried to keep in contact with Reg Calvert but, understandably, Calvert did not trust the Major and was sceptical about Smedley's ability to fund any promised new radio enterprise. According to Calvert's daughter Susan he simply did not like Smedley as a person and he found his upper-class scams and dodgy investment schemes distasteful.[2]

Having failed to raise any further capital from his usual chums in the city to keep Atlanta afloat Oliver Smedley was now starting to cast his net further afield. He was well known as an expert in, shall we say, tax-efficient and anonymous methods for individuals to hold offshore investments. His long-time personal assistant Aubrey Bountwood worked his way through a long list of individuals who had previously approached the pair seeking outlets for money which the authorities did not really need to know about. Bountwood, a former bankrupt who had served time for cheque fraud, had joined Smedley's investment advice and campaigning company Investment and General Management Services Limited as his accountant in the late 1950s and was his loyal fixer. On numerous occasions Smedley contacted Reg Calvert with news of potential investors, on one occasion going so far as to arrange for the investor to come to Radio City's Denmark Street office to look at the accounts, but nothing came of any of the approaches and Calvert was becoming impatient.

In the early summer of 1966 Reg Calvert's family noticed a change in his mood. Gone was his usual optimistic, and often misplaced, belief that he could make any enterprise work - to be replaced by some dark concerns that he would not share with his wife and daughters. Dorothy Calvert said that Reg seemed to be very worried. He wanted his wife and his daughters Susan and Candy to go abroad and stay there until a situation was sorted out but Dorothy refused. Later he told Dorothy that their lives had all been threatened, but he wouldn't give any more details. The Radio City project had been his pride and joy, largely superseding all his other music business activities, but now something had happened and he wanted rid of it, and quickly. Reg Calvert's passion for pirate radio was undiminished however, the only reason he was holding out for a better price for the Shivering Sands venture was in order to raise capital to set up a new station of his own on one of the other forts or in the Bristol Channel.

Major Smedley kept up the barrage of proposals, at one point suggesting that he and Reg Calvert form a joint stock company to run the fort and raise more capital from investors, but it seems the more Smedley and his contacts pushed Calvert the more worried he became and was soon desperate to find another way to get out of Shivering Sands.

Reg Calvert began negotiations to sell the whole enterprise to Radio London, initially expecting the station would move from the MV Galaxy onto the fort and make use of the new transmission mast. The businessman behind Radio London's commercial success, Philip Birch, mindful of the risk of future government legislation and the doubtful legality of the fort-based stations, had a better idea. Rather than risk or dilute the successful Radio London proposition they would jointly set up a new station called United Kingdom Good Music – or UKGM – to broadcast from the towers.

Under the deal Radio City would be replaced by UKGM and the new station would be managed by Radio London who would also handle all the advertising sales. Calvert would be free of any day-to-day management responsibilities but would still own 45% of the station and would receive a monthly income of £1,000. The agreement was set to commence on 1 June 1966 and the sweet music station would become operational on 1 July.

When Reg Calvert took a party of Radio London representatives out to Shivering Sands to look at their acquisition they were far from impressed. The group, including the Radio London office manager Dennis Maitland, engineer Martin Newton and Big L disc jockeys Duncan Johnson and Keith Skues, were quite appalled by the make-shift technical arrangements and bleak living conditions on the fort. Duncan Johnson commented 'it looked like a doss house compared to Radio London'. Still they managed to identify how they could re-develop the remaining towers, where they could place a new transmitter and build a new studio etc., and it looked like the deal could go ahead.[3]

Unfortunately, unaware of the arrangement with Radio London, Major Oliver Smedley had been pressing ahead with his own plans for the fort and had started making promises to some new investors. In early June, before the UKGM project had become public knowledge, Smedley rang Calvert to say he had finally firmed-up a deal for the fort. Whoever Smedley's mystery investors were it became clear that they were not the kind of people to take no for an answer and, when Calvert broke the news that he had entered into a separate deal with Radio London, Smedley rapidly became disturbed, angry and abusive.

The true meaning of a recent mysterious phone call to the Radio City office in Denmark Street suddenly became apparent. The anonymous caller had wanted to warn Reg and Dorothy Calvert that someone was planning to raid the Shivering Sands fort and take it over but would give no more information. The Calvert's had taken this to mean more trouble from Roy Bates, the boss of Radio Essex with whom they had already fought over occupation of the Knock John fort. Dorothy Calvert, who was now responsible for the routine management of the station, sent an urgent message to the station. They were to maintain a look-out and keep all the access hatches securely bolted.

It later emerged that the anonymous phone caller was Ted Allebury, then boss of rival fort-based station Radio 390, who maintained close contact with his former friends and colleagues in the British security services.

When the UKGM plan was made public in a newspaper article on 16 June Oliver Smedley realised that Shivering Sands was slipping from his grasp and his investors were not happy. Desperately needing to regain the initiative he decided to use the disputed transmitter as a pretext for direct action.

Major Smedley now finalised a plan to send a boarding party to take over the Shivering Sands fort by force. He contacted his former partners in Project Atlanta, Allan Crawford and Kitty Black for support. Allan Crawford did not want to be involved and warned Smedley against doing anything that would bring the stations into disrepute but Kitty Black, who believed that her money had been used to purchase the unwanted transmitter, said she would be happy to go along with the raid.

Oliver Smedley and Kitty Black, with the help of a couple of Trinity House pilots who had invested in Project Atlanta, quickly chartered a large tug and assembled a group of ten riggers, famously led by 'Big Alf' Bullen, from the London Docks. The party, including Smedley and Black, left Gravesend pier at midnight on Sunday 19 June.

Arriving just off the five Shivering Sands towers in darkness at about 3 am, when it was assumed everyone on board would be asleep, Alf Bullen and one of the other riggers were told they would have to climb each of the towers in turn until they found one with an open trapdoor. What happened next is difficult to believe. Transferred across to the foot of the first tower in a small motorboat they climbed to the top via an old rusty ladder to find the trap door into the chamber above had been left open. And, better yet, climbing inside they found this was the chamber they wanted, housing the all-important studio equipment. Signalling to the boat that the coast was clear the riggers waited while a second boat trip brought Oliver Smedley and Kitty Black across together with another two of the burly riggers.

Once the entire raiding party was assembled in the studio tower Smedley and Black crossed the narrow suspended walkway to the central tower which housed the sleeping accommodation. There were seven men sleeping on the fort that night: Engineers Paul Elvey, Ian West and Philip Perkins; Cook Leslie Dunne; DJs Alan Clark and Ian MacRae and a new boy, newsreader Peter Dolphin.

Alan Clark spoke about what happened next in an interview in 1997: 'They literally woke us in our beds (presumably all of us!) with flashing torches and implied threats. Some of the men wore knives in their belts, opposition was out of the question. There was no violence. They didn't hurt us or anything like that but they certainly kept us off the air for a few days. There was a feeling that it might well have been an 'inside job' in the sense that these marine structures are quite hard to gain access to. They are way, way above the surface of the sea and it was felt that someone must have helped them on board but who that person was I have no idea.'[4]

Paul Elvey was apparently the first awake and took the lead in everything that followed. Jumping out of bed he warned his colleagues not to resist and then went to start the generator so everyone would have light.

Elvey seemed to have a strange bond with the new guy, Peter Dolphin, who had only joined the fort two days earlier. Dolphin had an expensive professional camera with him with which he started to photograph the boarding party and their boats. When pursued by the raiders Dolphin passed the camera to Elvey to hide.

Meanwhile Smedley's gang removed the studio microphones and Kitty Black got Ian West to remove the crucial crystal from the transmitter and give it to her, without the crystal she evidently knew the transmitter could not produce the required frequency and would be useless. After a few hours Smedley, Kitty Black and some of the group returned to the mainland, leaving behind eight men to guard the studio and transmitter and prevent the station from broadcasting.

To Oliver Smedley's military mind it seemed that, having taken possession of the fort, he could now negotiate terms with its previous owners, although he was not sure if he was supposed to be dealing with Radio City or Radio London. Back on land first thing on Monday morning Oliver Smedley and Kitty Black drove from Gravesend to the Kent home of Radio London boss Philip Birch and asked him to come to an 11.30 meeting at the old Project Atlanta offices in Dean Street. They separately contacted Calvert and asked him to come to a meeting at the Atlanta offices at noon. Calvert may have known that Radio City had not come on the air at 6 am that morning, but technical breakdowns were not uncommon and he had no idea what had happened on the fort overnight.

At the meeting, also attended by Kitty Black and other former Project Atlanta shareholders Horace Leggett and Captain Sandy Horsley, Philip Birch was told that Smedley's group had taken over Shivering Sands and that they wanted to share in his deal with Radio City. If Birch agreed to their getting £5,000 compensation for the disputed transmitter and 50% of all future profits from UKGM the gang would be told to release the fort. Philip

Birch was appalled at the action and wanted nothing to do with it. He told the meeting that he would never be blackmailed into any agreement under duress and promptly walked out. Quite apart from the fact that Birch was, unlike Smedley, a businessman with some ethical principles, Radio London did not need this hassle. Big L was a profitable business facing pressure from hostile politicians, the last thing it needed was to be associated with this kind of skulduggery. Birch subsequently announced that Radio London would not be going ahead with the 'good music' project.

Reg Calvert arrived shortly after Birch had so suddenly left the shocked meeting. Smedley immediately told him what had happened. Radio City was off the air, and would stay that way unless he agreed to their terms. Reg Calvert bluntly refused and demanded that Smedley remove the boarding party immediately, threatening to take it back by force if necessary and, in a heated exchange allegedly threatening to use mortars and nerve gas against the invaders. Major Smedley responded by claiming that the men on the fort were armed and would destroy all the equipment if anyone tried to regain control. The meeting reached stalemate and Calvert stormed out of the building.

It would of course not have been practical for Calvert to mount any major physical attack on the tower while seven of his own people were still on board but those present at the meeting later described Reg Calvert's demeanour that day using words such as 'mental', 'threatening' and 'paranoiac'. However it was not uncommon for people to describe Calvert in similar terms, even when he was being sociable and friendly, he had a fertile imagination and loved sharing his often half-baked ideas with others. Radio London DJ Duncan Johnson has described how, sharing a car with three colleagues and Calvert on the way to visit the fort, the radio boss had talked about his 'hair-brain schemes' including pen-sized gas guns and 'how he was going to use a low frequency transmitter by sticking a copper tube down into the sea and send out low-frequency signals down through the water.... He was a nut case.'[5]

The papers were now full of the story and on Tuesday 21 June Reg Calvert formally reported the raid to the police. It was not clear what the police could do if, as the station had always claimed, the Shivering Sands fort was outside their jurisdiction but they duly listened to Calvert's side of the story. Unable to identify any UK law being broken the police could only suggest that Reg Calvert should sort out the dispute directly with the man who had obviously ordered the invasion, Oliver Smedley.

Having been unable to contact Major Smedley all day, on the Tuesday evening Reg Calvert accompanied by Alan Arnold (who had provided the new antenna) drove to Oliver Smedley's home, a cottage in Wendens Ambo a village some fifteen miles from Cambridge. He had taken a large amount of cash with him in the hope that he might be able to negotiate a deal to regain control of the fort, or if he could not, to bribe the boarding party the next day.

Reg Calvert and Alan Arnold arrived at the cottage at about 11 pm. The door was opened by Smedley's housekeeper Pamela Thornburn who refused them entry and a struggle ensued in the hallway as Calvert tried to push past her, insistent on seeing Oliver Smedley. As they pulled up in the lane the Major had gone to his bedroom, armed himself with a loaded shotgun and then dashed next door to tell his neighbours that there was going to be trouble and they should call the police. Returning he saw the scuffle in the entrance to his house and pointed the barrels at Calvert. Alan Arnold, fearing for his own life as well as Calvert's, turned and ran out of the front door to get help. As he left the cottage he heard a shot and turned to see Reg Calvert lying dead on the floor of the hallway. When the police arrived they charged Oliver Smedley with murder.

When Major Smedley made a brief appearance before Magistrates sitting in the Tudor gabled council chamber of Saffron Walden Town Hall the next day, press reports played up his military record and establishment contacts. The *Daily Express* started its report: 'Wealthy Major Oliver Smedley, paratrooper who won the Military Cross in Normandy, made a five minute appearance in court yesterday accused of murdering the "pop pirate" Radio City chief, Reg Calvert.' Just to make sure we had got the message the piece went on to point out that Smedley, once a prominent Liberal politician, was a chartered accountant and a director of 21 companies: 'He is now chairman of the "Keep Britain Out" campaign, founded in 1951 as an anti-Common Market movement. Other interests include the National Benevolent Fund for the Aged and Sound Money Research, an organisation set up this year to tackle inflation.'[6]

Oliver Smedley again appeared in court before magistrates on 18 July. Strangely, on the night of the second day of the hearing the Calvert's London home in Marylebone was expertly broken into but nothing appeared to have been stolen and the police dropped their enquiries almost immediately. At the same time, almost fifty miles away, Major Smedley's cottage at Wendens Ambo was also the subject of a similar mysterious and unexplained break in. It seemed someone was looking for something, or maybe just sending a warning.

The next day, having heard a very selective account of the events of 21 June, the magistrates decided that there was no case to answer on the murder charge and, releasing Smedley on £500 bail, committed him for trial to Chelmsford Assizes on a lesser manslaughter charge.

There are other books dealing with the murder and the subsequent court case in greater detail, and there probably should be more - as many questions remain unanswered. The prosecution was certainly half-hearted, they made a point of saying that a pen-sized gas gun was found on Calvert's body and that Major Smedley had seen Calvert picking up a bronze statuette with which he was threatening Pamela Thornburn. Peculiarly, far more time was spent examining the character and motivation of Reg Calvert, the victim, than on the recent activities and history of the defendant. Prosecution witnesses were not called or appeared too terrified to tell the truth, inconsistent evidence was not challenged and the prosecution appeared to deliberately weaken its own case by calling friends of Major Smedley, including Kitty Black, to give evidence against him. The jury was not allowed to hear the full story behind the dispute over the fort - instead being given a picture of an honourable senior military figure and businessman being spontaneously challenged by a reckless, crazed pirate.

On 11 October 1966, after a trial lasting just one and a half days and without retiring to consider their verdict, the jury stated that Smedley had acted in self-defence and found him not guilty. The judge said it was simply a case of aggravated burglary and awarded 250 guineas in costs to Smedley, who walked from court a free man.

Reg Calvert was buried on 1 July 1966 at St. Peter's, Dunchurch, near Rugby, with Screaming Lord Sutch among the mourners.

The day after the shooting word had reached the fort via a launch packed with journalists. Essex police sent officers out to Shivering Sands to interview the crew and the occupiers. Statements were taken but no arrests were made. The news came as a complete shock to everyone on the fort, according to DJ Tom Edwards: 'It was news that didn't sink in at first. There were police officers and newspaper reporters everywhere, both on and off the fort. The raiders were not happy and Big Alf, who seemed to be in charge, said to me that he didn't know anyone was going to get killed'.

Without warning, on the following Sunday afternoon, 26 June, a tug came alongside the fort and the boarding party suddenly left. The Radio City men found the microphones and a hidden spare transmitter crystal and were quickly back on the air. One of the departing boarders had suggested they might play them a song when they could so DJ Ian MacRae restarted broadcasts at 10 pm by playing Frank Sinatra's Strangers in the Night.

Reg Calvert's widow Dorothy took over the running of the station and said she was determined to see it continue. Ironically, while the police had been unable to help rid the fort of intruders their statement that this was because it was outside the territorial limit, and therefore outside the reach of UK law, heightened the value of Shivering Sands to those who wanted to control it.

Questions and recriminations began to circulate among the Radio City people, combined with plenty of conspiracy theories from those ashore. Ian MacRae later said: 'A question still haunts me about the incident. Who was it that left the trap door, that was normally always bolted, unlocked to allow the boarders access? I have my suspicions but no proof.'

Peter Dolphin left the fort on the first available boat and Paul Elvey was never allowed back on the fort. According to Adrian Johns Dorothy Calvert later said she believed Elvey to have been in contact with the Atlanta operation and 'suspected that he was responsible for leaving the trapdoor open that allowed Smedley's party to enter the fort.' Peter Dolphin told the press that, on his way back from Radio City, he had been kidnapped and interrogated about the station by unidentified men somewhere in the East End of London, only to deny that story when the police started to ask specific questions.[7]

Radio City was now on its own and Dorothy Calvert became the target of many offers of 'protection' for the fort and her people, some from legitimate security companies, some less so. Despite being so very recently bereaved, she bravely faced almost daily threats and more subtle harassment.

Reg and Dorothy's older daughter Susan Moore recently spoke to me about strange events surrounding the station at around that time: 'Many people after the shooting and trial wanted to write about it from my mother's perspective and reveal the truth behind it. Each time they were told they could not publish as there was a D-notice. Several people wanted to make a film and they were also stopped. At the time our telephones were constantly tapped. My mother thought she was being followed. She also had her life threatened several times.'

The idea of pirate stations having their telephones tapped was not far fetched. Quite apart from the activities of MI5 in Curzon Street from 1964, by the summer of 1966 most people who worked on the forts thought their telephones calls were being intercepted. According to Adrian Johns in *Death of a Pirate*, in January 1967 two jokers implicated in a further raid on

Shivering Sands tested their suspicions of phone-tapping by discussing, in a private telephone call, detailed plans to pick up an eight-man boarding party from the beach at Whitstable. At the appointed hour in the dead of night the harbour was swarming with Kent police constables.[8]

Whether a specific D-Notice was issued on the events surrounding the murder of Reg Calvert is not clear. The D-Notice system was set up in 1912 as a voluntary system distributing official government requests to news organisations not to publish or broadcast items on specified subjects for reasons of national security. The system is still in use in the United Kingdom as a DSMA-Notice (Defence and Security Media Advisory Notice). Hundreds of secret D-Notices were issued in the sixties and very largely obeyed by the media. They covered obvious things like military operations, plans, weapons, capabilities, nuclear facilities and the addresses and details of sensitive installations and key people. Others covered ciphers and secret communications and activities of the UK security and intelligence services. It was a D-Notice that prevented the location of MI5's HQ in Curzon Street from being public knowledge although another, ludicrously banning details of the location of the newly-built Post Office Tower (now BT Tower), was rather less successful!

It was to be two years before Paul Elvey's name next appeared in the press when it emerged that, since being sacked from Radio City, he had been working for the Kray twins as a contract killer. Early in 1968 the police arrested Elvey in Glasgow as he was about to board a flight to London with a number of sticks of dynamite intended to make a car bomb for the Krays.

Paul Elvey confessed to being involved in three murder attempts saying he had been employed by an American called Alan Bruce Cooper who in turn was working for the Kray gang. The increasingly implausible tale was that Cooper had chosen Elvey to construct complex killing devices to impress Ronnie Kray. Elvey met the Krays in pubs in London's East End on several occasions and discussed their needs. The first contraption was a small suitcase containing a hypodermic syringe filled with cyanide. The James Bond-style device had a catch which, when operated, made the needle protrude from the case. In a crowd the needle could easily be pushed into a target and the mechanism would release the almost immediately fatal poison. It was initially designed to assassinate a perceived enemy of the Krays, Leslie Payne, who was about to appear in a fraud case at the Old Bailey. Elvey was to get behind him in the crowded public lobby and operate the device. In the event the would-be assassin turned up but Payne did not, his case having been postponed after a tip-off. The second device supplied by Paul Elvey at the request of Alan Cooper was a specialist high-powered crossbow made of mahogany and steel with telescopic sights, which was designed for hunting in Africa. He claimed that it could silently kill a man at twenty-five yards.

If it seems unlikely that a skinny mild-mannered electrical engineer from Billericay should have been cast as a gangsters favoured hit-man, and if the elaborate technology seems far-fetched, the suitcase and crossbow in question are now on display in Scotland Yard's Black Museum, together with other materials confirming Paul Elvey's story.

Elvey's evidence was the beginning of the end for the Kray empire, once he started to put names, dates and places together for the police they could corroborate other evidence and other witnesses could be persuaded to talk. Unfortunately for the police however, when they questioned Alan Cooper he revealed that he was working for the United States Secret Service, investigating links between the Mafia in the USA and the Krays. Cooper said he had arranged a series of botched murder attempts in order to win the confidence of the twins and, even worse that a senior policeman at Scotland Yard had been secretly aware of his role all along.

On 8 May 1968 the Kray twins and 15 other gang members were arrested. Many other people were willing to come forward now that the Krays' powers of intimidation were restricted and the police were, for the first time, able to build a solid case with Paul Elvey and Alan Cooper as key prosecution witnesses. The charges involving the briefcase and crossbow was dismissed at the committal stage, but at the Old Bailey in 1969 the twins were found guilty of the murders of Jack 'The Hat' McVitie and George Cornell and sentenced to life imprisonment. Fourteen other members of 'the firm' were convicted of various offences.

The still unanswered question is how and when did Alan Cooper meet up with Paul Elvey? Was Elvey aware all along that he was bravely working for a secret intelligence service and, if so, had he done so before? Did Cooper come across Elvey in his earlier life, before he became a US secret agent, when Cooper was smuggling drugs across the Atlantic from France? Or was Elvey in fact already known to the Kray twins before Cooper came on the scene?

Back in 1966, when the Krays were still very much at large there was talk of their intention to get involved in gold smuggling and this was linked to some of the offshore forts, including Shivering Sands. There was a well-developed plan for a second raid on the fort in January 1967 and this was commonly linked to Smedley, Roy Bates of Radio Essex, unnamed underworld characters, or any permutation of the above.

By early February Dorothy Calvert had decided to close down Radio City. A combination of legal manoeuvres to put Shivering Sands within territorial waters and the government's upcoming Marine Broadcasting Offences Act was making it not worth facing the constant threats and the difficulties and costs of maintaining the station. Unexpectedly a man called in to the Radio City office in Denmark Street, he said his boss had been a professional associate of Reg Calvert's and would like to talk business with Mrs Calvert. That evening she was taken by a group of smartly dressed men with cockney accents to the Astor Club in Berkeley Square where she was introduced to a well-built man who she only later recognised as Reggie Kray. He told her that he wanted Radio City to continue operating, explaining that he had the government in his pocket. Alluding to the Boothby affair Kray said he knew influential people who would make sure the station was not harassed by the authorities. Dorothy Calvert, sensing that this man wanted to use the fort as a cover for other clandestine activities, refused, saying she would not break the law. After a few attempts to convince her to keep the station on the air Reggie Kray said he could see she was a lady who would not change her mind and politely arranged for his Rolls Royce to deliver her to her nearby home in Marylebone.

As it turned out after Radio City vacated the fort it was boarded by others who systematically stripped it of anything useful, although even they left behind the ancient transmitter supplied by Oliver Smedley.

The government, protective of its slender parliamentary majority, had been dragging its feet over introducing its legislation against the pirates but now Reg Calvert's death gave them every excuse to press ahead with the promised Marine Broadcasting Offences Act and other legal action.

Indeed a parliamentary debate on Pirate Radio legislation had been scheduled for 22 June 1966 and in his diary the Postmaster general, Tony Benn, summarised the position: 'It was a timely debate. Today a boarding party seized Radio City on Shivering Sands fort and the managing director was shot and killed. Gangsterism has moved into the pirates and the Government's failure to act is now an absolute disgrace.' In the House of Commons Benn confirmed his intention to act and discussed the problems associated with providing a replacement service.

The tragedy surrounding Shivering Sands was not born of gangsterism but from the collision of the two different types of capitalism prevalent in 1960s Britain. Faced with a business opportunity the likes of Major Oliver

Smedley would pass the word among his network of friends, perhaps even publish a political pamphlet or two, and hire the people and facilities to do the job. Reg Calvert was from the other end of the entrepreneurial spectrum, he would never think to set up an offshore company in the Bahamas to hide his earnings. As he had done in the dance halls he could achieve the same end using cash. Take money on the door, pay off the band and other costs, pocket the balance and, if the taxman asked, say you'd had a bad night. Seeing an opportunity Calvert would get a venue, a boat, a transmitter, whatever, and go and set it up himself. Ironically, what divided Smedley and Calvert was their mutual belief in free enterprise, a shared view that they should be allowed to get on with their own business. Laissez Faire.

CHAPTER TEN

MARINE OFFENCES

In the wake of the Radio City tragedy the government introduced into parliament its long-delayed legislation to ratify the 1965 Council of Europe Strasbourg Treaty, the 'European Agreement for the Prevention of Broadcasts Transmitted from Stations outside National Territories'. Explicitly intended to extend the government's control over broadcasting stations outside British territorial waters and airspace, The Marine Broadcasting Offences Bill was to make it illegal for persons subject to UK law to operate or assist offshore pirate radio or TV stations. Caroline's Ronan O'Rahilly was bullish. Back in 1965 he had told the *Daily Express*: 'We intend to carry on and we think we can. Legally. It would get tougher for us but not impossible. We could get our supplies from Spain, Portugal, North Africa, the United States or Ireland. 'We could get out food stocks once a fortnight instead of fresh food every day – or almost – and it might not cost that much more. We could use non-British crews and disc-jockeys and move administration to New York. And British advertisers might still be able to use Radio Caroline through New York agencies.'[1] However most commentators thought the ship-based stations would be forced to close down by the summer of 1967, and well before then the government started to tighten the noose around the fort-based pirates.

As early as September 1964 the Queen had approved an Order in Council which extended some of the UK's territorial waters. Until this point international waters were generally considered to start at a point three miles out from the low water line around the coast (this was said to be based historically on the reach of naval cannons fired from land). The government had come under pressure to update the definition not just because of the pirate radio stations but due to increasing pressure from other nations for agreements covering commercial fishing and oil exploration rights off the UK coast.

The Territorial Waters Order in Council 1964 created a series of straight 'baselines' which joined various islands, notably off the west coast of Scotland, and ran across the mouth of bays and estuaries, in particular the Thames estuary. Article 4 of the order specified that the baseline should 'if the bay has only one mouth and the distance between the low-water line of the natural entrance points of the bay does not exceed 24 miles, be a straight line joining the said low-water lines' or 'be a straight line 24 miles in length drawn from low-water line to low-water line within the bay in such a manner as to enclose the maximum area of water that is possible with a line of that length'.

The effect of this new interpretation, combined with some creative use of hydrographic surveys to put the low-water line further out to sea from the sand banks of the Thames estuary and Essex coasts, was that all but two of the wartime forts were declared to be inside territorial waters and therefore subject to prosecution under English law (some years later when the three mile limit was increased to twelve miles under international agreements the locations of the remaining forts. Rough Sands - 7 miles from the coast of Suffolk and Sunk Head – some 11 miles off the north Essex coast, would also become part of UK-controlled waters).

Then, as now, the United Kingdom operated a two-speed legal system - able to act immediately with an injunction if big money or powerful interests were threatened but also able to grind away excruciatingly slowly where that better suited the established order. So the Territorial Waters Order sat on the statute book for two years before being rolled out against any of the fort-based pirates.

First to be challenged was Ted Allbeury's Radio 390. In August 1966 two Post Office radio investigators went to Radio 390's London office and warned them that they could be prosecuted for broadcasting without a licence but the station maintained that it was, and had always been, outside territorial waters. A month later Ted Allbeury and David Lye, the company secretary of the Radio 390 company Estuary Radio, were issued with a summons for the unlawful use of wireless telegraphy equipment contrary to the 1949 Wireless and Telegraphy Act. The Act provided for a £100 fine or three months imprisonment, or both.

According to a front page lead story in the *Daily Express*: 'The move came as a shock to most of the pirate broadcasters – three on Thames estuary forts, six on ships well out to sea. They were not expecting any action until new legislation is passed through Parliament.' The paper quoted Radio City owner Dorothy Calvert as saying: 'We have heard nothing' while Don Robinson of Radio 270 said: 'There are 25 million people tuning into radio ships every day – they will never be stopped.'

The *Express*, always a fan of Radio 390, told its readers: 'It beams 17½ hours of continuous music daily to an audience claimed to be between 4 and 5 million, and it has taken £250,000 in advertising revenue.'[2]

Allbeury and Lye appeared at Canterbury magistrates court on 24 November where the Post Office gave evidence of using direction-finding equipment on the Essex and Kent coasts to pinpoint the source of the Radio 390 transmissions. The magistrates retired after Sir Peter Rawlinson, QC, a former Solictor General, defending, had submitted that Red Sands was outside British territorial waters and, therefore, that the court lacked jurisdiction in the matter. Later, in a prepared statement, the magistrates said: 'We find that Red Sands Tower is situated in territorial waters. The Wireless Telegraphy Act of 1949 is silent on the question of local jurisdiction but the territorial waters in question join the coast of Kent and for that reason we are of the opinion that the Justices of the County of Kent have jurisdiction in this matter.'

A key witness was Lieutenant Commander Peter Brian Beasley, head of the hydrographic department of the Ministry of Defence. He told the court that because a sandbank off the Isle of Sheppey was exposed at low water, Red Sands fort was within territorial waters. Mr. John Newey, prosecuting, said that taking the mouth of the Thames from the Naze to North Foreland, the Red Sands fort was within the court's jurisdiction.[3]

After two days of detailed debate about the extent of territorial waters Estuary Radio Limited was found guilty of broadcasting without a licence and fined £100. The two individuals were not penalised. An application to confiscate the equipment was denied but Ted Allbeury told the *Financial Times* that Radio 390 would stay off the air until an appeal was heard. He said if the appeal decision went against the company then he had other arrangements in mind for continuing broadcasting: 'In one way or another,' he said, 'we shall continue.'[4]

Estuary Radio set to work to challenge the evidence produced in court – which rested on whether the particular Thames sandbank, Middle Sands, which the prosecution had used as the baseline for the territorial limit, was ever exposed at low tide. Obtaining a hydrographers report stating that the sandbank was always under several inches of water and therefore that the Red Sands fort was at least one and a half miles outside UK jurisdiction, Allbeury felt confident enough to return to the air.

Radio 390 resumed broadcasting just before midnight on New Year's Eve with Ted Allbeury saying it was back to stay. When the Post Office responded by issuing further summons against Estuary Radio and everyone involved in running the company Allbeury resigned, as we've heard moving on to manage the ship-based Radio 355.

On 22 February 1967 magistrates at Rochford, near Southend, were told that the accused were involved in broadcasting without a licence on four specimen days in January. When the Navy was called to give evidence that Middle Sands was uncovered at low tide the magistrates were shown a photograph of a Lieutenant Commander John Mackay standing on the sands next to a Union Jack. Again found guilty, Estuary Radio Limited was fined £200, and the directors £40 each.

Now under the management of David Lye, Radio 390 decided to brave it out and stayed on the air despite a subsequent Post Office injunction and an application to the High Court for a ruling on whether Red Sands fort was within territorial waters. Finally, on 25 May Mr Justice O'Connor ruled that the station was transmitting illegally and, after an appeal was rejected by Lord Justice Sellers on 28 July Radio 390 was silenced. At 5.10 pm senior announcer Edward Cole read a formal farewell message and the station closed down with the national anthem.

The troublesome Roy Bates' Radio Essex was the government's second target. On 28 September 1966, a Post Office summons was served on Bates alleging that on 16 August he had contravened Section One of the 1949 Wireless Telegraphy Act by using a transmitter without a licence at Knock John Tower.

Against legal advice Roy Bates responded defiantly by one week later changing the name of the station to BBMS (Britain's Better Music Station) and saying that he was going to install a more powerful transmitter. At Rochford magistrates on 30 November Roy Bates entered a plea of guilty but claimed that the court had no jurisdiction over the matter as Knock John fort was in international waters. He quite reasonably asked why, if he had been breaking the law, it had taken so long to charge him. The magistrate was unimpressed and fined him £100 but refused a Post Office request to confiscate his broadcasting equipment, pending an appeal.

Bates said BBMS would stay on the air but the station closed at 4.30 pm on Christmas Day 1966. With no new advertising revenue coming in reports said that staff and bills had not been paid since the trial.

The appeal heard at Chelmsford Quarter Sessions on 17 January 1967 failed, the court finding that Knock John Tower was about one and a half miles inside territorial waters. But by this time most of the equipment had been transferred to the nearby Rough Sands Tower. There were reports of test transmissions from Roughs in early January but the station never re-emerged.

The transfer to Roughs tower did not go smoothly as by this point Radio Caroline had put two caretakers on board intending to convert it into an offshore supply base for the ship for use after the Marine Offences Act prohibited tender visits from the UK. Roy Bates deposed the caretakers but a series of violent skirmishes followed between men sent from Caroline and Bates' people over the next few months, some allegedly involving machine-gun fire and petrol bombs. In the end Roy Bates retained occupation of the tower and, in September 1967, he announced that the Roughs Tower was now 'The Principality of Sealand', a sovereign state with its own flag, passports, currency and postage stamps. Bates declared himself monarch and his son became Prince Michael.

Because he was not broadcasting from the Roughs Roy Bates and his family avoided the new legislation's ban on supplying the fort from the English coast and he therefore had no incentive to risk this lifeline by pursuing his radio ambitions.

The ongoing story of Sealand is covered elsewhere but it rumbles on to this day, an irritating issue of international law that successive governments have not felt the need to tackle. When in the early days a naval auxiliary vessel approaching the fort had warning shots fired across her bow Roy Bates was charged under the Firearms Act but the judge at Essex Assizes subsequently decided that the courts had no jurisdiction as the platform was outside territorial waters. And when in October 1987 Britain extended the limit of its territorial waters from 3 nautical miles to 12, bringing Rough Sands within its grasp, Bates responded by similarly extending Sealand's territorial waters. In such circumstances international law generally requires that the two countries divide the overlapping area down the middle. The UK government thought it best not to respond.

Other notable events on Sealand include a coup, when Dutch and German 'businessmen' took the fort by force, kidnapping Prince Michael, and when, at the height of the initial internet boom in June 2000, a company called HavenCo announced preliminary plans to locate its servers and satellite uplinks on Sealand, the idea being to avoid data scrutiny by government agencies.

Back in 1966 the Post Office held off taking any action against Radio City while the Oliver Smedley trial was taking place but at the end of January 1967 the station received a court summons for transmitting without a licence within UK territorial waters. On 8 February Rochford magistrates were shown the 'new' hydrographic information which proved that Shivering

Sands was within British waters. Despite Dorothy Calvert pointing out that the police had previously claimed the fort was outside the three mile limit the magistrates found that the transmitter was within their jurisdiction, found the company guilty and fined Dorothy Calvert the now standard £100. With no resources to fight the decision word was sent out to the fort that the station should close down at midnight. I and thousands of others listened as Radio City left the air with an emotional hour of nostalgic reminiscences, a recording of *The Party's Over* and the national anthem.

Seldom had the double standards at the heart of the British establishment been so clearly illuminated. When, just six months earlier, Reg Calvert had turned to the police for help when Shivering Sands had been seized by menacing invaders he had been repeatedly told, as was Dorothy Calvert after Reg's murder, that the fort was outside British jurisdiction. But the government had changed its attitude towards the station, and, with no change to maritime law or the position of the seabed in the meantime, Shivering Sands was now apparently clearly covered by English law.

So a few new lines drawn on Admiralty charts had put paid to the fort-based pirates and all that remained now was to deal with the radio ships. The Marine Offences Bill had its second reading in parliament and enjoyed majority support. Although the House of Lords wanted to delay implementation until an alternative, legal, pop music service could be established the Bill passed quickly through all its stages and the Marine, &c., Broadcasting (Offences) Act 1967 c.41, (usually shortened to the Marine Broadcasting Offences Act) received Royal assent on 14 July and became law one month later at midnight on Monday 14 August 1967. The Act stopped anyone in the UK from helping in any way with the operation or promotion of an unlicensed offshore broadcasting station. It made it illegal for British companies to buy advertising on the stations and crucially it also prohibited 'carrying by water or air goods or persons to or from it' which made tendering from the UK illegal.

As we've already heard Radio 355 (the former Britain Radio) was the first of the ship-based stations to close, it fell silent on 6 August at the end of its existing tendering contract. Three of the remaining stations defiantly hung on until 14 August.

Professional and determined to stay completely on the right side of the law to the end, Radio London announced that it would shut down at 3 pm on 14 August to enable staff to come ashore before the new law came into force. This would also give the final show a bigger audience. In a press statement managing director Philip Birch said: 'It is unfortunate that this government's attitude towards independent radio has consistently been one of suppression as part of a determined plan to continue the government's monopoly in radio broadcasting'.

Radio London showed great dignity in how it handled its final hour. To avoid any emotional outbursts and to help the DJs to make a speedy exit the programme was pre-recorded. It included specially recorded messages from top stars of the day, including such enduring names as Tom Jones, Cilla Black, Mick Jagger, Cliff Richard and Dusty Springfield, ending with Beatle Ringo Starr calling it 'a sad day for everybody.' In his recorded message Philip Birch thanked the DJs and everyone who had been involved with or supported the station as well as a claimed '12 million listeners in the United Kingdom and 4 million in the Netherlands, Belgium and France'. The final record was the Beatles *A Day in the Life* with that long final ominously decaying note allowed to run in full. This was followed by Paul Kaye's final announcement: 'Big L time is now three o'clock, and Radio London is now closing down'. The station's theme tune, the PAMS Sonowaltz jingle – famously dubbed *Big Lil* by Kenny Everett and Dave Cash - was played and engineer Russ Tollerfield switched off the transmitter on schedule just after 3 pm.

Along with thousands of others, this was the middle of the school holidays after all, I recorded that last hour on my reel-to-reel tape machine and I still have the tape to this day. That closedown was so classy that I still can't hear the *Big Lil* tune without getting a lump in my throat.

Just after Radio London transmitter had disappeared, leaving only background noise and static, I tuned across to Radio Caroline South just in time to hear DJ Robbie Dale broadcast a brief eulogy for the station, he sincerely thanked its DJs and staff and observed a minute's silence.

Four days later the Radio London ship sailed to Hamburg. Despite several proposals to use her for another Europe-wide radio project she remained there until 1975 when she was moved to a shipyard in Kiel where she sank in 1979. The Galaxy was finally cut up for scrap in 1986.

Meanwhile off the Yorkshire coast Radio 270 was still on the air having chosen to close down at one minute to midnight after abandoning a plan to stay on the air by being supplied and managed from the Netherlands. It was originally intended that the entire DJ team should be on board for a goodbye party but stormy seas prevented their trip out to the Ocean 7 and it fell to a very nervous programme director Vince 'Rusty' Allen to handle the official closedown at 23.59 pm after reading a message from Radio 270 chairman

Leonard Dale. A brief recorded message from Wilf Proudfoot advised the audience that free radio would eventually come once 'the socialists' had been 'drummed out of office.'[5]

Demonstrating Radio 270's somewhat different agenda to that of Radio London, the final record played was wartime favourite Vera Lynn singing *Land Of Hope And Glory* followed by Rusty Allen saying 'God bless and God speed. Goodnight and goodbye. Radio 270 is now closing down' and, finally, the national anthem.

The Ocean 7 sailed up to Whitby the next day where it was laid up while a buyer was sought without success. Eventually the transmitter and much of the broadcasting equipment was removed from the ship and put in storage. The ship was broken up for scrap in 1969 the proceeds being used to pay off outstanding creditors. It is unlikely that any of Wilf Proudfoot's shareholders ever saw a return on their investment.

North of the border Radio Scotland similarly hung on until the last moment and closed at midnight on 14 August. The last six hours of the station had largely been pre-recorded because most of the DJs had gone ashore to attend a closedown ball in Glasgow's Locarno ballroom - where an estimated 2,000 fans turned up to mourn the station's passing. The closing sequence was overseen by DJs Tony Allan and Mark West (Mark Wesley) who had volunteered to stay on board the Comet. The final hour contained messages from present and former staff and the managing director Tommy Shields who said it was the saddest day of his life. He told listeners that the station had lost £100,000 but thought that if it had been allowed to keep going until the end of the year it could have started to pay its way. Appropriately, Radio Scotland closed down with a bagpipe lament. Tommy Shields died six months later aged just 49.

After spending some days at anchor in the Firth of Forth the Comet was put up for sale in Dunbar Harbour. As with Radio 270's Ocean 7 this was not a good time to be selling a radio ship and with no buyers on the horizon a month later the Comet was towed to the port of Methil in Fife where the antenna mast and broadcasting equipment was removed before she was taken to Holland, where she was broken up and sold for scrap in 1969.

As befits its murky origins much greater secrecy surrounds the fate of the Radio England and Britain Radio ship which was now known as the Laissez Faire. According to an article in the Texas newspaper *The Abilene Reporter*, dated 15 September 1967, right-wing wheeler-dealer Don Pierson had been instructed by the owners to find a buyer. He had placed a classified advertisement in the *Wall Street Journal* which read, in part: 'Pirate radio – 50,000 watt commercial radio station, mobile. Lease negotiable.'

'She can go anywhere in the world and broadcast whatever the owner wants as long as she stays in international waters.' Pierson told the Texas paper. 'So far I've had responses to the ad from a foreign government, a large industry and two men.'[6] The identity of the 'two men' might be deduced from the next chapter but, whoever the parties were, they were not regarded as suitable purchasers by his backers and Pierson did not take the offers any further.

Towed to Miami, USA, the Laissez Faire became the subject of a court case for unpaid bills and the transmitters were reclaimed by Continental Electronics. The ship itself appeared to still be owned by Pierce Langford III but its history then becomes confused as its identity appears to have been switched at the Lloyds Registry with that of its sister ship the Olga Princess.

We know that one ship was renamed Akuarius II in 1970 and was sold to the giant Zapata Corporation, becoming the MV Earl J. Conrad Junior in 1974, but the other ship mysteriously disappeared from the records.

Zapata Oil was an oil exploration business set up by George H W Bush (George Bush senior) with assistance from Allen Dulles the then Director of the CIA. The company was never particularly profitable and appears to have worked primarily as a front for a range of espionage and covert operations. It is commonly assumed that the Zapata Corporation acted as a conduit for CIA funding. George H W Bush went on to become Director of the CIA himself and then, in 1989, the 41st President of the United States.

In the 1980s Don Pierson was quoted as saying that the radio ship went on to do clandestine work in the Caribbean, and other reports said it had been used in the 1970s as a radio station or relay station off the coasts of Vietnam and Cuba.[7]

1967's celebrated 'Summer of Love' was not working out very well for the UKs pirate radio stations. At the end of 1966 there had been ten stations broadcasting regularly off Britain's beaches but now, on 15 August 1967, there were only the two Radio Caroline transmitters operating.

For the government there was still one loose end to be tied up before the Marine Broadcasting Offences Act could become completely effective. By ancient tradition laws applying on the Isle of Man had to be passed by the island's own parliament, The High Court of Tynwald. Founded over one thousand years ago, Tynwald has a reasonable claim to be the oldest continuously existing parliament in the world and had demonstrated its

MARINE OFFENCES

independence of thinking on local radio broadcasting by approving the establishment of a legal, land-based, commercial radio station as early as June 1964. Much to the annoyance of the UK government, Manx Radio, based in Douglas, had been licenced as the island's national public service broadcaster, supported by commercial advertising. The Isle of Man is a crown dependency and the extent of its legislative competence is ambiguous but the UK government did not choose this issue as sufficient cause to challenge centuries of peaceful co-operation between the parliaments.

Radio Caroline North had ensured that it was seen as a useful asset to the Isle of Man economy and was very popular on the island. For a while it seemed that Tynwald would demand an exemption from the new law but this would of course have rendered it useless as the ships could then have continued to operate, managed and serviced from the island. In the end the Marine Broadcasting Offences Act became law in the Isle of Man a fortnight after the rest of the UK, on 1 September.

By the end of 14 August 1967 the only disc jockeys left on the Radio Caroline South ship were Johnnie Walker and Robbie Dale, along with newsreader Ross Brown. Faced with the threat of a large fine and possibly a period in jail all the other presenters had left, although a few did return later.

22 year-old Johnnie Walker had already prepared for a long exile by throwing a party for some of his friends and fans at his home in Hampton-in-Arden. He told Birmingham's Evening Mail that the new law brought penalties of up to three months imprisonment or a £400 fine, or both. For conviction on indictment the penalty was a maximum of two years in jail. 'The Act also says that a Briton cannot return to England for two years after the first offence – that is why I am giving the party' said Johnnie.

At exactly midnight the station changed its name to Radio Caroline International and Johnnie Walker addressed the nation: 'This is your radio station, this is Radio Caroline and it is now twelve midnight.' After singing along to the anthem of the civil rights movement *We Shall Overcome* he played the familiar *Caroline* by the Fortunes in the background while giving an unexpected interpretation of the situation in almost Churchillian tones: 'Radio Caroline would like to extend its thanks to Mister Harold Wilson and his Labour government for at last, after over three and a half years of broadcasting, recognising this station's legality. It's right to be here, it's right to be broadcasting to Great Britain and the continent. It's right to give the music and service to the peoples of Europe which we have been doing since Easter Sunday 1964, and we in turn recognise your right as our listener to have freedom of choice in your radio entertainment and of course that Radio

Caroline belongs to you. It is your radio station even though it costs you nothing. And, as we enter this new phase in our broadcasting history, you, naturally, have our assurance that we intend to stay on the air. Because we belong to you. And we love you. Caroline continues.'

On 1 September the senior Radio Caroline North DJ, the Canadian Don Allen, made a similar announcement and that station continued with a skeleton crew of just four DJs, an engineer and five seamen supplied by the Dutch Wijsmuller company. The tender for the north ship brought supplies and crew changes from Dundalk in the Irish Republic, a port quite near to where the Caroline ships had been originally fitted out.

In preparation for the change in law Radio Caroline had wound up the Planet Productions operation in Britain, closed down the offices at Caroline House in London and set up a new office at Singel 160 in Amsterdam. Partly due to the popularity of their Radio Veronica the Dutch were the only North Sea country not to have yet introduced similar legislation against the pirates. Ronan O'Rahily had US and Irish citizenship and Philip Solomon now had an Irish passport so they were both legally able to continue to direct operations from a base abroad.

How the two men expected to maintain the Radio Caroline operation is a mystery. Even before the Marine Offences Act blocked their main source of income the two ships had been running at a loss. An August 1967 article in the *Financial Times* gave the example of a shareholder in Planet Productions who originally bought 500 'one shilling' shares for £750, equivalent to 30 shillings (£1.50) a share. He had never received any dividend and, on 21 April 1967, the company sent him a letter which said that Philip Solomon, one of its directors, was offering to purchase the shares of the company for a price of just sixpence a share (2.5p).[8]

For the year ended 31 May 1966 Planet showed a loss of £2,204 following a loss of £8,899 in 1965. The *Financial Times* concluded: 'Planet Productions, in fact, is in a bad way, and according to the company's accounts the popular impression that Radio Caroline is a great money-spinner is far from correct... the prospect of legislation has been putting advertisers off since the peak months of last year, and it is common knowledge that advertisers have been able to secure pirate radio advertising at a fraction of the official rates'

Caroline continued to broadcast advertisements, mainly for international brands, but it was not clear how many of these, if any, had been paid for. A spokesman for Horlicks, Ian Bruce, told the *Daily Express*: 'We cancelled our advertising and had an assurance from the station that it would cease. These commercials still being broadcast were not booked by us.' A Beecham official stressed: 'Radio Caroline is not authorised to use these advertisements – all our contracts ended in November last year.'

The station was playing cat and mouse with the authorities and making it difficult to trace whether anyone with UK connections was actually paying anything for airtime. Similarly the blatant plugging of certain records and recording labels continued, including Major Minor releases. However it seems little money was reaching the ships and by the end of the year supplies were getting low. In December 1967 Johnnie Walker showed his disdain by throwing all the pay-for-play records overboard and telling the listeners that the ship was getting short of food and drinking water, saying that he had been stuck on the ship for almost a month with no contact from shore.[9]

The stations maintained their precarious existence with Ronan O'Rahilly and his money-man Philip Solomon secretly controlling them from London. The audience had been dented by the launch of the BBC's answer to the pirates, Radio One, but the real problem for Caroline was the lack of advertising revenue.

Wijsmuller had been supplying crews for the ships for some time and had provided the tender boats for Radio London and Radio England ships as well as Caroline. Being a company based in the Netherlands they were not affected by the new UK law after August but it appears that Philip Solomon, faced with little or no income, had stopped paying their bills. When another month had passed without the promised payments Wijsmuller decided to take the law into their own hands. On 3 March 1968, in a co-ordinated commando-style operation in the early hours of the Sunday morning while both ships were off the air, workers from the Dutch company arrived by tug, cut the heavy anchor chains, locked the studios, removed the transmitter crystals and towed the ships to Amsterdam.

Radio Caroline, not the first, not the biggest, and probably not the best of the offshore radio stations, was nevertheless the broadcaster the general public most associated by with the pirate radio boom of the 1960s, and it had now been silenced after barely four years.

During the introduction of the anti-pirate legislation, postmaster general Edward Short announced that the BBC had agreed to launch a new 'pop music' station – which was to become Radio One. The old Light Programme was to be split in two, continuing as 'Radio Two' on long wave and FM frequencies while Radio One would take over its 247 metres medium wave transmitters. At the same timr the Third Programme was to become 'Radio Three' and the Home Service 'Radio Four'.

Radio One launched on 30 September 1967 with many of the familiar pirate DJ voices in its schedule, particularly those from Radio London. The breakfast show was presented by Tony Blackburn. However budget limitations and needle-time restrictions meant that Radio One had to share many programmes with Radio Two, only providing something like a 'pop' service for some five or six hours per day.

While this book is primarily about the British pirate phenomenon of the 1960s it would be remiss to stop without mentioning that the Caroline brand was to return to the air several more times, firstly as a temporary identity for a political campaign from another station in strange circumstances detailed in the next chapter and then while attempting to run its own ship in the face of increasingly united opposition from northern European governments.

When, after they had been rusting in the harbour for over four years, the Wijsmuller company decided to auction off the two former Caroline ships, the MV Caroline was sold for scrap but the Mi Amigo, previously home to Radio Nord, Radio Atlanta and Radio Caroline South was sold to a Dutch free radio organisation to be converted into an offshore radio museum. Volunteers cleaned and painted the old ship, restoring the studios and accommodation. But secretly Ronan O'Rahilly had arranged to use the Mi Amigo for its originally intended purpose and, in late 1972 anchored off the Dutch coast, it again started to transmit Radio Caroline.

The lack of finance and problems with the ship again silenced the station on several occasions and Radio Caroline was forced to share the transmitters with Dutch and Belgian stations. When in 1974 the Dutch government joined most of the rest of Europe in making support for offshore radio illegal the Caroline offices moved to Spain and the Mi Amigo moved back close to the Essex coast, where she was supplied illegally from the Netherlands, Belgium, France and Britain. The Mi Amigo struggled along for a further six years but, on the night of 20 March 1980, losing her anchor in a storm, she began taking in water and was lost at sea just after the crew were rescued by lifeboat.

Radio Caroline returned to the air on 20 August 1983 using a newly converted radio ship, the MV Ross Revenge, a factory fishing trawler previously based in Grimsby and used in the North Sea by Ross Fisheries. Initially fitted out with a 50 kW transmitter and a 300 foot antenna in Santander, Spain, she became Europe's last surviving offshore radio ship but yet again the financial model was baffling, possibly non-existent. There were many lengthy periods when the station was off the air due to money, fuel and staff shortages, raids by the Dutch and British authorities or serious weather damage.

The final pirate broadcast from the Ross Revenge was on 5 November 1990. However the ship survives to this day and is maintained by a group of Radio Caroline supporters and enthusiasts while Radio Caroline still continues to broadcast on the web and other digital platforms.

With the passage of the Marine Broadcasting Offences Act in 1967 and the government's much delayed determination to make life impossible for fort-based radio stations you might have thought that big money would have turned away from funding any further expensive North Sea pirate radio projects. But there were still hidden overseas agendas at work and, as we will see in the next chapter, they were not only based in the USA.

The final rebirth of Radio Caroline in 1983 coincided with the preparation of a new American-style radio ship which was to become a spectacularly successful attempt at regenerating the excitement of the sixties offshore era. Laser 558 was an excellent music station and, despite the considerable development of commercial and BBC radio since the 1960s managed to gain a respectable share of the listening audience. The story of this project is told in some detail by Paul Rusling in his recent book *Radio Adventures of the MV Communicator*,[10] but a brief summary makes a fascinating historical footnote. The idea of setting up a new offshore station five years after they had become illegal was born of a marriage of individuals linked to the then thriving Irish land-based radio pirates and US individuals who had still not fully given up on the idea. The capital funding was said to have come from a mysterious Irish millionaire, and a number of UK passport holders were very involved in the setting up of the station. In order to throw the authorities off the scent Laser encouraged the press to believe that the station was being controlled from New York, where an advertising office was being run by Roy Lindau, and that it had American backing. Paul Rusling has written extensively about his involvement in the setting up of the station and the fitting out of the ship, a former trawler the Gardline Seeker. In August 1983 the ship quietly headed across the Atlantic from Lowestoft to the shipyards in Florida, like so many well-funded radio ships previously. Renamed MV Communicator and registered in Panama the ship was fitted out with two 25 kW medium wave transmitters and, despite Rusling's advice, a 350 foot long wire antenna to be suspended from a helium balloon. The Americans insisted that this had worked well for the CIA ship-based stations in the Caribbean, the Mediterranean and the Far East and ignored the experience of those who had tried, and spectacularly failed, to make the system work in the very different waters of the North Sea.

There were in fact two groups planning to share the Communicator, one owning the station which was to become Laser 558 playing a hot hits format and a separate group intending to run a gold hits service called Radio Waves. While the ship was being fitted out in Florida the mysterious American backers of the second station walked away from the project, concerned at the complete lack of advertising sales by the New York office. With the equipment for the second service hastily removed the Communicator left Florida in November and crossed the Atlantic with a full team of American disc jockeys and an experienced US radio engineer on board.

By the time the Laser ship arrived in the Thames estuary, having stopped in the Azores and Ireland for further supplies and equipment, other members of the original team had left after losing confidence in the project. Nevertheless by New Year 1984 the ship had moved to its intended anchorage, near to Radio Caroline's Ross Revenge 12 miles off the Essex coast.

As might have been expected the balloon idea failed and there was a further delay while two 100 foot lattice masts were fitted to the ship fore and aft and an 'inverted L' wire antenna was rigged between them. Although this was only capable of taking half the power of one of the transmitters it was able to put out a signal with decent range on the unusually low medium wave frequency of 558 kHz.

Eventually launching on 24 May 1984, Laser 558 was an almost instant success. Partly this was due to the sheer amount of uninterrupted pop music it was playing. The BBC's replacement for the pirates, Radio One, had some pretty verbose disc jockeys in those days and the growing number of licenced local commercial radio stations were each restricted by a specific 'promise of performance' typically calling for some 25 per cent of airtime to be devoted to speech. Laser 558 proudly announced that it was playing 'all the hits, all the time' and promised the listeners 'you're never more than a minute away from music'. However another crucial factor was that the music was a well chosen and carefully programmed sequence of high quality recent oldies and only the hottest current hits.

A few years after this, when I was working at Tyneside-based commercial station Metro Radio, I discussed this music policy with the former Laser 558 disc jockey and programme manager Dave Lee Stone. I commented that whenever I had been in the south of England I had listened to Laser and I had, quite literally, never heard the station playing a duff record. How was such control – which had eluded all the previous pirates – possible?

'It was easy' laughed Dave, 'there were no turntables in the studios, the only songs that they could play were the ones we had recorded onto carts'. These 'carts' were tape cartridges loaded with a long loop of recording tape which were widely used in UK commercial radio for short audio items like jingles and advertisements. At the end of each playback the loop would run on and cue itself back at the precise start of the audio ready for the next time it was needed on-air. Many stations in the USA were now using cartridges for all their music, ensuring repeated undamaged and click-free playback of a popular disc. On a radio ship they also avoided all the issues of needles bouncing out of the groove in a rough sea. So the DJs were constrained to play only the biggest hits and, unlike most of its predecessors, the station was not being paid by any record companies to plug second-rate material. All the hits, all the time.

Laser 558's 'more music' policy was also helped by the complete lack of any commercials, Roy Lindau's expensive Madison Avenue office in New York having sold none at all. But while a financial crisis was looming the station was soon reported to have gained a UK audience of nearly five million listeners. The public fiction that the operation was run by an American consortium was maintained, and given the suspicious CIA-related funding of so many previous radio ships this was easy to believe. It was said that by using only American staff and supplying the ship directly from Spain the station was completely legal.

The British authorities knew otherwise, they had been monitoring the comings and goings from the Communicator from the start and were well aware that she was being tendered illegally from Whitstable in Kent, indeed they had already made some arrests under the Marine Broadcasting Offences Act and other prosecutions were to follow. Laser 558 was plainly not broadcasting any advertisements and it was thought that it could be costing someone about £15,000 a week to keep the ship on the air. Who was paying the bills, and why? Press speculation started to grow about who was really behind the Laser project with, as Paul Rusling remembers, some pointing out that the name Communicator contained the letters CIA![11]

In August 1984 the London *Evening Standard* named the then BBC journalist Roger Parry as a leading figure in the Laser 558 consortium and identified Irish multi-millionaire Philip Smythe as the ultimate owner of the station.[12] Roger Parry CBE, denied the reports, calling them 'bizarre' and 'nonsense', but never sued the *Evening Standard*. He left the BBC and went on to become CEO of Clear Channel International, at one point the world's largest owner of commercial radio stations and, among many other senior media positions, has been Chairman of regional newspaper group Johnston Press plc and is currently chairman of market research firm YouGov.

In early 1985 Laser faced repeated serious problems with storm damage to its antenna and generator faults which frequently took it off the air. Then in August the government launched a blockade of the Communicator and the nearby Caroline ship, with a small boat, the Dioptic Surveyor being chartered by the Department of Trade And Industry's' radio regulatory department to spy on all their activities, the police prosecuting anyone who helped or promoted the stations from the UK.

Suffering from serious generator problems and starved of supplies and fuel Laser 558 closed down on 5 November 1985 and the Communicator was escorted into Harwich by a DTI ship where she was impounded by the authorities. Laser was to return briefly a year later when the ship was purchased by a new owner and then passed to a Panamanian company with connections to an agency in, guess where, Dallas, Texas. The station relaunched as Laser Hot Hits on 576 kHz but the same set of problems and government pressure forced the final closure of Laser at the end of April 1987.

CHAPTER ELEVEN

RED SIGNALS

By 1970 I was supposed to be studying for a degree in Electronics at the University of Essex (in reality spending more time helping to set up a legal medium wave radio station for the campus) and found myself living in student digs near the seafront in Clacton-on-Sea. I couldn't help wishing I had been here five years earlier, able to look out and see Radio Caroline and Radio London ships and, later, Radio England and Britain Radio.

As the swinging sixties had drawn to an end it was assumed that so too had the era of what Kenny Everett liked to call 'watery wireless'. It was therefore a surprise when, looking out from the clifftop promenade, a very brightly coloured ship with a tall mast could be seen on the horizon. There had been stories of Radio Caroline returning, but this ship was plainly, even from that distance, in another league.

The mystery radio ship had been broadcasting off the Dutch coast for about six weeks since mid-February with an American-style hits format hosted by English and German presenters at different times of day. What made this station different was the apparent scale of the operation, this was by far the most elaborately equipped of all the pirate radio ships. Identifying itself as Radio Northsea International, or RNI, the ship had been fitted out with two large studios and no fewer than five broadcast transmitters. The most powerful, now broadcasting on 1610 kHz, was twice as powerful as anything used in the North Sea previously. Specially built by RCA in the States it was capable of producing 105 kW and was constructed from combined modules from two RCA 50 kW transmitters, that being the largest size allowed for AM commercial radio in the USA. There was also a standby medium wave transmitter, a 10 kW RCA unit purchased from the now closed down Radio 390, which was sometimes used to transmit a second medium wave service simultaneously on another frequency.

The ship was also equipped to broadcast on the VHF FM band, a first for a pirate station aimed at a British audience, using a 1.2 kW Rhode & Schwarz VHF transmitter, initially operating on 102 MHz. But what provoked most interest, and concern in high places, was the inclusion of two powerful short wave transmitters: another RCA 10 kW unit set for the 31 metre band and a Brown & Boveri transmitter for the 49 metre band. Each studio was beautifully equipped with top of the range broadcast-quality gear, including two EMT turntables, two Revox A77 tape recorders and three Spotmaster cartridge players. It was said that the ship was capable of simultaneously transmitting four different programmes on four different frequencies.

It was not just the technical specifications that exceeded anything else to have hit the airwaves from the North Sea, by the standards of the previous pirate stations the ship was lavishy appointed with fitted carpets, clean and comfortable cabins, a pleasant television lounge and spacious showers. The hull was painted in a colour scheme often described as psychedelic but which, to me, looked more like a fragment of a 'WHAM!' from a comic book – a colourful, jagged pattern on each side of the hull. This ship wanted to be noticed. Originally built in 1948 in the Netherlands and called the Silvretta, the 630 tonne 174 foot coaster had been newly fitted out in Rotterdam and renamed, after the company who now owned her, the Mebo II.

The burning question was WHY?

Why, two years after the Marine Broadcasting Offences Act had made it illegal to support or work with such stations, and professional outfits like Radio London and Radio 390 had concluded that they had to close, invest so lavishly in a new radio ship?

Why expensively equip the station for short wave broadcasting if the target audience was in the countries surrounding the North Sea? Short wave retained a value for world-wide broadcasting, for example to ex-pats abroad, and was still popular in the third world where the local, or even national, broadcasting infrastructure was more sparse and often dominated by a dictatorial government. But very few English listeners, apart from radio hams and assorted geeks like me, ever listened on short wave, most homes did not even possess a radio capable of short wave reception. How was this a commercial proposition?

Why bother with a local-scale FM transmitter which, off Essex with a mast reaching only 150 feet above sea level was not going to make any impact in London, or any other European capital for that matter?

Nevertheless on the morning of 24 March 1970 the Mebo II left the Dutch coast and took up her prominent position a few miles off the beaches of Clacton-on-Sea broadcasting loud and clear (in Clacton anyway) on 1610 kHz (186 metres) and 100 MHz FM. The trouble was that these channels were not empty.

While it was not the first time a well-designed and fully-financed radio ship had made some fundamental errors in the choice of its broadcast frequency, it became clear that RNI's frequencies seemed specifically chosen to annoy the authorities in their target areas. The chosen medium-wave frequency was in fact slightly above the official broadcast band and when the powerful transmitter was switched on in international waters off Noordwijk, Holland on 11 February 1970 it immediately started to cause interference to ship-to-shore radio services on both sides of the North Sea.

Similar frequencies slightly beyond the top on the AM broadcast band had been used by other pirates, notably Radio City for its religious programming and most cheap transistor radios could, just, tune to them but above 1602 kHz the frequencies were officially reserved for maritime radio communications. However this was the first time that such a high-power broadcast transmitter had been used right on top of a ship-to-shore frequency. The situation was not helped by the fact that the RNI transmitter had been set up to broadcast higher quality audio than most European AM transmitters and therefore occupied a greater bandwidth, well in excess of 5 kHz either side of the stated frequency. Further there were obvious problems in setting up and maintaining the tuning of the Ampliphase transmitter, often resulting in considerable 'splatter' audible on my receiver on land some distance either side of the intended channel.

Walton-on-the-Naze coastguards, who had generally been very helpful towards the previous pirate stations, complained of interference to the frequencies they used to communicate with lightships and Trinity House vessels. Specious complaints of unlicensed stations interfering with vital ship-to-shore links or unidentified emergency services had always been trotted out by government spokesmen to justify action against the pirates, but on this occasion I was inclined to believe them. Although all such communication has now switched to the VHF maritime band, in the sixties coastguard and lifeboat radios were equipped for several frequencies in the 1605 – 1699 kHz range. Certainly 1647.5 kHz was used by a number of coastguard stations in south east England at that time and 1621.5 kHz is still listed as a Norwegian ship-to-shore channel.

In 1969 the archaic role of postmaster general had gone the same way as the outdated powers of the Lord Chamberlain to censor theatre productions the year before. The office was abolished by the Post Office Act 1969, the Post Office becoming a public corporation and the remaining powers of the PMG being transferred to a minister of posts and telecommunications, a post first held by Labour's John Stonehouse. Initially under the Board of Trade the Ministry of Posts and Telecommunications became part of the powerful new Department of Trade and Industry when that was set up in October 1970.

Seizing the excuse to take early action against this unexpected blossoming of new pirate activity the newly empowered Ministry of Posts and Telecommunications immediately arranged to 'borrow' from the BBC (under a promise of strict secrecy) the 10 kW trailer-mounted emergency transmitter kept in reserve at their Brookmans Park transmission site in north London for deployment as part of the Wartime Broadcasting Service. Quickly and quietly pressed into service on 25 March at the navy radio station at Beacon Hill, Chattenden near Rochester in Kent, the high power transmitter replaced the navy's equipment which had been transmitting continuous Morse code on 1612 kHz in an attempt to keep their channel clear.

One of the RNI short wave frequencies was equally provocatively chosen. The short wave frequencies between about 2 MHz and 30 MHz are carved up between different users and there are a number of broadcast bands suitable for different purposes at varying times of day. The 49 metre broadcast band officially stretched from 5900 and 6200 kHz so RNI's selected frequency of 6210 kHz put it outside the band, similarly to the medium wave transmitter, and too close for comfort to a long-distance international distress frequency of 6215 kHz. A Norwegian ship-to-shore radio station, Rogaland Radio, almost immediately responded by jamming the RNI frequency with announcements and loud tones. The main concern at this stage was to keep the shipping channel clear and when RNI later moved further away from the distress frequency to 6205 kHz the jamming stopped.

Similarly the FM transmissions to the Clacton coast on 100 MHz clashed with frequencies then in use by Essex Police as well as the Suffolk and Essex fire brigade transmitters on 100.1 and 100.15 MHz respectively. Emergency service frequencies were reallocated after 1987 but in those days the UK's FM broadcast band only stretched from 88 to 97.7 MHz even though most FM radios on sale, as now, covered the more common international allocation of 88 to 108 MHz. Tuning around the top half of the dial above 97.7 one would hear the repeated bleeping of police transmitters and where, as in Essex, they used FM transmission, you could clearly but illegally listen in to the base station end of conversations with police cars. The mobile units generally used other frequencies outside the broadcast band and the base station sent 'pip tones' every couple of seconds to indicate that someone else was transmitting to the control room. Mobile units would request 'talk-through' if they needed to speak directly to another unit and in those cases you heard the mobile ends of the call as well. The fire brigades generally operated in talk-through mode and you could therefore hear the fire crews as well as the control room. It was clear to any FM listener that Radio Northsea International was indeed disrupting emergency frequencies.

After a few days RNI closed down the offending transmissions on the coastguard and police frequencies and when it returned on 10 April it was using the more sociable 1578 kHz (190 metres) medium wave and 102 MHz FM. The programmes were now in German from 5.30 in the morning until 7 am, then in English throughout the peak times of the day until 8 pm. In the evenings German programmes ran until 11 pm with the English Service returning until closedown at 2 am.[1]

The programming was a little reminiscent of Swinging Radio England but without the American excesses and with a distinctly pan-European flavour. The English service DJs were mainly familiar voices from previous pirate ventures, competent presenters like Roger Day, Andy Archer, Mark Wesley and Carl Mitchell. The music was well-chosen, lively and uplifting. At the top of each hour RNI played its strident theme tune: *Man Of Action* by the Les Reed Orchestra which always, to my ears, seemed to be running at slightly the wrong speed. But my recollections of RNI during the hot and sunny summer of 1970 are dominated by the sound of Mungo Jerry's *In The Summertime*, which also seemed to be played once every hour. Apart from the jamming and frequent frequency changes the only issue preventing the station from gaining a big audience was the frequent technical problems with the medium wave transmitter. Living in Clacton I was one of the few with the luxury of listening to RNI on the FM band. Although not in stereo (the owners correctly felt this would reduce the effective range of the transmitter) the high quality music was a novelty to hear from a UK radio ship - but it was always possible to hear when the power-hungry AM transmitter unexpectedly shut down. Suddenly without its major load the ship's generator would speed up for a few seconds, taking the turntables with it. Even more pronounced was the enormous 'wow' created when the records slowed down as the big transmitter came back on air.

Although the station was no longer broadcasting on shipping frequencies the government had the scent of blood and, fuelled by concern from the security services about the purpose of the ship, the Ministry of Posts and Telecommunications was encouraged to continue to jam the new Radio Northsea frequency in the medium wave broadcast band. On 15 April the transmitter at Rochester started to broadcast a 800 Hz tone on 1578 kHz blocking the RNI signal near to the Thames and making it unpleasant to listen to further afield.

This was the first time a broadcast signal had been jammed during peacetime in Britain. Although common practice in the communist bloc and among despotic governments elsewhere not even the German Lord Haw-Haw broadcasts during the Second World War had been jammed in the UK. None of the earlier pirate broadcasts had attracted such attention, although it had been discussed and ruled out on numerous occasions from Radio Atlanta onwards. Indeed the later transmissions from Radio Caroline and Laser 558 ships were not subjected to jamming. The government plainly knew there was something very different about Radio Northsea International.

The two people behind the ship were Swiss entrepreneurs Erwin Meister and Edwin Bollier whose surnames were reflected in the name of the ship and their Zurich-based company Mebo Telecommunications AG. Still in their early thirties the pair had become millionaires by trading internationally in electronics, telecommunications and radio equipment from a base in Switzerland. Their story was that they had made money from a lucrative deal selling Japanese radio equipment to the Roman Catholic charity Caritas for use in war-torn Biafra where over a million civilians died from starvation. The morality of pocketing millions from a charity trying to help desperate people in the breakaway Nigerian state apparently did not concern the duo.

In fact they were known to the security services for some time to have been exploiting Switzerland's neutral political position and central geographic location to run a lucrative business importing and exporting high-tech electronics. The pair had both started out fitting and repairing car radios and moved into the two-way radio business, establishing offices at Albisriederstrasse 13 in Zurich.

When, in an era of guided weapons and the space race, it looked like the most technologically advanced nation would win the 'cold war', the United States had introduced an embargo on selling a wide variety of high-tech equipment and expertise to the communist countries, similar to an arms embargo already in place. The restriction encompassed a wide range of the new computer, satellite and communication systems as well as the new integrated circuit 'chips'. The USA had also pressed its allies in the west to apply similar blockades.

This was the time of transition to transistors. By 1969 my electronics department at the go-ahead University of Essex had proudly eradicated all references to valve technology from its courses but my short wave receivers and home-made experimental transmitters still used valves. There was amusement when the Americans got their hands on a downed Soviet military aircraft and delighted in telling the world that the Russians still relied on old valves in their radio sets. The glee turned to embarrassment when they realised that the old vacuum tube technology was far more immune to the effects of the huge electromagnetic pulse of energy (EMP) which would be released after a nuclear explosion than the tiny transistors used by the Americans, which would be fused immediately.

The Swiss entrepreneurs were happy to find ways round the American technical blockade, for a price. They would order sophisticated electronic equipment from the west, for delivery to their offices in Switzerland, and could then legally sell it on for use in a communist country.

Meister and Bollier also started to manufacture their own electronic devices, specialising in things that could, using new transistors and with the introduction of integrated circuits, be miniaturised onto a small single printed circuit board. One lucrative product was their line of tiny spy bug transmitters which proved very popular with their clients in the communist east.

Off the Essex coast in April 1970, faced with continued interference from the UK government's jamming transmitter, Radio Northsea International again closed down on medium wave and at the end of the month a game of cat-and-mouse began with the station frequently changing its position on the dial, the jamming transmitter chasing after it.

RNI reappeared on 1385 kHz (217 metres) but disappeared again due to transmitter problems, subsequently testing on other frequencies and finally settling on approximately 1232 kHz (244 metres) by mid-May. Inexplicably the FM service returned to 100 MHz at the same time. The Ministry of Posts and Telecommunications now claimed to have received a complaint of interference to a station in Czechoslovakia and John Stonehouse ordered the BBC emergency transmitter installed at Rochester to continue to block the 244 metres broadcasts. How adding another noisy transmitter to the same frequency would help the Czechs was never made clear. It was true that 1232 kHz was exclusively allocated to Czechoslovakia, for four separate stations, under the European Broadcasting Convention (the Copenhagen Plan) signed in September 1948. However, twenty years on from the Copenhagen conference around half of all the medium wave radio stations in Europe were using channels not allocated to them under the plan and all the previous UK pirates had equally squatted on frequencies allocated to other nations without that justifying jamming by the UK government.[2]

The jamming transmitter was now modulated with loud pulses of tone sounding like the bleeps from pedestrian traffic lights but this time the frequency chosen by RNI was, cunningly, separated by only one channel from BBC Radio One's famous '247 metres' transmissions on 1214 kHz. As a result the jamming signal from Beacon Hill also swamped out reception of BBC Radio One on the average transistor radio across much of Kent and the south of Essex. The audio modulation of the transmitter was quickly removed and instead its radio frequency was rapidly varied up and down by a few hundred Hertz two or three times per second to give a rapidly varying, and very annoying, heterodyne whistle when received alongside the RNI signal. While many listeners found that, due to the very directional properties of an internal ferrite-rod antenna, the interfering signal could be minimised by rotating their transistor radio, the jamming was obviously effective as, by 28 May, RNI had adopted a strategy of slightly changing its transmission frequency every fifteen minutes or so, the jamming engineers having to follow behind.

Why was the government so concerned about Radio Northsea International? We have seen throughout this book that some of the self-serving or promotional stories promulgated at the time by those involved with the pirates have passed into folklore and become the accepted version of history. In this case many believe that the unprecedented peacetime jamming of an incoming broadcast signal began when RNI started to interfere in the UK General Election in June 1970, however it started well before that, indeed before the ship even anchored off the English coast.

The authorities had always had their suspicions about the source of finance for the station, and for once the evidence did not point towards a consortium of CIA agents in Texas. This time it seemed pretty clear that the station had been set up, funded, or at least encouraged, by the secret intelligence services of one or more eastern European communist states.

Communist controlled countries on the other side of the 'iron curtain' were ostensibly independent entities but on most political issues they were expected to toe a line set by Moscow. However they all had their own secret police forces which seemed to pursue different agendas requiring varying degrees of repression of their own people. Some of the worst included the Soviet Union's KGB and the East German Stasi, others such as the Czechoslovakian Statni Bezpecnost (StB) were more subtle but equally focussed on controlling their population.

The man leading the government operation against Radio Northsea International, the new minister of posts and telecommunications John Stonehouse, was in a very interesting position. It is known that the home secretary, Jim Callaghan, was against the jamming of the broadcasts but it was Stonehouse who pushed the idea and won over the support of prime minister Harold Wilson, although Wilson had stipulated that it should be done without publicity. What was not publicly known at the time was John Stonehouse's involvement with the Czechoslovakian government.

Wilf Owen, the Labour MP for Morpeth, had been charged under the Official Secrets Act in March 1970. He was alleged to have been passing secret documents to the Czechs for most of the last ten years. The problem for the government was that during the trial his Czech handler, Robert Husak, would be named. MI5 was aware that while John Stonehouse had been at the Ministry of Technology, with access to sensitive material, Stonehouse and Husak used to meet regularly. The intelligence service brought this to the attention of Stonehouse's new boss Tony Benn and said they had transcripts of these conversations.[3]

It was not until some years later that a fuller account appeared when the first official history of MI5, *The Defence of the Realm*, was written by Cambridge historian Christopher Andrew, who had been given access to secret files. Published in 2009 the book revealed that then prime minister, Margaret Thatcher, had agreed in 1980 to cover up evidence that John Stonehouse had been a Czech spy since the 1960s. MI5 held extensive files on Stonehouse and he was named as a spy by a Czech defector in 1969, but he managed to convince MI5 and Harold Wilson that he was innocent.

Stonehouse faked his own suicide in Miami, Florida, in 1974 by leaving his clothes on a beach and fled to Australia with his mistress and secretary, Sheila Buckley.[4] He was finally exposed as a spy five years later when another Czech defector provided convincing evidence of his activities.[5]

What exactly was expected of a Czechoslovakian spy during this turbulent period of the nation's history is not clear. In January 1968, Alexander Dubcek had become head of the Communist Party, and during the 'Prague Spring' started to reform the way the country was governed. While keeping the one-party state and the centrally planned economy he wanted to give it a human face and fix the ailing economy. The leaderships of the USSR and the neighbouring Soviet bloc countries were worried that, were Dubcek to succeed, the movement would inevitably spread to their countries. Throughout the summer Soviet president Brezhnev tried to exert political pressure on Dubcek with no success.

On August 21 1968 Soviet tanks had rolled into the Czechoslovakia, accompanied 165,000 troops from the Warsaw Pact countries, with the intention of crushing the democratic reforms of the Prague Spring. Shocked citizens took to the streets in protest and over a hundred were killed. It emerged that most of the invading soldiers had no idea of why they were there and many had not even been told where they were going. The peaceful protests in the street grew and were centred around the headquarters of Czech radio in Prague which had continued to broadcast honest accounts of the Soviet-led invasion.

For several days not only the Czech domestic services but a skeleton TV news service and the overseas services of Radio Prague in English continued to broadcast using the Czech equivalent of the secret British Wartime Broadcasting Service. Ironically the Soviet Union had insisted that Czechoslovakia should set up an underground radio network in order that it could continue informing the public in the event of a western invasion, but the Czech government had never given the details to the USSR. I was able to listen to Radio Prague on medium wave and short wave as they described what was happening in the streets and appealed for international support. The domestic service was, we were told, appealing for peaceful, non-violent protest, suggesting places where people could gather and giving out the registration numbers of cars being used by the secret intelligence services.

Protesters formed a human shield around the radio and TV building in Prague and prevented the invading forces from getting to the studios. When they eventually stormed the building fifteen people lost their lives at the broadcasting centre and, while radio transmissions continued for a while from secret locations, the media rebellion and public protest was soon suppressed. In the wake of the uprising a Soviet puppet regime was installed and hundreds of state broadcasting employees were purged from the organisation. The StB quickly restored a climate of fear with individuals not trusting their friends and family and again becoming unwilling to speak up against the repressive state.

So why was the UK government minister in charge of broadcasting, who had been in the pay of the Czechoslovak government for several years so keen to break with tradition and jam this one offshore station? It could not have been due to the alleged interference with the Czech frequency as the jamming started before Radio Northsea International moved to 244 metres. Plainly the Czechs were not behind Radio Northsea International, they had bigger issues to deal with in 1969, so suspicion turned towards Meister and Bollier's other friends in eastern Europe.

The British press was preoccupied with talk of a general election and there was little coverage of the unprecedented jamming of a broadcast frequency. But when, on 18 May 1970, prime minister Harold Wilson announced the date of the election supporters of the offshore stations were galvanised into action. On Sunday 31 May a protest rally was held outside the gates of the Beacon Hill transmitter. It was organised by the Campaign for Independent Broadcasting, a breakaway group from the Free Radio Association, and created a lot of press interest, alerting many of the public for the first time to the government's action in setting up a jamming transmitter.

The Free Radio Association had campaigned against the introduction of the Marine Broadcasting Offences Act in 1967, many of its members naively believing that the government could, instead, simply 'let the pirates come ashore'. Now they felt that the only way to preserve what they perceived as free radio was to ensure that the Conservatives won the election and replaced the Labour government which had introduced the Act. They believed that the Tories, being fans of free enterprise, would stop the jamming and let Caroline and RNI sail up the Thames broadcasting all the way.

The Free Radio Campaign had organised big protest rallies in London at the time of the Marine Broadcasting Offences Act and equated the campaign for free radio with contemporary battles for sexual equality, gay rights and nuclear disarmament, and against apartheid and the Vietnam war. I am still haunted by the memory of all these young people styling themselves as freedom-loving hippies, fighting for a new kind of alternative media, who were encouraging others to vote for the Conservatives. This was the first time 18 year olds had been given the vote in a general election (previously the minimum age had been 21) and pirate radio was bound to be a factor in the election campaign.

Unimpeded by the Representation of the People Act or any requirement for political balance in its broadcasts, Radio Northsea International had been suggesting that its listeners should make sure they were voting for someone who supported free radio. Initially they avoided mentioning specific political parties but, as the jamming from Kent continued, they started to specifically promote the Conservatives. Then, just five days before polling day, RNI's frequency appeared to have been taken over by something called Radio Caroline International. Edwin Bollier and Erwin Meister had agreed with the founder of Radio Caroline, Ronan O'Rahilly, to mount a joint campaign, supported by the Free Radio Association, against the Labour Party. As already mentioned, Caroline was the brand most associated with the golden age of the radio ships by the general public and the name was seen as packing more political punch, particularly among those no longer teenagers, than RNI.

Ronan O'Rahilly was no fan of Labour Party leader Harold Wilson. When the Marine Offences Act was going through parliament he had told the press that he intended to broadcast a recorded programme called *The Private Life of Harold Wilson* which would he claimed reveal shocking facts about the prime minister.[6] The programme has never been heard, it may never have existed, but it is known that the security service had always had their doubts about Wilson, to the extent of tapping his phone calls.[7] Harold Wilson resigned as PM, suddenly and without giving a reason, a few years later.

The British broadcast media were not then, and are not today, allowed to cover political news stories on polling day, they are limited to talking about things like the weather and the size of the turnout. Faced with the prospect that, while the polling stations were open, a powerful broadcaster could be telling its listeners to vote Tory, the government felt it had to act more decisively. Too many people were beyond the range of the Beacon Hill navy transmitter site and others could nullify the interference by carefully positioning their radios, what was needed was a more powerful transmitter located so that the signal, in the main population centre, was coming from the same direction as the pirate.

It is frequently suggested that the more powerful jamming of Radio Northsea International was provoked by the station's intervention in the 1970 election campaign, in fact we know it was being prepared at least two weeks earlier perhaps because the security service moles were well aware of the Radio Caroline plan in advance. At the start of June RNI had written to the ministry threatening to start jamming the transmissions of Radio One on the day before the election if the interference with the RNI frequency was not stopped and this also galvanised the government into action.

John Stonehouse instructed officials at the Ministry of Posts and Telecommunications to identify a suitable transmission site on the east coast and to find a more powerful transmitter. For security and to avoid alerting the press the site ideally needed to be a government controlled location and sites like Orford Ness, Bradwell nuclear power station and Shoeburness firing range were considered. In the end the site of the former RAF 'Chain Home' radio station at Canewdon near Southend Airport was selected. Chain Home was a forerunner of radar and used multiple transmitter and receiver masts to detect the approach of enemy aircraft in the second world war and only one of the 250 foot high wooden masts remained on site, occasionally used by the Marconi company for equipment test transmissions.

There were no spare high-power AM broadcast transmitters installed or under construction in the UK at this time other than the BBC's secret 'contingency' and the BBC was understandably unwilling to become further involved in the jamming of broadcasts for political reasons in the run-up to a general election. There was however a transportable 50 kW transmitter complete with its own diesel generator stationed as a standby unit at the giant Foreign Office 'Diplomatic Wireless Service' transmitter site at Crowborough in Sussex. Although the site was used to carry some BBC External Service transmissions it was not under the Corporation's control and the transmitter could be borrowed by another government department with no questions asked.

The transmitter in question was a well-travelled device with a surprising history. It was a Continental Electronics CE 317C, serial number 12, which had been built to order in Dallas in 1965 specifically for Radio Caroline. It had been needed to give Radio Caroline South on the Mi Amigo a power boost to compete with the more successful Radio London.

At around the same time, in November 1965, the Rhodesian prime minister, Iain Smith, had issued a 'Unilateral Declaration of Independence', withdrawn from the British Commonwealth and broken diplomatic relations with London. The government urgently needed to step up the BBC World Service broadcasts targeting Rhodesia. The Foreign Office funded BBC overseas broadcasting and were happy to pay to install new transmitters in a country neighbouring Rhodesia but there were no suitable transmitters available in the UK and the only powerful units they could find were under construction by Continental in the USA.

The Continental factory had nearly completed two 50 kW transmitters, the one ordered by Project Atlanta for Radio Caroline and a second one, serial number 13, for another customer. The US military and intelligence services were major clients of Continental and when the British government brought diplomatic pressure to bear on the USA it was quickly decided that the two almost finished transmitters should be crated up and despatched to Francistown in the soon to be republic of Botswana.

The new BBC World Service relay station beaming into Rhodesia went on the air at the end of 1965 and Radio Caroline's replacement transmitter was ready in early 1966. The delay was probably fortunate for Caroline as in January the Mi Amigo had been washed up on Frinton beach and was put out of service for two months. While programmes continued from the temporary ship the Continental Electronics transmitter, serial number 14, was installed on the Mi Amigo in Holland and was ready for her return to the Essex coast.

When the BBC relay station was no longer required transmitter serial number 12 was sent to the UK where it became the standby transmitter owned by the secretive Diplomatic Wireless Service at Crowborough, and was now to be used to jam Radio Northsea International.[8]

In a secret military-style operation the transmitter and its accompanying diesel generator were set up in a marquee in the empty field rented from Marconi at Canewdon and Post Office engineers strung an inverted V antenna over the remaining radio tower. Unlike Beacon Hill this was no longer a military base so Securicor guards were employed to protect the site against any prying eyes or protestors.

Without any pre-publicity the powerful Canewdon transmitter joined Beacon Hill in the fight for the RNI frequency on the eve of the general election. Its frequency-modulated carrier was more powerful than the Mebo II transmitter and obliterated RNI for most of the UK. Whether the 'free radio' campaign made any difference to the outcome we will never know but, despite the opinion polls predicting a comfortable Labour victory, a late swing gave the Conservatives a small lead and ended almost six years of Labour rule. The Conservatives were elected and formed a new government.

One day after the election Radio Northsea International dropped the Radio Caroline identity and returned to normal programming but, much to the amazement of the free radio campaigners, the jamming signals did not stop. The new Minister of Posts and Telecommunications, former athlete and ITN newscaster Christopher Chattaway, perhaps now in possession of a security briefing which he had not seen in opposition, announced that the transmissions on RNI's frequency would continue indefinitely. Following representations from members of parliament from Kent and Essex, and aware of the widespread interference with Radio One reception, the high power transmitter at Canewdon was shut down, although it remained on stand-by for a few more weeks and the previous jamming from Beacon Hill in Kent continued.

It is implausible to think that Radio Northsea International was ever a commercial proposition, but the months of frequency changes, breaks in transmission, jamming and, now, political propaganda had not helped. Neither had there been any sign of Erwin Meister and Edwin Bollier attempting to sell advertising on the station anyway. Mebo II's British expedition seemed to be over and, on 23 July, the Mebo II made the journey back to the Netherlands, anchoring off Scheveningen - and the UK government's jamming ceased immediately.

The question was now not only who had paid to set up this wandering ship but, in the absence of advertising, who was paying to keep it on the air?

Before buying the Silvretta and transforming her into the splendid Mebo II the two Swiss businessmen had already converted a much smaller vessel for radio use, in April 1969 purchasing a 124 foot 374 ton Norwegian ship and spending nearly £60,000 on renovations and installing studios. The Bjarkoy had previously been used for work in the Norwegian fjords and was totally unsuitable for use as a radio ship in the open waters of the North Sea. Nevertheless she was registered in Panama as the Mebo I and formed the basis of the plans for the new station until Meister and Bollier suddenly found the cash to pay for a much bigger and better ship.

Meister and Bollier claimed to have spent some £400,000 of their own money on the Mebo II and never identified any other investors or shareholders. The two have always remained intensely proud of RNI and are quite happy to keep all the credit for themselves. But these were shrewd entrepreneurs who made their money by purchasing or making products and selling them on to people who otherwise would not have access to them. If they invested in a radio ship it would be with a specific client or clients in mind, so the question becomes who wanted a broadcasting platform and was willing to pay good money for a turnkey project to deliver one?

If we believe that Edwin Bollier and Erwin Meister made millions of Swiss francs from Biafran charity work then it is possible that they decided to take the opportunity to deal in something larger than the small transmitters and receivers which had been the staple of their business so far. But, having completed the first ship they found that the clients wanted something bigger and better and would pay big money for it to be built.

Mebo II was unique in that it was conceived as a multi-purpose, go anywhere, broadcasting platform. All the previous ships had been designed primarily for a single purpose, a specific broadcasting band and a particular transmission range, with or without on-board studios as required. This vessel offered a full range of capabilities, from ultra-local FM transmission to worldwide short wave broadcasting, it had the highest power medium wave transmitter and two versatile studios, one equipped for production work. The Mebo II was a ship named after the company that owned and operated it, not identified with a romantic notion, station name, political statement, or previous ships registration like the Galaxy, Laissez Faire, Caroline, Veronica or Comet. This was a taxi for hire, available to do a radio job anywhere in the world.

The temporary change of identity to Radio Caroline emphasised that for Meister and Bollier this enterprise was not really about Radio Northsea International, it was about marketing the Mebo II as a radio ship capable of being whatever you wanted it to be.

If we benevolently discount the story that the pair made a lot of money out of the charity Caritas and other work related to the Biafran war, we also need to identify who paid for the first ship which never saw service as a broadcasting platform and was simply used as a long-distance tender for the Mebo II. It is quite possible that there was more than one mysterious overseas investor in this project.

One of the biggest customers for Meister and Bollier's export of high-tech electronics from Switzerland was in communist East Germany. The Institut fur Technische Untersuchungen (Institute for Technical Research) in East Berlin bought hundreds of items from Mebo, including the spy bugs, full size radio communications equipment and coding and decoding devices. The Institute was in fact a front for the East German secret police, the Ministerium für Staatsicherheit, or Stasi, devising and supplying advanced electronic devices for its agents.

Responsible for both internal security and foreign espionage, the Stasi was the most feared branch of the East German state, it infiltrated every organisation and all aspects of daily life in the German Democratic Republic (DDR). People were frightened that their workmates, friends or even family members might denounce them to the Stasi, it was said to have relied on a million informants in addition to its 100,000 staff. After the collapse of the Berlin wall it was discovered that the Stasi had kept files on around six million East Germans, more than one third of the population.[9]

The Stasi was equally ferocious in its foreign espionage activities. Although mainly concerned with spying on NATO and its neighbours in West Germany it also encouraged and supplied a wide range of terrorist groups who were hell-bent on the destruction of various western governments. It was linked to the Palestine Liberation Organization, Abū Niḍāl the founder of Fatah, the Baader-Meinhof Group (Red Army Faction) in West Germany, and Ilich Ramírez Sánchez (Carlos the Jackal). It reads like a list of all the seventies' international bad guys. When Colonel Muammar Gaddafi took power in Libya following a military coup in 1969 the Stasi was immediately supportive, even allowing Libyan agents to use East Berlin as a base when launching terrorist attacks on the west. But mainly the Stasi was the go-to supplier for any organisation needing high-tech help to destabilise the west - a sort of Maplin or Radio Shack store for terrorists worldwide.

The Institut fur Technische Untersuchungen was far more than simply a warehouse for dodgy electronic devices however. One of the surprises for the western intelligence community following the re-unification of Germany was the extent to which the West Germans, the CIA and MI6 had underestimated how technically advanced the Stasi had become.

In a thesis titled *Control Through Constant Knowledge: An Analysis of the Stasi's Effects on Audio Technology*, John Gieger of Belmont University, Nashville, Tennessee, wrote in 2009: 'During the cold war era, also the heyday of magnetic recording development, the Stasi created technologies that have continued to impact today'. Gieger explains that the intelligence battle between east and west was one of micro-engineering, meaning an effort to put ears where traditionally it was thought impossible 'such as pockets, walls and remote locations'. He also sheds light on the Stasi's SIGINT (signals intelligence) operation which he describes as one of the biggest in the world. Having no idea of the communist state's technical progress the West Germans' telecommunications links were insecure or at best poorly protected.[10]

Former CIA counterintelligence officer Ben Fischer has written about the huge Stasi SIGINT operation, quoting one senior agent as saying 'all we had to do was stick a finger in the air and we were able to grab everything because nothing, absolutely nothing, was encrypted or protected.' Rich sources of intelligence were car telephones, fax machines and early computer networks used by politicians, senior government officials, industrial managers and journalists.

Fischer also writes about the Stasi's Institut fur Technische Untersuchungen's success in cracking the codes and ciphers being used for secret communications in other western countries. He claims that 'An HVA (foreign intelligence branch of the Stasi) agent codenamed "'Rubin", a business manager at the Swiss firm Mebo AG, reportedly obtained a cipher machine from the Swiss company Crypto AG on orders from the KGB.'[11]

'Rubin' was Edwin Bollier, apparently registered at Stasi headquarters under file number 2550/70. Bollier provided the East Germans with two-way radios, special antennas, coding equipment and data terminals in exchange for huge amounts of cash, paid in West German marks, perhaps explaining why the staff on the Mebo II were often paid in Deutschmarks.

Western intelligence services must have been aware of Mebo's activities and Bollier seems to have had good contacts in the western security industry. Internal reports found after the fall of East Germany showed that, when he was able to supply the communists with a top secret 'Mark' voice analyser, a kind of polygraph for the human voice, some people in the Stasi started to become suspicious that he might even be working for the CIA.

According to Ben Fischer: 'In addition to fixed sites, (the Stasi) used a plane, a helicopter and a ship as dedicated mobile (SIGINT) collection platforms.' He says it also used East German merchant ships and fishing fleets as required.

According to an article published in the leading Dutch newspaper *De Telegraaf* on 8 July 1971, the Institut fur Technische Untersuchungen had ordered the construction of ten pirate radio ships, based on the design of the Mebo II, in Gdansk in Poland. The report suggested that this was a response to the US-funded Radio Free Europe and Radio Liberty, broadcasting propaganda into the communist east from mainland transmitters. It was also presumed that such vessels would incorporate secret SIGINT facilities.

This seemed plausible, it followed the established practice where Mebo would supply samples of western technology to the Stasi's technical institute - which enabled them to make their own, often improved, copies. It is also likely that the story, whether accurate or not, was a bargaining chip in the Soviet bloc's continuing diplomatic negotiations to get the American cross-border transmitters closed down. It is suspected that one of these ships was completed and used by the Soviet Union around this time to broadcast Russian propaganda into China.

The sudden influx of capital enabling Meister and Bollier to build their second, larger and more versatile, radio ship coincided with Colonel Gaddafi seizing power in the Libyan bloodless military coup of 1969. Gadaffi immediately tackled the international oil companies, demanding a higher price for Libyan oil and a much larger share of the revenue, thus instantly gaining personal access to an enormous amount of foreign currency. The Stasi was very supportive of the new leader, helping him to channel funds to mutually useful causes and equipping him to set up his own state intelligence services. In later years the Stasi assisted Gaddafi in openly supporting rebel movements like Nelson Mandela's African National Congress, the PLO and the IRA.

Either directly or indirectly, some of Gaddafi's oil money had been channelled into the Mebo II, and later, when the Mebo II was no longer required to do whatever it was doing in the North Sea, it became the property of Libya.

After leaving British shores the Mebo II had an eventful life off the Dutch coast, becoming embroiled in a pirate power struggle and further cloak-and-dagger happenings. When the ship anchored off Scheveningen on 24 July

1970 the transmissions continued without any interference from the British government stations. But within days the Dutch telecommunications authority complained that the Radio Northsea programmes on 244 metres were interfering with the main Dutch Hilversum 3 service on 240 metres and that the FM signal was interfering with bus communications. It seemed like history was repeating itself as the station went off air while frequencies were changed only to be interrupted again when storm damage silenced the station in mid-August.

Radio Northsea International remained that strangest of animals - a commercial radio station without any firm arrangements for selling airtime - until an Amsterdam night club owner Kees Manders announced that he was the RNI's new 'commercial director' and would be selling advertising on the station. A few weeks later, after Meister and Bollier had denied any knowledge of the deal, Mebo I, now used as a tender, was impounded by court order in Scheveningen harbour after Manders claimed he was owed advertising commission.

On 29 August Kees Manders hired two boats to go out to the Mebo II and insisted on talking to the captain. He offered cash if the captain would sail the ship into Scheveningen or threatened to cut the anchor chain and tow it into harbour himself. While RNI broadcast frantic calls for help a battle ensued in which Manders' crew attempted to board Mebo II, missiles were thrown from the deck of the radio ship and the attackers threatened to fuse the antenna mast by targeting it with a water cannon. The would-be invaders left before a Dutch naval frigate arrived on the scene and stood by the Mebo II for twenty four hours.

Programming continued until 24 September when Radio Northsea International broadcast a statement that it was voluntarily closing down. On-air the stated reason was to prevent the Dutch government from taking action against Radio Veronica but Meister and Bollier told the press that the ship had been sold to 'an African country' and would shortly be broadcasting in the Mediterranean. In fact, it later emerged, the owners of long-established Dutch pirate Radio Veronica had paid Mebo Telecommunications a reported one million Dutch Guilders to stop broadcasting in order to protect Veronica's own investment.

However it appears that Colonel Gaddafi did not yet need the ship to be broadcasting off the Libyan coast and the Swiss were offered more money to keep it on air in the North Sea, because in December Meister and Bollier offered to repay the bribe to Radio Veronica in order that they could restart transmissions from the Mebo II. In January 1971, Radio Veronica having refused the cash, the RNI owners tricked the Mebo II's captain (now in the pay of Radio Veronica) into going ashore while they took over the ship and moved it to a new position off the Dutch/Belgian border at Cadzland. The itinerant radio ship now appeared to have been hired by a Belgian station called Radio Marina but, after some test transmissions, nothing came of the project and by February the Mebo II was back off the Dutch coast at Scheveningen.

Much to the annoyance of Radio Veronica a new independent company was formed to operate a Dutch language service from the Mebo II, Radio Noordsee NV, while the ship remained the property of Mebo. The new Dutch service started on 7 March while Radio Veronica pushed ahead with legal action to enforce their agreement with RNI in the Dutch courts. When the court found in favour of RNI the now furious Veronica management decided to take matters into their own hands.

The continued broadcasts of Radio Noordzee in Dutch and RNI in English were also an embarrassment to the western security services who were pretty clear on who was ultimately responsible for funding the operations. *Why* remained a harder question. Theories ranged from the ship being a clandestine SIGINT listening platform (unlikely considering the interference from its own powerful transmitters), a short wave 'numbers station' sending secret messages to KGB and Stasi agents in the west (unlikely as these could just as easily have been sent directly from stations on land in the GDR), or (most likely) a sleeper resource available for deployment where and when needed (as in the case of the UK election). Some DJs who worked on the ship, like Steve Merike and Roger Day, pour scorn on the spy-ship stories while others, like Andy Archer, say they were aware of strange coded overnight transmissions. Others point out that it is possible to convey a simple command to a large number of people by simply and discreetly including, or not, certain words or a particular piece of music at a fixed time in a broadcast.

During the second world war the BBC frequently included 'personal messages' in its broadcasts to occupied-Europe which were in reality coded messages intended for secret agents. The pirate Radio City always had a copy of *You've Got Your Troubles* by the Fortunes in the studio to be broadcast as a secret signal in the event that they were under attack or broadcasting under duress. Radio Moscow's short wave English language service used to play an instrumental version of *Moscow Nights* as an interval signal before the hourly news to signify to overseas agents that everything was okay, the absence of the tune meant they should go to ground and await new orders.

When, on the night of 15 May 1971, the Mebo II was attacked and set ablaze by frogmen who arrived silently in a rubber dinghy it was widely interpreted as the work of the Dutch secret service, the BVD, under pressure from their western counterparts. Two men were said to have boarded the ship and quietly made their way down to the engine room where they attached an explosive device to the fuel line.

At 10.50 pm DJ Alan West interrupted his programme to say that there had been an explosion and the ship was on fire: 'Mayday. Mayday. Mayday. This is Radio North Sea International from the Mebo II at exactly 52°11' latitude, 40°16' longitude, four miles from the coast of Scheveningen, Holland, one mile from the radio ship Norderney, Veronica. We are having to abandon ship very soon. The bridge and the engine room are on fire. The fire is taking control of the ship. The fire was caused by a bomb thrown on board from a small motor launch with an outboard motor. The Mebo II is now abandoning ship.'

Forty five minutes after the explosion the transmitters were shut down and Captain Hardeveld gave the order to abandon ship. A firefighting tug and the Radio Northsea International tender Eurotrip arrived on the scene and, together with other ships and lifeboats, they managed to tackle the blaze extinguishing it after a couple of hours. At daybreak it was possible to see that the whole stern section of the Mebo II, including the bridge, had been gutted in the fire. But with the studios, transmitters and crew cabins unaffected RNI was soon back on the air from the stricken vessel.

Another Dutch navy frigate took up station beside the ship while Dutch police began an investigation. On 16 May, following a tip-off, the three members of the boarding party were arrested and the following day the police also arrested the Radio Veronica advertising manager Norbert Jurgens. Radio Veronica told the press that they had nothing to do with the firebomb attack but the next day Veronica director Bull Verweij appeared on Dutch television and admitted paying a man to force Mebo II into territorial waters - where the ship would have been liable to arrest or confiscation by court order. Verweij was immediately arrested for conspiracy in planning the attack.

For some reason Meister and Bollier told the police that they did not want to prosecute the offenders, but nevertheless the case came to trial in September and all five defendants were sentenced to one year in prison. Whether Radio Veronica was behind the attack or not the incident did not end well for the veteran radio ship, within weeks the Dutch prime minister announced that his government would, finally, join the other countries round the North Sea and introduce legislation to ratify the 1965 Strasbourg Convention and outlaw support for offshore broadcasting.

The Mebo II was repaired while still at sea and continued broadcasting in Dutch and English for the next couple of years with only occasional breaks in transmission when she lost her anchor in storms and entered Dutch territorial waters. There was still little commercial justification for the English language broadcasts, but when in October 1972 the Dutch service director, reasoning that they attracted very little advertising revenue, decided to cease the English programmes his instruction was immediately countermanded by Erwin Meister and Edwin Bollier.

In 1973 with the legislation making slow progress through the Dutch parliament and the Swiss government having already introduced a similar law, RNI's Zurich office had to be closed and responsibility for all programming was passed to the Dutch airtime company. There was a suggestion that Dutch pirates might be given access to legal frequencies in the Netherlands after the introduction of the new laws so both Veronica and RNI needed to hang on for another year.[12]

The Netherlands' Marine Offences Act was to come into force on 1 September 1974 and all programmes from the Mebo II ended at 8 pm on 31 August. Under the new law the pirates were supposed to be entitled to airtime on the Dutch broadcasting system, under a strange arrangement in which different broadcasting organisations time-shared state controlled radio and TV channels, but the government denied this to both RNI and Radio Veronica. Some staff set up the VOO (Veronica Broadcasting Organisation) and were eventually able to become a recognised Dutch broadcasting group while Meister and Bollier looked elsewhere for the next opportunity to use their radio asset.

By September 1974 both Mebo vessels were laid up at Slikkerveer in the Netherlands. They were expensively dry docked and were cleaned, repainted and fully refitted. The Mebo II transmitters were stripped and overhauled, the antenna system improved while a new record library and three replacement studios were built. Apparently the intention was to start a new Europe-wide, multi-language, broadcasting operation from a position off Genoa on the Italian coast in the northern Mediterranean.

When Meister and Bollier attempted to move the ships to their new anchorage the Mebo II was detained by the Dutch authorities. A court hearing was not convinced by the suggestion that the transmitters were simply cargo and held that they had been installed illegally under the new Dutch Marine Offences Act.

The Swiss businessmen were told they could not take the Mebo II out of port until the transmitters had been removed from the vessel. After a long legal battle stretching through most of 1975 and 1976 it was agreed that the owners had to pay a fine for the broadcasting offence and pay a returnable deposit to the court as a guarantee that the ship would not be used for broadcasting, anywhere in Europe, within the next two years. The two ships had to leave the Netherlands within three months.

Erwin Meister and Edwin Bollier's European initiative would have to be put on hold for at least two years so, in January 1977, the two ships each set sail with a crew of nine and headed for a friendly welcome from Colonel Gaddafi in Libya. Arriving in Tripoli on 14 February the newly refurbished ships changed their names, Mebo II becoming El Fatah and the former Mebo I renamed Almasira.

Throughout the remainder of the 1970s the El Fatah broadcast programmes from the government controlled and snappily titled Socialist People's Libyan Arab Jamahiriyah Broadcasting Corporation, more often referred to as LJB or Radio Jamahiriyah. But it seems that by this time, like the East German Stasi, Colonel Gaddafi was himself developing doubts about the motivation of Meister and Bollier and after 1980, concerned that El Fatah might have been fitted out as a spy ship for the CIA, he ordered that she was stripped of all her broadcasting equipment and used for target practice by the Libyan navy and air force. She sank in the Mediterranean in 1984.

On the night of 21 December 1988 a Boeing 747 bound for Detroit was destroyed by a bomb over the Scottish town of Lockerbie. All 259 passengers and crew aboard Pan Am flight 103 were killed and large sections of the aircraft crashed onto homes in Lockerbie killing a further eleven people on the ground.

It soon emerged that a bomb had been loaded onto the jumbo jet in Frankfurt, in an unaccompanied suitcase transferred from an Air Malta flight. Investigators established that the bomb used Semtex explosive hidden inside a Toshiba radio cassette recorder, the same as a device found two months earlier which had been built by a group of Palestinian terrorists in the German city of Neuss.

However, in November 1991, following one of the world's biggest ever terrorism-related investigations, undertaken jointly by the Scottish police and the United States FBI, it was announced that NOT the Palestinians but two Libyan secret agents, Al Amin Khalifa Fhimah and Abdelbaset Al Megrahi were suspected of being behind the attack.

The US Justice Department demanded the extradition of the two suspects with no success, but in 1999, after lengthy negotiations and UN sanctions, Libyan leader Muammar Gaddafi handed over the two men for trial at a special court presided over by three Scottish judges at Camp Zeist in the Netherlands.

After a trial which took evidence from 230 witnesses over 84 days, Al Amin Khalifa Fhimah, was found not guilty and acquitted on the 270 counts of murder. Libyan intelligence agent Abdelbaset Al Megrahi was found guilty by unanimous decision of the court and sentenced to life imprisonment. The judges recommended a minimum sentence of 20 years in view of the 'horrendous nature' of the crime but in 2009 Al Megrahi was controversially released by the Scottish government on compassionate grounds after being diagnosed with prostate cancer. He died in 2012 after always having protested his innocence, the only person to be convicted for the attack.

The case against Al Megrahi rested heavily on the discovery in the wreckage of a tiny fragment of circuit board from an electronic timer said to have been used to detonate the bomb on board the aircraft. The timer was identified as being a MST-13 device a number of which, the investigators said, had been supplied only to Libya through Tripoli or via the Libyan embassy in East Berlin.

The CIA directed Scottish police to the manufacturers of the MST-13 timers, the electronics company Mebo AG in Zurich. Mebo co-owner Edwin Bollier is to this day adamant that the fragment of circuit board (of which he had been shown a photograph by Scottish police during the investigation) was not from the batch sold to Libya but rather from a batch of prototype timers he had sold to the Stasi's Institut fur Technische Untersuchungen's in East Germany. Called to give evidence at the trial, Bollier says he was then asked to identify a timer fragment from a different board, the later version delivered to Libya.

Little was heard from Erwin Meister, who chose to stay in the background, and Edwin Bollier remained enigmatic. Mebo's involvement with the suspicious radio ship was referred to in the Lockerbie trial but its owners' relationship with the intelligence community was not explored. Bollier was only willing to travel to the Netherlands to give evidence on the condition that he was given immunity from prosecution for his involvement in the events leading up to the attack on Pan Am flight 103, which duly arrived in a letter from the Scottish Crown Office dated 9 June 2000. He had previously told investigators that, if he were to be charged with any offence, he would call some very high-ranking witnesses to appear in his defence, including ex-President George H W Bush, a former Director of the CIA, and Lieutenant Colonel Oliver North, the former deputy-director of the US National Security Council.

Was it possible that the Americans also had a hand in the operation of the Mebo radio ship? When asked by the German news magazine *Der Spiegel* about his alleged CIA contacts, Bollier said simply: 'No comment'.

REFERENCES

BRITANNIA WAIVES THE RULES
1. *Offshore Radio Museum*. www.offshoreradiomuseum.co.uk/page496.html Accessed Feb 2017.
2. Alasdair Glennie. *Daily Mail*. 23 July 2013. http://www.dailymail.co.uk/news/article-2375551/Paul-Gambaccini-claims-BBC-labelled-camp-Christmas.html. Accessed December 2015
3. Interview with John Hiscock. The Real Casino Royale: gangsters in a class of their own. *Daily Telegraph*. 24 February 2009. http://www.telegraph.co.uk/culture/film/4735580/The-Real-Casino-Royale-gangsters-in-a-class-of-their-own.html Accessed February 2017.
4. John Pearson. *Notorious. The Immortal Legend of the Kray Twins*. Arrow Books London 2019]
5. BBC *On This Day* http://news.bbc.co.uk/onthisday/hi/dates/stories/september/1/newsid_2969000/2969846.stm
6. Decca Aitkenhead. Mayfair's wheel of fortune, *Guardian* 16 July 1999. https://www.theguardian.com/theguardian/1999/jul/16/features11.g21. Accessed February 2017

THE VOICE OF AMERICA
1. Lawrence W Lichty and Malachi C Topping. *American Broadcasting*. Hastings House Publishers. New York. 1975. p401.
2. *The Offshore Radio Museum*. www.offshoreradiomuseum.co.uk/page10.html. Accessed Feb 2017]
3. Martin J. Manning, Herbert Romerstein. *Historical Dictionary of American Propaganda*. Greenwood Publishing Group.
4. CIA memo to Allen Dulles, Director CIA, June 1 1961. References to Radio Broadcasting to Cuba. Marked SECRET. Approved for release 2008: CIA-RPD80B01676R002700020032-8

THE VOICE OF SLOUGH
1. Curran and Seaton. *Power without Responsibility*. Routledge. p. 117
2. John Reith. *Broadcast over Britain*. Hodder and Stoughton Limited, 1924
3. *BBC Handbook 1929*. BBC. London. p55
4. Martin Cloonan. *Negotiating needletime: the Musicians' Union, the BBC and the record companies, c. 1920–1990*. Taylor and Francis Group 2016

5. Robert Chapman. *Selling the Sixties. The Pirates and Pop Music Radio.* Routledge, London and New York 1992. p43
6. *The Offshore Radio Museum.* www.offshoreradiomuseum.co.uk/page942.html. Accessed Feb 2017
7. *Hans Knot's International Radio Report - June 2008* www.hansknot.com/2008-06.htm Accessed March 2017
8. GBOK. *The Offshore Radio Museum.* www.offshoreradiomuseum.co.uk/page622.html. Accessed March 2017
9. Jan van Heeren. *The broadcast revolution of CNBC.* Soundscapes.info www.icce.rug.nl/~soundscapes/VOLUME05/Radiorevolutie_CNBCUK.shtm Accessed March 2017

CONS PIRACY
1. Interview with Kitty Black. Ray Clark. *Radio Caroline: The True Story of the Boat that Rocked.* The History Press, Stroud 2014
2. Major Oliver Smedley. This man swore to kill me...personally! *The People.* Sunday 6 November 1966
3. Allan Crawford – The unsung Offshore Radio Pioneer. *Offshore Echos.* www.offshoreechos.com/Allan%20Crawford.htm. Accessed March 2017
4. Radio Caroline in the Sixties. Part One: The Beginning. http://www.offshoreradio.co.uk/car61.htm. Accessed March 2017
5. The Pirates. *World In Action.* 1 May 1964. You Tube. www.youtube.com/watch?v=06i9ddAOhyQ. Accessed March 2017
6. Major Oliver Smedley. *The People.* Sunday 6 November 1966
7. Sir Jocelyn Stevens – obituary. *The Telegraph.* 13 October 2014. www.telegraph.co.uk/news/obituaries/11158471/Sir-Jocelyn-Stevens-obituary.html
8. Ray Clark. *Radio Caroline: The True Story of the Boat that Rocked.* The History Press, Stroud 2014. p38
9. Andrew Lownie. *The Spectator.* 5 November, 1988
10. Chapman Pincher. *Their Trade is Treachery.* Sidgwick & Jackson London 1981
11. Kim Philby. *My Silent War: the Soviet Master Spy's Own Story.* Grove Press New York 1968
12. Robert Chapman. *Selling the Sixties. The Pirates and Pop Music Radio.* Routledge, London and New York 1992. p99
13. *The Pirate Radio Hall of Fame.* Part Four: The sounds of '65. http://www.offshoreradio.co.uk/odds04.htm Accessed March 2017
14. *Hansard.* Pirate radio ships and local sound broadcasting. HC Deb 02 June 1964 vol 695 cc933-8 933

199

hansard.millbanksystems.com/commons/1964/jun/02/pirate-radio-ships-and-local-sound-1

TOWERS OF POWER
1. Allan Crawford in conversation with Colin Nicol. *The Pirate Radio Hall of Fame.* www.offshoreradio.co.uk/odds37.htm Accessed March 2017
2. Hans Knot. *The legal battle against offshore radio and television. Some reflections on the REM Island Project.* Soundscapes. info Volume 14. September 2011 www.icce.rug.nl/~soundscapes/VOLUME14/Rem_Reflections.shtml Accessed January 2017
3. Susan Moore. Clifton Hall, School of Rock 'n' Roll. Kindle Edition. May 2016.
4. Radio man fined. *Daily Express.* 21 April 1965
5. Pop radio gets pigeon post. *Daily Express.* 23 April 1965
6. Author's converstion with Susan Moore. March 2017.
7. *The Journal of the Reading and District Amateur Radio Club* December 1999. www.radarc.org/Newletter/winter99%20-%20PoP%20Pirates-Copy%20Updated.pdf Accessed March 2017
8. Sixties City. *The History of Pirate Radio.* sixtiescity.net/Radio/PirateRadio2.shtm Accessed January 2017
9. Frank Howitt. Pop radio drowning drama. *Daily Express.* 18 December 1964
10. John Venmore-Rowland. *Radio Caroline.* The Landmark Press, Lavenham, Suffolk 1967
11. Merrick Winn and Christopher Rowlands. *Daily Express.* January 1965

OIL ON THE WATER
1. Jack Adrian. Obituary: Ted Allbeury. Thriller-writer and spy. *Independent.* 15 December 2005
2. Radio Pirates Prepare for a Benn Broadside. *Financial Times.* 15 January 1966
3. Radio 390 goes off the air. *Financial Times.* 26 November 1966. Front page.
4. Philip Radcliffe. *The Piccadilly Story.* Blond & Briggs. London 1979. p48
5. John Venmore-Rowland. *Radio Caroline.* The Landmark Press, Lavenham, Suffolk 1967. P36.
6. Robert Chapman. *Selling the Sixties. The Pirates and Pop Music Radio.* Routledge, London and New York 1992. p78
7. Merrick Winn and Christopher Rowlands. *Daily Express.* January 1965.
8. William Keegan. Who made the profits-and the losses. *Financial Times.* 5 August 1967
9. John Venmore-Rowland. *Radio Caroline.* The Landmark Press, Lavenham, Suffolk 1967. P100

10. Ray Clark. *Radio Caroline: The True Story of the Boat that Rocked*. The History Press, Stroud 2014. P104
11. Major Oliver Smedley. *The People*. Sunday 6 November 1966
12. Tony Benn. *Out of the Wilderness. Diaries 1963-67*. Arrow Books Limited, London 1987. p164
13. Norman Hare. Radio pirates to pay composers. *Daily Telegraph*. Date uncertain, in author's own cuttings.
14. Asa Briggs. *The History of Broadcasting in the United Kingdom: Volume V: Competition*. Oxford University Press, 1995. p33

CASH CASINO
1. Robert Chapman. *Selling the Sixties. The Pirates and Pop Music Radio*. Routledge, London and New York 1992. p118.
2. Stuart Henry and Mike von Joel Ed. *Pirate Radio Then and Now*. Blandford Press, Dorset 1984
3. Paul Denver. *Radio Caroline Annual*. World Productions, Manchester 1965
4. Radio Pirates Prepare for a Benn Broadside. *Financial Times*. 15 January 1966]
5. Obituary. David Hart. *Telegraph* 5 January 2011
6. MP 'spied on by the state'. BBC News. 1 November 2002. news.bbc.co.uk/1/hi/programmes/true_spies/2378459.stm Accessed May 2017
7. Peter Barberis, John McHugh, Mike Tyldesley. *Encyclopedia of British and Irish Political Organizations: Parties, Groups and Movements of the 20th Century*. A&C Black, 2000
6. Martin Childs. Obituary. David Hart. *Independent*. 11 January 2011
8. Obituary. David Hart. *Telegraph*. 5 January 2011
9. A useful tool is the *Distance to the Horizon Calculator*. www.ringbell.co.uk/info/hdist.htm. Accessed March 2017
11. *Hans Knot's International Radio Report - September 2005* www.hansknot.com/sept2005b.htm. Accessed April 2017
12. Joseph Progler. *American Broadcasting to Cuba: The Cold War Origins of Radio and TV MARTI*. Ritsumeikan International Affairs Vol.10 2011. pp.159-182 www.ritsumei.ac.jp/acd/re/k-rsc/ras/04_publications/ria_en/10_09.pdf Accessed April 2017

LAISSEZ FAIRE
1. Martin Tolchin. Obituary. John G. Tower, 65, Longtime Senator From Texas. *New York Times*. 6 April 1991 www.nytimes.com/1991/04/06/obituaries/john-g-tower-65-longtime-senator-from-texas.html

2. Stuart Henry & Mike von Joel Ed. *Pirate Radio Then and Now*. Blandford Press, Dorset. 1984. p 71
3. Website. broadcasting-fleet.com/olga-patricia-laissez-faire. Accessed April 2017
4. *The Pirate Radio Hall of Fame*. Boss Radio and the Hallmark of Quality: Memories of Swinging Radio England and Britain Radio www.offshoreradio.co.uk/sre1.htm Accessed March 2017
5. John Venmore-Rowland. *Radio Caroline*. The Landmark Press, Lavenham, Suffolk 1967. p109
6. Derek Burroughs Jr. *The Radio Rose of Texas*. Chapter 12. stellamaris.no/chapter12.htm

SHIVERING SANDS

1. Sixties City. *The history of pirate radio*. sixtiescity.net/Radio/PirateRadio3.shtm Accessed April 2017
2. Author's converstion with Susan Moore. March 2017
3. Duncan Johnson writing in *Pirate Radio Then and Now* Stuart Henry, Mike von Joel. Blandford Press, Dorset 1984. p86.
4. *The Pirate Radio Hall of Fame*. The raid on Shivering Sands and the death of Reg Calvert. www.offshoreradio.co.uk/raid.htm Accessed February 2017
5. Duncan Johnson writing in *Pirate Radio Then and Now*. Stuart Henry, Mike von Joel. Blandford Press, Dorset 1984.
6. David Thurlow. Smedley denies murder in Duck Street. *Daily Express*. 23 June 1966
7. Adrian Johns. *Death of a pirate: British radio and the making of the information age*. W M Norton & Company Ltd. New York. 2011 p216
8. Adrian Johns. *Death of a pirate*. p235

MARINE OFFENCES

1. Merrick Winn and Christopher Rowlands. *Daily Express*. January 1965.
2. Martin Jackson. Pop Pirate Summons. *Daily Express*. 22 September 1966. Front page lead.
3. Girls picket court as 'pirates' go on trial. *Daily Express*. 25 November 1966
4. Radio 390 goes off the air. *Financial Times*. 26 November 1966. Front page
5. Robert Chapman. *Selling the Sixties. The Pirates and Pop Music Radio*. Routledge, London and New York 1992. p195
6. Wanta Pirate Radio Station? *The Abilene Reporter – News*. Abilene, Texas. 15 September 1967.

7. Derek Burroughs Jr. May 11th, 2006. Written in connection with the Radio England & Britain Radio reunion, May 12th-14th, 2006, London. www.stellamaris.no/perspectives.htm. Accessed April 2017
8. William Keegan. Who made the profits - and the losses. *Financial Times*. 5 Aug 1967
9. Ray Clark. *Radio Caroline: The True Story of the Boat that Rocked*. The History Press, Stroud. 2014
10. Paul Rusling. *Radio Adventures of the MV Communicator*. World of Radio Limited. 2016.
11. Paul Rusling. *Laser 558*. paulrusling.com/Laser_558.html Accessed May 2017. See also: Paul Rusling. *The Lid Off Laser 558*. Pirate Publications 1984
12. Stuart Henry and Mike von Joel. *Pirate Radio Then and Now*. Blandford Press, Dorset 1984. p116

RED SIGNALS
1. *Offshore Radio Museum*. Radio North Sea International (RNI) www.offshoreradiomuseum.co.uk/page671.html Accessed April 2017
2. Copenhagen Plan. European Broadcasting Convention. Copenhagen 1948.
3. Tony Benn. *Office Without Power. Diaries 1968-72*. Arrow Books, London 1988. p252
4. Arthur Martin. Former Labour minister who faked his own death was communist spy. *Daily Mail*. 6 October 2009. www.dailymail.co.uk/news/article-1218373/Former-Labour-minister-faked-death-Communist-spy.html#ixzz4gL8OcoiI
5. Christopher Andrew. *The Defence of the Realm: The Authorized History of MI5*. Allen Lane/Penguin 2009
6. Robert Chapman. *Selling the Sixties. The Pirates and Pop Music Radio*. Routledge, London and New York 1992. p210
7. Peter Wright interview. *Panorama*. BBC TV. 13 October 1988
8. www.rossrevenge.co.uk/tx/othertx.htm Accessed May 2017
9. Joel D. Cameron. Stasi. *Encyclopædia Britannica*. Encyclopædia Britannica, inc. www.britannica.com/topic/Stasi Accessed May 2017
10. John Gieger. *Control Through Constant Knowledge: An Analysis of the Stasi's Effects on Audio Technology*. Belmont University. Nashville 2009
11. Ben Fischer. *One of the Biggest Ears in the World: East German SIGINT Operations*. 2001
12. *Offshore Radio Museum*. RNI History. www.offshoreradiomuseum.co.uk/page142.html Accessed May 2017

INDEX

Abilene, Texas, 55, 138, 163
Allbeury, Ted, 81-2, 84, 157-8
Al Megrahi, Abdelbaset, 195-6
Ampliphase, 89, 110, 175
Amplitide modulation (AM), 38
Archer, Andy, 177, 192
Armstrong, Garner T, 61, 83, 86, 93, 113, 132
Armstrong, Herbert W, 23, 34, 44, 86, 139
Arnold, Alan, 143, 149
Aspinall, John, 11-12
Atlanta, Texas, 20, 48
Bate, Terry, 104
Bates, Roy, 106-9, 118, 145, 154, 159-60
BBC Light Programme, 8, 32-3, 82-3, 89, 112, 167
BBC Radio 1, 33, 38, 92, 167, 170, 180, 184, 186
BBC Radio 2, 92, 113, 167-8
Beacon Hill, 176, 180, 183-4, 186
Beatles, the, 17, 50, 70, 89, 162
Bell Laboratories, 16
Benn, Anthony Wedgewood (Tony), 84, 96-7, 154, 181
Bevins, Reginald, 59
Biafra, 178, 187
Big Lil, 162
Birch, Philip, 87-8, 90, 96, 144, 147, 162
Black, Kitty, 42, 44, 95, 140, 146-7, 150
Blunt, Sir Anthony, 54-5
Board of Trade, 105, 175
Bollier, Edwin, 178-9, 182-3, 186-96.
Boothby, Lord Robert, 11, 13-15, 154
Bridlington, 115
British Broadcasting Corporation (BBC), 3-12, 26-9, 31-4, 37-8, 40-1, 45, 52, 70, 73, 81-2, 84, 89, 92, 97, 102, 111, 114, 123, 135, 137, 167, 170, 176, 179, 185, 192
BBC Television, 12, 70, 125
BBC World Service, 10, 20, 185
Britain Radio, 40, 90, 105, 131-8, 163, 173
Britain's Better Music Station (BBMS), 159
Broadcasting House, 8, 29, 32-3
Brookmans Park, 176
Bullen,'Big Alf', 146
Burgess, Guy, 10, 54-5
Burghead, 8
Bush, President George H W, 132, 164, 197
Calvert, Dorothy, 144-5, 151, 154, 157, 161
Calvert, Reg, 66-72, 106, 108, 118, 124, 140-5, 148-55, 161
Campaign for Independent Broadcasting, 183
Canewdon, 184, 186
Caroline House, 55, 58, 90, 101, 166
Caroline Television, 128
Caribbean, 25, 130, 164, 170
Cash, Dave, 89, 93, 136, 162
Cash Casino, 104-5
Castro, Fidel, 23-4, 126, 130
CBC (Plays) Limited, 42, 44
Central Intelligence Agency (CIA), 3, 23-5, 34, 47, 86, 116, 122, 126, 130, 132, 164, 169, 171, 180, 189-90, 195-7
Ceto (ship), 4
Chattenden, 176
Cheetah (ship), 18-19
Cheetah II (ship), 19, 99-101, 123

204

INDEX

Chesterfield Gardens, 53-6, 90
Christmas tree files, 9, 10
Clacton-on-Sea, 99, 104, 117, 120, 122, 173-4, 176-7
Clark, Alan, 70, 146
Clark, Ray, 47
CNBC, 36-7, 110
Campaign for Nuclear Disarmament (CND), 9
Collins Electronics Manufacturing Company, 18, 134
Comet (ship), 110-12, 163, 187
Communicator (ship), 169-72
Continental Electronics, 22, 47, 100, 130-1, 133, 164, 185
Cooper, Alan, 153
Copyright, 7, 32-3, 60-1, 96
Courier (ship), 18
Crawford, Allan, 37, 42-5, 48-9, 52, 56, 58, 62, 94, 101-2, 140-1, 143, 146
Crawford Committee, 27
Cuba, 23-4, 44, 126-8, 130, 164
Curzon Street, 12, 55, 90, 132-3, 138, 151-2
Czechoslovakia, 179-82
D notices, 151-2
Daily Mail, 4
Daily Telegraph, 10, 95, 122
Dale, Leonard, 111-3, 115, 163
Dallas, 4, 20-1, 47-8, 51, 85, 87, 90, 131, 135, 172, 185
Day, Roger, 135, 137, 192
Dean Street, 37, 49, 50, 52, 61, 110, 147
Decca, 31-2, 41
Dee, Simon, 50, 57
Denmark, 20, 42
Denmark Street, 68, 70, 144-5, 154
Der Spiegel, 197
Dolphin, Peter, 146-7, 151

Driberg, Tom, 14
Droitwich, 8
Dublin, 35, 46-7
Dulles, Allen, 164
Duncan, Peter, 114
East Berlin, 188, 196
East Germany, 23, 81, 188-9, 196
Ellen (ship), 34-6
Elvey, Paul, 69, 71, 143, 146-7, 151-3
EMI, 31-2, 41
Esmerelda's Barn, 12, 107
Essex University 8, 10, 173, 178
Estuary Radio Limited, 82-3, 157-9
Everett, Kenny, 89, 93, 136, 162, 173
Evesham, 8
Faversham, 72, 74-5
Fisher, Anthony, 41
Florida, 87, 93, 130, 133, 136, 169-70, 181
Ford, Anna, 10
Fortunes, the, 50, 66, 71, 165, 192
Free Radio Association, 183
Frinton-on-Sea, 51, 88, 99-100, 103, 141, 185
Gaddafi, Colonel Muammar, 188, 190-1, 195-6
Galaxy (ship), 87-8, 93, 99, 101, 130, 144, 162
Gale, Roger, 116
GB-OK, 35-6, 51, 69, 110
Gambaccini, Paul, 10
Gardiner, Gerald QC, 14
General Post Office (GPO), 26-7, 29, 46, 55-6, 96, 98, 101, 117
General Strike, 27-8
Goodman, Arnold, 14
Greene, Sir Hugh, 10, 81
Greenore, 46-7, 49, 51
Grey broadcasting policy, 24-5, 86

205

INDEX

Guardian, The, 122
Hair (the musical), 6
Harris, Tomás, 53-5
Hart, David, 121-2
Harwich, 53, 93, 99, 105, 172
Heath, Edward, 36
Herne Bay, 65, 102-3
Hilversum, 15, 19, 191
Home Office, 8, 97
Home Service (BBC), 15, 32, 167
Independent Broadcasting Authority (IBA), 5, 9
Independent Television Authority (ITA), 123
Institut fur Technische Untersuchungen, 188-90, 196
Institute for Economic Affairs, 41, 43
International Broadcasting Company (IBC), 29, 30
IRA, 46, 190
Isle of Man, 49, 51, 56, 58, 97, 116-7, 164-5
Jamming, 19, 176-186
Joffe, Roland, 10
Kennedy, President John F, 3-4, 48, 87, 126
KGB, 54, 122, 180, 189, 192
King Radio, 74, 76, 81-83
KLIF, 3, 20, 51, 87-92, 135
Knock John (fort), 64, 106-9, 118, 143, 159
Kotschack, Jack, 21
Kray, Reginald, 11-12, 14, 107, 154
Kray, Ronnie, 11-12, 14, 107, 152
Lady Chatterley's Lover, 6, 7, 68
Lady Dixon (ship), 35, 51, 69
Laissez Faire (ship), 137-8, 155, 163-4, 187
Langford, Pierce, 131, 138, 164

Laser 558, 169-72, 178
Lawrence, D H, 6
Leconfield House, 55, 90, 133
Liberal Party, 41- 43, 96
Liberty Broadcasting System, 20
Libya, 188-91, 195-6
Liechtenstein, 11, 22, 45, 56
Light Programme (BBC), 8, 32-3, 82-3, 89, 112, 167
Lindau, Roy, 169, 171
Lockerbie, 195-6
Lord Chamberlain, 5-6, 175
Lye, David, 76-7, 82, 157, 159
Maclean, Donald, 54
Macmillan, Harold, 12, 59
Major Minor Records, 102, 167
Manders, Kees, 191
Manx Radio, 116, 164
Marconi Company, 26, 184, 186
Margate, 37, 64, 118
Marine Broadcasting Offences Act, 127-8, 154, 156, 161, 164-5, 169, 171, 174, 183
Martin, Eric, 70
Maudling, Caroline, 48
Maunsell, Guy, 64
Mayfair, 11-13, 53, 77, 90
McLendon, Gordon, 3, 20-1, 43-4, 48, 51, 85-90, 92
Mebo I (ship), 187, 191, 195
Mebo II (ship), 174, 186-95
Mebo AG, 189, 196
Mechanical Copyright Protection Society (MCPS), 33
Medium wave, 8, 15, 18-9, 29-31, 38-40, 72-3, 82, 95, 117, 119, 123, 135, 167. 170, 173
Megrahi, Abdelbaset Al, 195, 196
Meister, Erwin, 178, 183, 186-7, 194-6

INDEX

Merike, Steve, 192
Metropolitan Police, 14
MI5, 9-10, 47, 54-5, 81, 90, 121, 133, 151-2, 181
MI6, 81, 189
Mi Amigo (ship), 23, 43-4, 47-9, 51, 56-7, 85, 99-101, 125, 130, 141, 168, 185
Ministry of Defence, 65, 67, 140, 158
Ministry of Posts and Telecommunications, 175-7, 179, 184
Moore, Chris, 47, 50
Moscow, 180, 192
Murchison, Clint, Jr., 21-2, 44, 48
Musicians Union, 33, 89
Needle time, 33, 45
Netherlands, 19, 37, 63, 78, 112, 123, 125, 162, 167-8, 174, 186, 194-6
Newcastle-upon-Tyne, 26, 114
News of the World, 53, 108, 120
Nicaragua, 22
Nore (fort), 34-6, 64-5
North, Lieutenant Colonel Oliver, 197
Norway, 19
Observer, The, 9-10
Ocean 7 (ship), 112, 114-6, 162-3
Official Secrets Act, 10, 181
Offshore I (tender), 105, 119, 142
O'Quinn, Ron, 133-6
O'Rahilly, Ronan, 4, 34, 45-52, 56, 58, 61, 65, 88, 94, 100-2, 127-9, 143, 156, 167-8, 183-4
Oswald, Lee Harvey, 3
Owen, Wilf, 181
PAMS (jingles), 85, 135, 162
Pan Am, 195-6
Panama, 22, 44, 112, 125, 130, 169, 172, 187
Parry, Roger, 171
Peel, John, 89, 93, 136

Penguin Books, 6-7
Pepper, Tom, 72, 74-6
Performing Right Society (PRS), 32, 60-1, 96
Philby, Kim, 54, 81
Phonographic Performance Limited (PPL), 32, 61
Pierson, Don, 85-8, 90, 131, 133-4, 136-8, 163-4
Pitsea, 35, 69
Plugge, Captain Leonard Frank, 29, 30, 37
Post Office (see also GPO), 6-7, 26, 36, 50, 55, 56, 59, 96, 98, 157-60, 175, 186
Postmaster general, 6, 26, 59, 84, 95, 97, 116, 154, 167, 175
Prague, 181-2
Profumo, John, 13, 47, 59, 95
Project Atlanta, 44-5, 47-9, 53, 56, 58, 62, 94, 100-1, 106, 140-3, 146-7, 185
Proundfoot, Wilf, 111-6, 163
Pye, 41
Queen magazine, 46-8, 53-4
Radex TV, 124-5
Radio 270, 113-6, 130, 157, 162-3
Radio 390, 83-4, 96, 101, 135, 137-8, 146, 157-9
Radio Atlanta, 43-5, 48-50, 52-3, 56, 59, 61, 65-6, 73, 76-7, 85, 102, 106, 168
Radio Caroline, 3, 39, 47-61, 76-8, 85, 93-4, 96-7, 99-106, 116, 118, 125, 137, 140-3, 156, 162, 164-170, 183, 185-6
Radio Church of God, 25, 35, 44, 86, 93, 113, 132, 138
Radio City, 70-1, 74, 106-9, 118, 124, 140-54, 156-7, 161, 192
Radio Corporation of America (RCA), 18, 73, 82, 87, 110, 112, 127, 173

INDEX

Radio England, 90, 105, 131-8, 163
Radio Essex, 106, 109-10, 143, 159
Radio Free Europe, 23, 190
Radio Invicta, 36, 72-6, 81, 101
Radio Liberty, 190
Radio London, 77, 85, 88-95, 99, 101, 104, 131, 135-8, 141, 144-5, 147-8, 162
Radio Luxembourg, 29-31, 34-6, 38, 45, 84, 137
Radio Mercur, 18-9, 42-3
Radio Moscow, 24, 192
Radio Noordzee, 62, 192
Radio Nord, 20, 22-3, 36, 42-5, 47, 132, 168
Radio Normandie, 29
Radio Northsea International (RNI), 173-7, 179-80, 183-4, 186-7, 191-4
Radio Scotland, 110-2, 120, 137, 163
Radio Swan, 23, 34, 126
Radio Tower (Tower Radio), 117, 119-21
Radio Veronica, 19, 36-7, 42, 45, 47, 84, 166, 191-4
Radlon Sales Limited, 87, 112
Raven, Mike, 76-7, 84
Red Sands (fort), 64, 72, 74-6, 78, 82-4, 158-9
Reith, John, 27-8, 32
REM Island, 62-3, 123
Rice-Davies, Mandy, 13
Robinson, Don, 111-13, 115, 157
Rochford, 159-60
Rosko, 'the Emperor' (Michael Pasternak), 102
Ross, Carl (Jimmy), 46, 94, 168
Ross, Ian, 46-7
Ross Revenge (ship), 168-70
Rotterdam, 47, 174
Rough Sands (fort), 64, 118, 157, 159-60
Royal Navy, 15, 50, 64, 122, 159, 176

Ruby, Jack, 3, 20-1
Rusling, Paul, 169, 171
Scarborough, 106, 111-5
Scheveningen, 37, 186, 190-3
Sealand, 160
Security Service, 14, 54-5, 91, 146, 177-8, 184
Sheffield, John, 47, 94
Sherrin, Ned, 12
Shields, Tommy, 109-11, 120, 163
Shivering Sands (fort), 65, 67, 71-2, 108, 118, 141-8, 150-4, 161
Short, Edward, 116, 167
Short wave, 18, 23, 174, 176, 187, 192
SIGINT, 189-90, 192
Slough, 34-5
Smedley, Major William Oliver, 41-4, 53, 76, 86, 106, 122, 140-50, 155
Smythe, Philip, 171
Solomon, Philip, 76, 101-2, 104, 166-7
Sony, 17
Southend, 34, 67, 76, 108-9, 118, 184
Soviet Union, 10, 54, 180, 182, 190
Spain, 23, 43, 49, 86, 156, 168, 171
Special Branch, 121
Stasi, the, 180, 188-90, 192, 196
Stevens, Jocelyn, 46-8, 53
Stonehouse, John, 175, 179-81, 184
Storz, Todd, 20, 89
Strasbourg Convention, the, 156, 194
Stratovision, 126-8
Sullivan, Eric, 117-9
Sunday Mirror, 13-14
Sunk Head (fort), 64, 117-22, 157
Sutch, David, Screaming Lord, 66-70, 150
Swan Island, 23
Swanson, Arnold, 34-5, 69, 110
Sweden, 18, 20-23, 45, 123

INDEX

Switzerland, 178-9, 188, 196
Television, 5-9, 12, 31, 62, 100, 117, 123-8
Texas Instruments, 16
Thames estuary, 7, 15, 63-4, 67, 88, 103, 106-7, 125, 140-1, 156-7
That Was The Week That Was, 12, 70, 114
The World Tomorrow, 23, 34, 61, 83, 113, 138-9
Theatres Act, 5
Thompson, John, 34, 36, 71, 75-6
Thornburn, Pamela, 149-50
Tollerfield, Russ, 162
Tongue Sands (fort), 64-5, 118
Top 40, 20, 89-90, 94, 113, 131-2, 134-5
Torr, Reg, 117
Tottenham Court Road, 15, 67
Tower, Senator John, 131-2
Tower Television, 117, 119, 123
transistor radio, 15-17, 31, 38-9, 52, 73, 102, 123, 175, 180
Trinity House, 44, 62, 65, 146, 175
Trodd, Kenith, 10
TV Noordzee, 63, 123, 128
Tynwald, 97, 164-5
UKGM, 145-7
VHF (see also FM), 18, 38-9, 97-8, 173, 175
Vick, William E, 133, 138
Vietnam, 24, 127, 164, 183
Vision Projects, 117-20
Voice of America, 18, 24
Voice of Slough, 34-7, 72
Wadner, Britt, 19, 100
Walker, Johnnie, 102-4, 133, 135, 165, 167
Walton-on-the-Naze, 99, 104, 119, 121, 130, 175

Ward, Stephen, 13
Wartime Broadcasting Service (WTBS), 7-9
Washington DC, 18
Wendens Ambo, 149
West, Alan, 193
Whitstable, 65, 67-72, 74-5, 107-8, 125, 152, 171
Wichita Falls, Texas, 131, 138
Wijsmuller, 100, 105, 119, 166-8
Wilson, Harold, 14, 43, 60, 165, 181-2, 184
Wireless Telegraphy Act 1949, 36, 48, 97, 112, 157-9
Wood Norton, 8-9
Zurich, 178, 194, 196